Multimedia Systems and Digital Processing

Multimedia Systems and Digital Processing

Edited by Susan Gibbs

LANRYE
INTERNATIONAL
www.clanryeinternational.com

Clanrye International,
750 Third Avenue, 9ᵗʰ Floor,
New York, NY 10017, USA

ISBN: 978-1-63240-716-0

Cataloging-in-Publication Data

Multimedia systems and digital processing / edited by Susan Gibbs.
p. cm.
Includes bibliographical references and index.
ISBN 978-1-63240-716-0
1. Multimedia systems. 2. Image processing--Digital techniques. 3. Digital media.
I. Gibbs, Susan.
QA76.575 .M85 2018
006.7--dc23

For information on all Clanrye International publications
visit our website at www.clanryeinternational.com

Contents

Permissions

Index

Preface

The technology of the world changed considerably after the advancement of multimedia. Today, we can text, call, send a video, chat, etc. to anyone from any part of the world because of multimedia. The use of multimedia is not only limited to the day-to-day life but is crucial in fields like robotics, medical diagnosis, military, digital forensics, quality inspection, etc. This textbook provides in-depth information about the different technologies and concepts used in this field. Such selected concepts that redefine multimedia processing have been presented in it. Those in search of information to further their knowledge will be greatly assisted by this textbook.

A foreword of all Chapters of the book is provided below:

Chapter 1 - Multimedia is a content that is formed after combining audio, text, video, animation, etc. in a synchronized manner. This synchronization is extremely significant as uncoordinated multimedia signals can reduce or obliterate the meaning of the transmitted message. This is an introductory chapter which will introduce briefly all the significant aspects of introduction to multimedia technology; **Chapter 2 -** Image compression is a form of data compression by the use of which photos can be made compact. To compress an image, redundancies are exploited. If an image has fewer details, it implies that it has more redundancies and hence can be made more compact than an image with more details. Images with textures have less redundancy and its compression is comparatively difficult. This section discusses the methods of image compression system in a critical manner providing key analysis to the subject matter; **Chapter 3 -** There is a need to have uniformity in encoding and decoding so that products are less complex and users need not install separate decoders. This has given birth to coding standards. A few examples of image compression standards are JBIG, JPEG, and JPEG 2000. This chapter has been carefully written to provide an easy understanding of the varied facets of still image compression standards; **Chapter 4 -** A video codec is a form of encoder that compresses or decompresses a digital video. A few examples of video codecs are MPEG-1, MPEG-2, and MPEG-4. An audio codec is an encoder that compresses and decompresses digital audio data as per an audio coding format. A content representation format for transmitting and soring audio is known as audio coding format. MP3 is its most popular form. Audio and video coding is best understood in confluence with the major topics listed in the following section; **Chapter 5 -** Wavelet is a wave-like oscillation, created to be used in signal processing. They can be used to examine spatial frequency contents at different resolutions. Due to this, they can perform multi-resolution analysis of images. Multi-resolution analysis is a design method of discrete wavelet transforms and justification for fast wavelet transforms' algorithm. The chapter on wavelet and wavelet coding offers an insightful focus, keeping in mind the complex subject matter.

I would like to thank the entire editorial team who made sincere efforts for this book and my family who supported me in my efforts of working on this book. I take this opportunity to thank all those who have been a guiding force throughout my life.

Editor

Introduction to Multimedia Technology

Multimedia is a content that is formed after combining audio, text, video, animation, etc. in a synchronized manner. This synchronization is extremely significant as uncoordinated multimedia signals can reduce or obliterate the meaning of the transmitted message. This is an introductory chapter which will introduce briefly all the significant aspects of introduction to multimedia technology.

Multimedia

Multimedia is content that uses a combination of different content forms such as text, audio, images, animations, video and interactive content. Multimedia contrasts with media that use only rudimentary computer displays such as text-only or traditional forms of printed or hand-produced material.

Multimedia can be recorded and played, displayed, interacted with or accessed by information content processing devices, such as computerized and electronic devices, but can also be part of a live performance. Multimedia devices are electronic media devices used to store and experience multimedia content. Multimedia is distinguished from mixed media in fine art; for example, by including audio it has a broader scope. The term "rich media" is synonymous with interactive multimedia.

Terminology

The term *multimedia* was coined by singer and artist Bob Goldstein (later 'Bobb Goldsteinn') to promote the July 1966 opening of his "LightWorks at L'Oursin" show at Southampton, Long Island. Goldstein was perhaps aware of an American artist named Dick Higgins, who had two years previously discussed a new approach to art-making he called "intermedia."

Multimedia (multi-image) setup for the 1988 Ford New
Car Announcement Show, August 1987, Detroit, MI

On August 10, 1966, Richard Albarino of *Variety* borrowed the terminology, reporting: "Brainchild of songscribe-comic Bob ('Washington Square') Goldstein, the 'Lightworks' is the latest *multi-media* music-cum-visuals to debut as discothèque fare." Two years later, in 1968, the term "multimedia" was re-appropriated to describe the work of a political consultant, David Sawyer, the husband of Iris Sawyer—one of Goldstein's producers at L'Oursin.

In the intervening forty years, the word has taken on different meanings. In the late 1970s, the term referred to presentations consisting of multi-projector slide shows timed to an audio track. However, by the 1990s 'multimedia' took on its current meaning.

In the 1993 first edition of *Multimedia: Making It Work*, Tay Vaughan declared "Multimedia is any combination of text, graphic art, sound, animation, and video that is delivered by computer. When you allow the user – the viewer of the project – to control what and when these elements are delivered, it is *interactive multimedia*. When you provide a structure of linked elements through which the user can navigate, interactive multimedia becomes *hypermedia*."

The German language society Gesellschaft für deutsche Sprache recognized the word's significance and ubiquitousness in the 1990s by awarding it the title of German 'Word of the Year' in 1995. The institute summed up its rationale by stating "Multimedia has become a central word in the wonderful new media world."

In common usage, *multimedia* refers to an electronically delivered combination of media including video, still images, audio, and text in such a way that can be accessed interactively. Much of the content on the web today falls within this definition as understood by millions. Some computers which were marketed in the 1990s were called "multimedia" computers because they incorporated a CD-ROM drive, which allowed for the delivery of several hundred megabytes of video, picture, and audio data. That era saw also a boost in the production of educational multimedia CD-ROMs.

The term "video", if not used exclusively to describe motion photography, is ambiguous in multimedia terminology. *Video* is often used to describe the file format, delivery format, or presentation format instead of *"footage"* which is used to distinguish motion photography from *"animation"* of rendered motion imagery. Multiple forms of information content are often not considered modern forms of presentation such as audio or video. Likewise, single forms of information content with single methods of information processing (e.g. non-interactive audio) are often called multimedia, perhaps to distinguish static media from active media. In the fine arts, for example, Leda Luss Luyken's ModulArt brings two key elements of musical composition and film into the world of painting: variation of a theme and movement of and within a picture, making *ModulArt* an interactive multimedia form of art. Performing arts may also be considered multimedia considering that performers and props are multiple forms of both content and media.

Major Characteristics

Multimedia presentations may be viewed by person on stage, projected, transmitted, or played locally with a media player. A broadcast may be a live or recorded multimedia presentation. Broadcasts and recordings can be either analog or digital electronic media technology. Digital online multimedia may be downloaded or streamed. Streaming multimedia may be live or on-demand.

Multimedia games and simulations may be used in a physical environment with special effects, with multiple users in an online network, or locally with an offline computer, game system, or simulator.

The various formats of technological or digital multimedia may be intended to enhance the users' experience, for example to make it easier and faster to convey information. Or in entertainment or art, to transcend everyday experience.

A lasershow is a live multimedia performance.

Enhanced levels of interactivity are made possible by combining multiple forms of media content. Online multimedia is increasingly becoming object-oriented and data-driven, enabling applications with collaborative end-user innovation and personalization on multiple forms of content over time. Examples of these range from multiple forms of content on Web sites like photo galleries with both images (pictures) and title (text) user-updated, to simulations whose co-efficients, events, illustrations, animations or videos are modifiable, allowing the multimedia "experience" to be altered without reprogramming. In addition to seeing and hearing, haptic technology enables virtual objects to be felt. Emerging technology involving illusions of taste and smell may also enhance the multimedia experience.

Categorization

Multimedia may be broadly divided into linear and non-linear categories:

- Linear active content progresses often without any navigational control for the viewer such as a cinema presentation;

- Non-linear uses interactivity to control progress as with a video game or self-paced computer-based training. Hypermedia is an example of non-linear content.

Multimedia presentations can be live or recorded:

- A recorded presentation may allow interactivity via a navigation system;

- A live multimedia presentation may allow interactivity via an interaction with the presenter or performer.

Usage/Application

A presentation using Powerpoint. Corporate presentations
may combine all forms of media content.

Virtual reality uses multimedia content. Applications and delivery
platforms of multimedia are virtually limitless.

VVO Multimedia-Terminal in Dresden WTC (Germany)

Multimedia finds its application in various areas including, but not limited to, advertisements, art, education, entertainment, engineering, medicine, mathematics, business, scientific research and spatial temporal applications. Several examples are as follows:

Creative Industries

Creative industries use multimedia for a variety of purposes ranging from fine arts, to entertainment, to commercial art, to journalism, to media and software services provided for any of the industries listed below. An individual multimedia designer may cover the spectrum throughout their career. Request for their skills range from technical, to analytical, to creative.

Commercial Uses

Much of the electronic old and new media used by commercial artists and graphic designers is multimedia. Exciting presentations are used to grab and keep attention in advertising. Business to business, and interoffice communications are often developed by creative services firms for advanced multimedia presentations beyond simple slide shows to sell ideas or liven up training. Commercial multimedia developers may be hired to design for governmental services and non-profit services applications as well.

Entertainment and Fine Arts

Multimedia is heavily used in the entertainment industry, especially to develop special effects in movies and animations (VFX, 3D animation, etc.). Multimedia games are a popular pastime and are software programs available either as CD-ROMs or online. Some video games also use multimedia features. Multimedia applications that allow users to actively participate instead of just sitting by as passive recipients of information are called *interactive multimedia*. In the arts there are multimedia artists, whose minds are able to blend techniques using different media that in some way incorporates interaction with the viewer. One of the most relevant could be Peter Greenaway who is melding cinema with opera and all sorts of digital media. Another approach entails the creation of multimedia that can be displayed in a traditional fine arts arena, such as an art gallery. Although multimedia display material may be volatile, the survivability of the content is as strong as any traditional media. Digital recording material may be just as durable and infinitely reproducible with perfect copies every time.

Education

In education, multimedia is used to produce computer-based training courses (popularly called CBTs) and reference books like encyclopedia and almanacs. A CBT lets the user go through a series of presentations, text about a particular topic, and associated illustrations in various information formats. Edutainment is the combination of education with entertainment, especially multimedia entertainment.

Learning theory in the past decade has expanded dramatically because of the introduction of multimedia. Several lines of research have evolved, e.g. cognitive load and multimedia learning.

From multimedia learning (MML) theory, David Roberts has developed a large group lecture practice using PowerPoint and based on the use of full-slide images in conjunction with a reduction of visible text. The method has been applied and evaluated in 9 disciplines. In each experiment, students' engagement and active learning has been approximately 66% greater, than with the same material being delivered using bullet points, text and speech, corroborating a range of theories presented by multimedia learning scholars like Sweller and Mayer. The idea of media convergence is also becoming a major factor in education, particularly higher education. Defined as separate technologies such as voice (and telephony features), data (and productivity applications) and video that now share resources and interact with each other, media convergence is rapidly changing the curriculum in universities all over the world.

Journalism

Newspaper companies all over are trying to embrace the new phenomenon by implementing its practices in their work. While some have been slow to come around, other major newspapers like *The New York Times*, *USA Today* and *The Washington Post* are setting the precedent for the positioning of the newspaper industry in a globalized world.

News reporting is not limited to traditional media outlets. Freelance journalists can make use of different new media to produce multimedia pieces for their news stories. It engages global audiences and tells stories with technology, which develops new communication techniques for both media producers and consumers. The Common Language Project, later renamed to The Seattle Globalist, is an example of this type of multimedia journalism production.

Multimedia reporters who are mobile (usually driving around a community with cameras, audio and video recorders, and laptop computers) are often referred to as mojos, from *mo*bile *jo*urnalist.

Engineering

Software engineers may use multimedia in computer simulations for anything from entertainment to training such as military or industrial training. Multimedia for software interfaces are often done as a collaboration between creative professionals and software engineers.

Mathematical and Scientific Research

In mathematical and scientific research, multimedia is mainly used for modeling and simulation. For example, a scientist can look at a molecular model of a particular substance and manipulate it to arrive at a new substance. Representative research can be found in journals such as the *Journal of Multimedia*.

Medicine

In medicine, doctors can get trained by looking at a virtual surgery or they can simulate how the human body is affected by diseases spread by viruses and bacteria and then develop techniques to prevent it. Multimedia applications such as virtual surgeries also help doctors to get practical training.

Associations and Conferences

In Europe, the reference organisation for the multimedia industry is the European Multimedia Associations Convention (EMMAC).

Scholarly conferences about multimedia include:

- ACM Multimedia

- IEEE International Conference on Multimedia & Expo (ICME)

Interactive Media

Interactive media normally refers to products and services on digital computer-based systems which respond to the user's actions by presenting content such as text, moving image, animation, video, audio, and video games.

Definition

Interactive media is a method of communication in which the output from the media comes from the input of the users. Interactive media works with the user's participation. The media still has the same purpose but the user's input adds interaction and brings interesting features to the system for better enjoyment.

Development

The analogue videodisc developed by NV Philips was the pioneering technology for interactive media. Additionally, there are several elements that encouraged the development of interactive media including the following:

- The laser disc technology was first invented in 1958. It enabled the user to access high-quality analogue images on the computer screen. This increased the ability of interactive video systems.

- The concept of the graphical user interface (GUI), which was developed in the 1970s, popularized by Apple Computer, Inc. was essentially about visual metaphors, intuitive feel and sharing information on the virtual desktop. Additional power was the only thing needed to move into multimedia.

- The sharp fall in hardware costs and the unprecedented rise in the computer speed and memory transformed the personal computer into an affordable machine capable of combining audio and color video in advanced ways.

- Another element is the release of Windows 3.0 in 1990 by Microsoft into the mainstream IBM clone world. It accelerated the acceptance of GUI as the standard mechanism for communicating with small computer systems.

- The development by NV Philips of optical digital technologies built around the compact disk (CD) in 1979 is also another leading element in the interactive media development as it raised the issue of developing interactive media.

All of the prior elements contributed in the development of the main hardware and software systems used in interactive media.

Terminology

Though the word *media* is plural, the term is often used as a singular noun.

Interactive media is related to the concepts interaction design, new media, interactivity, human computer interaction, cyberculture, digital culture, interactive design, and includes augmented reality.

An essential feature of interactivity is that it is mutual: user and machine each take an active role. Most interactive computing systems are for some human purpose and interact with humans in human contexts. Manovich complains that 'In relation to computer-based media, the concept of interactivity is a tautology. .... Therefore, to call computer media "interactive" is meaningless – it simply means stating the most basic fact about computers.' Nevertheless, the term is useful to denote an identifiable body of practices and technologies.

Interactive media are an instance of a computational method influenced by the sciences of cybernetics, autopoiesis and system theories, and challenging notions of reason and cognition, perception and memory, emotions and affection.

Any form of interface between the end user/audience and the medium may be considered interactive. Interactive media is not limited to electronic media or digital media. Board games, pop-up books, gamebooks, flip books and constellation wheels are all examples of printer interactive media. Books with a simple table of contents or index may be considered interactive due to the non-linear control mechanism in the medium, but are usually considered non-interactive since the majority of the user experience is non-interactive reading.

Advantages

Effects on Learning

Interactive media is helpful in the following four development dimensions in which young children learn: social and emotional, language development, cognitive and general knowledge, and approaches toward learning. Using computers and educational computer software in a learning environment helps children increase communication skills and their attitudes about learning. Children who use educational computer software are often found using more complex speech patterns and higher levels of verbal communication. A study found that basic interactive books that simply read a story aloud and highlighted words and phrases as they were spoken were beneficial for children with lower reading abilities. Children have different styles of learning, and interactive media helps children with visual, verbal, auditory, and tactile learning styles.

Intuitive Understanding

Interactive media makes technology more intuitive to use. Interactive products such as smartphones, iPad's/iPod's, interactive whiteboards and websites are all easy to use. The easy usage of these products encourages consumers to experiment with their products rather than reading instruction manuals.

Relationships

Interactive media promotes dialogic communication. This form of communication allows senders and receivers to build long term trust and cooperation. This plays a critical role in building relationships. Organizations also use interactive media to go further than basic marketing and develop more positive behavioral relationships.

Types

Distributed Interactive Media

The media which allows several geographically remote users to interact synchronously with the media application/system is known as Distributed Interactive Media. Some common examples of this type of Media include Online Gaming, Distributed Virtual Environment, Whiteboards which are used for interactive conferences and many more.

Examples

A couple of basic examples of interactive media are video games and websites. Websites, especially social networking websites provide the interactive use of text and graphics to its users, who interact with each other in various ways such as chatting, playing online games, sharing posts that may include their thoughts and/or pictures and so forth. Video games are also one of the common examples of Interactive Media as the players make use of the joystick/controller to interactively respond to the actions and changes taking place on the game screen generated by the game application, which in turn reacts to the response of the players through the joystick/controller.

Technologies for Implementation

Interactive media can be implemented in a wide variety of platforms and applications encompassing virtually all areas of technology. Some examples include mobile platforms such as touch screen smartphones and tablets, was well as other interactive mediums that are created exclusively to solve a unique problem or set of problems. Interactive media is not limited to a certain field of IT, it instead encompasses any technology that supplies for movie parts or feedback based on the users actions. This can include javascript and AJAX utilization in web pages, but can further be extended to any programming languages that share the same or similar functionality. One of the most recent innovations to supply for interactivity to solve a problem the plagues individuals on a daily bases is Delta Airlines "Photon Shower." This device was developed from Delta's collaboration with Professor Russell Foster of Cambridge University. The device is designed to reduce the effect of jet lag on customers that often take long flights across time zones. The systems interactivity is evident because of the way in which it solves this commonplace problem.. By observing what time zones a person has crossed and matching those to the basic known sleep cycles of the individual, the machine is able to predict when a persons body is expecting light, and when it is expecting darkness. It then bombards the individual with the appropriate light source variations for the time, as well as an instructional card to inform them of what times their body expects light and what times it expects darkness.Growth of interactive media continues to advance today, with the advent of more and more powerful machines the limit to what can be input and manipulated on a display in real time is become virtually non-existent.

Multimedia Signal

So, are we now in a position to formally define a multimedia signal? At first, let us digress from multimedia and only try to define "signal". Signal is something that varies with respect to time and/or space, or with respect to some other quantity and represents something that is meaningful. It is very difficult, if not impossible to arrive at a definition that is complete, but we can accept the above definition to ease our understanding. If we can accept the above definition of "signal", we can attempt to define "multimedia signal" in the following way:

A multimedia signal is one that integrates signals from several media sources, such as video, audio, graphics, animation, text in a meaningful way to convey some information.

In the above definition, the stress is on the word "meaningful". For example, you may pick up different words at random from a dictionary one after the other and try to compose a sentence, but we can't call it a sentence unless it conveys a meaning. Same is the case with "multimedia signal". We can't just create a random mixture of audio, video, graphics, animation etc. in any manner we like and claim it to be a multimedia presentation. The integration of different media must be done with some definite objective. And then, just like definite grammatical rules must be followed in a sentence, integration of different media must necessarily follow some rules and regulations, which are specified in the standards.

Elements of Multimedia Communication Systems

For multimedia communication, we have to make judicious use of all the media at our disposal. We have audio, video, graphics, texts - all these media as the sources, but first and foremost, we need a system which can acquire the separate media streams, process them together to make it an integrated multimedia stream.

Devices like cameras, microphones, keyboards, mouse, touch-screens, storage medium etc. are required to feed inputs from different sources. All further processing till the transmission is done by the computer. The data acquisition from multiple media is followed by data compression to eliminate inherent redundancies present in the media streams. This is followed by inter-media synchronization by insertion of time-stamps, integration of individual media streams and finally the transmission of integrated multimedia stream through a communication channel, which can be a wired or a wireless medium.

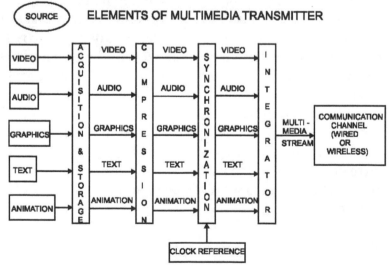

Elements of Multimedia Transmitter

The destination end should have a corresponding interface to receive the integrated multimedia stream through the communication channel. At the receiver, a reversal of the processes involved during transmission is required.

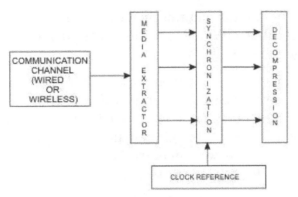

Elements of multimedia receiver

The media extractor separates the integrated media stream into individual media streams, which undergoes de-compression and then presented in a synchronized manner according to their time-stamps in different playback units, such as monitors, loudspeakers, printers/plotters, recording devices etc.

Challenges in Multimedia Communication

Today, multimedia communication is no longer a dream, but a reality, although the technology is yet to reach its maturity. It has become possible to overcome some challenges, but still many challenges remains to be solved satisfactorily. The challenges involved with multimedia communication are listed below:

(i)   Bandwidth limitations of communication channels.

(ii) Real-time processing requirements.

(iii) Inter-media synchronization.

(iv) Intra-media continuity.

(v)   End-to-end delays and delay jitters.

(vi) Multimedia indexing and retrieval.

We now discuss each of these points separately and understand the technical aspects of these challenges.

Bandwidth Limitations

Limited bandwidth of communication channels poses the most serious challenge in multimedia communication. Some of the media streams, such as video sequences, large-sized still images, even stereo quality audio require large volumes of data to be transmitted in a short-time, considering real-time requirements. A few typical examples will make things clear.

Suppose, we want to transmit a color image of 1024 x 768 picture elements (called pixels, or pels) through a telephone channel, supported with modem, having a speed of 14.4 Kbits/second. Assuming 24-bits for each pixel, i.e., 8-bits for each color components (Red, Green and Blue), the total number of bits to be transmitted for the entire image is given by

Total number of bits, B = 1024 x 768 x 24 = 18.8 x 10^6

Therefore, the total time required to transmit this image is ($18.8 \times 10^3 / 14.4$), i.e., approximately 22 minutes, which is excessively high. The total time will be halved, if we double the modem speed, but 11 minutes of transmission time is still too high.

Let us now consider the example of a video sequence to be used for video conferencing. We consider a fairly small frame size of 352 x 288 pixels and a colored video sequence having 24-bits / pixel, acquired at a frame rate of 30 frames per second, which is to be transmitted through a leased line of bandwidth 384 Kbits/second. From the given data, the raw video bit rate is (352 x 288 x 24 x 30), i.e., 72.9 Mbits/second. Hence, we cannot transmit the video through the given channel bandwidth, unless the data is significantly compressed.

The actual situation is not as bad as we may conclude from the above discussions.

You can observe that most of the pixels have almost the same intensity as those of the neighbors. Only at the boundaries of the objects, the intensities change significantly. Thus, there is considerable redundancy present in the images, since the pixels are spatially correlated to a great extent. If this redundancy could be exploited, significant data compression can be achieved.

We can observe that the redundancies are not only present within a frame (which we can call as the spatial redundancy), but also between successive frames (which can call as the temporal redundancy).

Can you now see that the successive frames are very similar to each other? It is because of the fact that between successive frame time, only a limited movement of the moving objects is possible and if the background is stationary, then most of the pixels do not exhibit any change at all between successive frames. In this example, you can only see lip movements and eye movements between successive frames. Thus, although the data to be handled is much more in video, there is a scope to exploit both spatial and temporal redundancy.

We are definitely convinced that data compression is an essential requirement for images and video. In case of CD-quality stereo audio sampled at 44.1 KHz, the raw data rate is 192 Kbps, which is also somewhat high, if we consider leased line bandwidth or wireless channel bandwidth. Hence, audio compression is also a requirement. Other media streams (text, graphics, animation etc) have relatively less data content in most of the applications and may not require compression.

However, we should not think that we can perform data compression to whatever extent possible. Most of the data compression techniques that achieve significant compression are irreversible. These therefore lead to loss of data and quality degradation. There is always a trade-off that is present between compression, i.e, bandwidth reduction and quality.

Real-time Processing Requirements

Whichever techniques we may adopt to exploit the redundancies and achieve data compression, significant amount of processing will be involved. If the processing time is high, the advantage of data compression may be lost. In our still image example, if we are able to achieve a compression of 20:1, the entire image can be transmitted in one minute. If however, the processing time to achieve this compression had been in the order of minutes (imagine that a very old computer of the `60s is used to do the processing), the advantage of compression would have been lost. Challenges are much more in the case of video. Video frames are captured at a rate of 30 frames per second and this leaves a time of 33 milliseconds between successive frames. Hence, video compression and whatever additional processing are required, needs to be completed within one frame time. This is very often the problem. Although today's processors, operating at GHz rate are extraordinarily fast, quite often even such high speed processors are unable to perform real-time processing and high-speed, dedicated parallel processing hardware may be required. Development of multimedia processing hardware with real-time capability is a highly challenging research topic of today.

Inter-media Synchronization

As already outlined briefly, inter-media synchronization is another challenging requirement in multimedia communication. The media streams are available from different and independent sources and are asynchronous with respect to each other. Lack of lip-synchronization is a commonly observed problem in multimedia systems involving audio and video. Lack of synchronization between the different media may even defeat the purpose of multimedia presentation. Multimedia standards have addressed this problem and adopted "time-stamping" to ensure synchronization. Time-stamps, with respect to a system clock reference (SCR) are appended with the different media (audio, video etc) packets before integrating the individual streams into a multimedia one. At the receiver end, the individual media streams are decoded and presented to the playback units in accordance with the time-stamps obtained from the pack and packet headers.

Intra-media Continuity

The extent of data compression with acceptable reconstruction quality is highly data-dependent. Wherever redundancy is more, high compression ratios are achievable, but redundancy may vary. Take the example of a video sequence. Each frame will undergo different extent of compression and this in turn will vary the bit rate (i.e., the number of bits to be transmitted per second) from one frame to the other. If we use a channel that supports constant bit rate, accommodating a variable bit rate source will be a challenging task. This is achieved by providing a buffer before the bit-stream generation. The buffer may be filled up at variable rate, but emptied during transmission at a constant rate. One must therefore ensure that at no instant should the buffer be completely emptied and the channel starves for data (this is known as buffer underflow problem). On the other hand, at no instant should the buffer be completely filled up and further incoming data is lost (this is known as buffer overflow problem). In both these extreme situations of buffer overflow and underflow, the continuity is lost during presentation. The question is, to what extent can we tolerate such discontinuities? This depends upon the medium under consideration. If it is a video and you occasionally lose a frame, your eyes may not even notice that, whereas any discontinuity in the audio stream will be immediately detected by your ears. It is because our ears are more sensitive than our eyes as the ultimate detector. We can say that it is easy to fool our eyes, but it is not easy to fool our ears.

However, it must not be misunderstood that intra-media discontinuity can happen only due to the buffer overflow / underflow problems. It may happen because of inadequate processing speed, packet loss, channel errors and many other conditions.

End-to-end Delays and Delay Jitters

This is yet another important consideration. In a multimedia broadcast or multimedia conferencing, if the users receive the multimedia contents after considerable delays or different users receive the same contents at different times, the interactivity is lost. The multimedia standards available till date have addressed this problem and specified what is acceptable.

Multimedia Indexing and Retrieval

As the price of digital storage media decreases, the storage capacity increases and multimedia applications gain more popularity, there is a requirement to store large number of multimedia files. Unless these files are properly indexed, retrieval of desired multimedia file becomes a tough task, in view of the search complexities. If the multimedia files are based on their contents and then a content-based query system is developed, efficient retrieval can be obtained. Often, for quick browsing of multimedia files, video summaries are needed and automated generation of video summaries is a very challenging task. All these issues are being addressed in the upcoming MPEG-7 multimedia standards.

2

A Comprehensive Study of Image Compression

Image compression is a form of data compression by the use of which photos can be made compact. To compress an image, redundancies are exploited. If an image has fewer details, it implies that it has more redundancies and hence can be made more compact than an image with more details. Images with textures have less redundancy and its compression is comparatively difficult. This section discusses the methods of image compression system in a critical manner providing key analysis to the subject matter.

Image Compression

Image compression is a type of data compression applied to digital images, to reduce their cost for storage or transmission. Algorithms may take advantage of visual perception and the statistical properties of image data to provide superior results compared to generic compression methods.

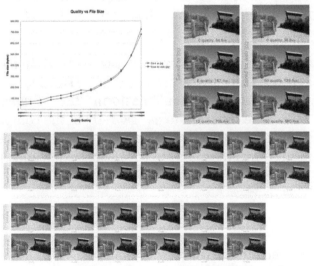

Comparison of JPEG images saved by Adobe Photoshop at
different quality levels and with or without "save for web"

Lossy and Lossless Image Compression

Image compression may be lossy or lossless. Lossless compression is preferred for archival purposes and often for medical imaging, technical drawings, clip art, or comics. Lossy compression methods, especially when used at low bit rates, introduce compression artifacts. Lossy methods are especially suitable for natural images such as photographs in applications where minor (sometimes imperceptible) loss of fidelity is acceptable to achieve a substantial reduction in bit rate. Lossy compression that produces negligible differences may be called visually lossless.

Methods for lossless image compression are:

- Run-length encoding – used in default method in PCX and as one of possible in BMP, TGA, TIFF

- Area image compression

- DPCM and Predictive Coding

- Entropy encoding

- Adaptive dictionary algorithms such as LZW – used in GIF and TIFF

- Deflation – used in PNG, MNG, and TIFF

- Chain codes

Methods for lossy compression:

- Reducing the color space to the most common colors in the image. The selected colors are specified in the color palette in the header of the compressed image. Each pixel just references the index of a color in the color palette, this method can be combined with dithering to avoid posterization.

- Chroma subsampling. This takes advantage of the fact that the human eye perceives spatial changes of brightness more sharply than those of color, by averaging or dropping some of the chrominance information in the image.

- Transform coding. This is the most commonly used method. In particular, a Fourier-related transform such as the Discrete Cosine Transform (DCT) is widely used: N. Ahmed, T. Natarajan and K.R.Rao, "Discrete Cosine Transform," *IEEE Trans. Computers*, 90-93, Jan. 1974. The DCT is sometimes referred to as "DCT-II" in the context of a family of discrete cosine transforms; e.g., discrete cosine transform. The more recently developed wavelet transform is also used extensively, followed by quantization and entropy coding.

- Fractal compression.

Other Properties

The best image quality at a given bit-rate (or compression rate) is the main goal of image compression, however, there are other important properties of image compression schemes:

Scalability generally refers to a quality reduction achieved by manipulation of the bitstream or file (without decompression and re-compression). Other names for scalability are *progressive coding* or *embedded bitstreams*. Despite its contrary nature, scalability also may be found in lossless codecs, usually in form of coarse-to-fine pixel scans. Scalability is especially useful for previewing images while downloading them (e.g., in a web browser) or for providing variable quality access to e.g., databases. There are several types of scalability:

- Quality progressive or layer progressive: The bitstream successively refines the reconstructed image.

- Resolution progressive: First encode a lower image resolution; then encode the difference to higher resolutions.

- Component progressive: First encode grey; then color.

Region of interest coding. Certain parts of the image are encoded with higher quality than others. This may be combined with scalability (encode these parts first, others later).

Meta information. Compressed data may contain information about the image which may be used to categorize, search, or browse images. Such information may include color and texture statistics, small preview images, and author or copyright information.

Processing power. Compression algorithms require different amounts of processing power to encode and decode. Some high compression algorithms require high processing power.

The quality of a compression method often is measured by the Peak signal-to-noise ratio. It measures the amount of noise introduced through a lossy compression of the image, however, the subjective judgment of the viewer also is regarded as an important measure, perhaps, being the most important measure.

Redundancies

As already discussed, image compression is largely possible by exploiting various kinds of redundancies which are typically present in an image. The extent of redundancies may vary from image to image.

(A) Image at the left has less details and more Redundancy than the image at the right

It may be observed that Fig B has much higher degree of details and hence less redundancies, as compared to Fig A. Example of two synthetic images will exaggerate the situation.

To represent an image without incurring any loss of data, we need to include only the following information:

- Background intensity.

- Foreground intensity.

- Size and position of the foreground object.

If the intensity levels are represented by one byte, size (height and width) by two bytes and position (x-y coordinates of a reference corner point) by two bytes, we require just 6 bytes of data, as compared to the original 256 x 256 pixel array, consisting of 65536 bytes. In this case, very high compression is achievable. Now, look at Fig C. It is a synthetically generated random-dot image. Can you perceive any redundancy? There is hardly any It is not possible to predict any pixel from its immediate neighbors. To represent this image without incurring any loss, we need to include each pixel value individually and hence, there is no redundancy.

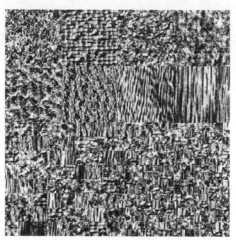

(B) Texture image examples. Contains less redundancy

Natural images however are not as complex as that of Fig C. Definitely, the extent of redundancy varies from image to image.

(C) Random Dot Image

Classification of Redundancies

Redundancies in images may be categorized as follows –

Statistical Redundancy

Statistical redundancy occurs due to the fact that pixels within an image tend to have very similar intensities as those of its neighborhood, except at the object boundaries or illumination changes. For still images, statistical redundancies are essentially spatial in nature. For natural two-dimensional images, redundancies are present along both the x- and y-dimensions. Video signals exhibit yet another form of statistical redundancy and that is temporal. For video, intensities of same pixel positions across successive frames tend to be very similar, unless there is large amount of motion present. In this chapter however, we focus our attention to only one form of statistical redundancy and that is spatial redundancies of images. Presence of statistical redundancies in natural images allows efficient representation in the transformed output.

Psychovisual Redundancy

Psychovisual redundancy arises due to the problem of perception. Our eyes are more responsive to slow and gradual changes of illumination than perceiving finer details and rapid changes of intensities. Hence, to what extent we should preserve the details for our perception and to what extent we can compromise on the quality of reconstructed image that we perceive is essentially carried out by exploiting the psychovisual redundancy. Psychovisual redundancy has been well studied and its exploitation has been included within the multimedia standards.

Lossy Compression

Low compression (high quality) JPEG   High compression (low quality) JPEG

In information technology, lossy compression or irreversible compression is the class of data encoding methods that uses inexact approximations and partial data discarding to represent the content. These techniques are used to reduce data size for storage, handling, and transmitting content. Different versions of the photo of the cat above show how higher degrees of approximation create coarser images as more details are removed. This is opposed to lossless data compression (reversible data compression) which does not degrade the data. The amount of data reduction possible using lossy compression is often much higher than through lossless techniques.

Well-designed lossy compression technology often reduces file sizes significantly before degradation is noticed by the end-user. Even when noticeable by the user, further data reduction may be desirable (e.g., for real-time communication, to reduce transmission times, or to reduce storage needs).

Lossy compression is most commonly used to compress multimedia data (audio, video, and images), especially in applications such as streaming media and internet telephony. By contrast, lossless compression is typically required for text and data files, such as bank records and text articles. In many cases it is advantageous to make a master lossless file which is to be used to produce new compressed files; for example, a multi-megabyte file can be used at full size to produce a full-page advertisement in a glossy magazine, and a 10 kilobyte lossy copy can be made for a small image on a web page.

Types

It is possible to compress many types of digital data in a way that reduces the size of a computer file needed to store it, or the bandwidth needed to transmit it, with no loss of the full information contained in the original file. A picture, for example, is converted to a digital file by considering it to be an array of dots and specifying the color and brightness of each dot. If the picture contains an area of the same color, it can be compressed without loss by saying "200 red dots" instead of "red dot, red dot, ...(197 more times)..., red dot."

The original data contains a certain amount of information, and there is a lower limit to the size of file that can carry all the information. Basic information theory says that there is an absolute limit in reducing the size of this data. When data is compressed, its entropy increases, and it cannot increase indefinitely. As an intuitive example, most people know that a compressed ZIP file is smaller than the original file, but repeatedly compressing the same file will not reduce the size to nothing. Most compression algorithms can recognize when further compression would be pointless and would in fact increase the size of the data.

In many cases, files or data streams contain more information than is needed for a particular purpose. For example, a picture may have more detail than the eye can distinguish when reproduced at the largest size intended; likewise, an audio file does not need a lot of fine detail during a very loud passage. Developing lossy compression techniques as closely matched to human perception as possible is a complex task. Sometimes the ideal is a file that provides exactly the same perception as the original, with as much digital information as possible removed; other times, perceptible loss of quality is considered a valid trade-off for the reduced data.

The terms 'irreversible' and 'reversible' are preferred over 'lossy' and 'lossless' respectively for some applications, such as medical image compression, to circumvent the negative implications of 'loss'. The type and amount of loss can affect the utility of the images. Artifacts or undesirable effects of compression may be clearly discernible yet the result still useful for the intended purpose. Or lossy compressed images may be 'visually lossless', or in the case of medical images, so-called Diagnostically Acceptable Irreversible Compression (DAIC) may have been applied.

Transform Coding

More generally, some forms of lossy compression can be thought of as an application of *transform coding* – in the case of multimedia data, *perceptual coding:* it transforms the raw data to a domain that more accurately reflects the information content. For example, rather than expressing a sound file as the amplitude levels over time, one may express it as the frequency spectrum over time, which corresponds more accurately to human audio perception. While data reduction (compression, be it lossy or lossless) is a main goal of transform coding, it also allows other goals: one may represent data more accurately for the original amount of space – for example, in principle, if one starts with an analog or high-resolution digital master, an MP3 file of a given size should provide a better representation than a raw uncompressed audio in WAV or AIFF file of the same size. This is because uncompressed audio can only reduce file size by lowering bit rate or depth, whereas compressing audio can reduce size while maintaining bit rate and depth. This compression becomes a selective loss of the least significant data, rather than losing data across the board. Further, a transform coding may provide a better domain for manipulating or otherwise editing the data – for example, equalization of audio is most naturally expressed in the frequency domain (boost the bass, for instance) rather than in the raw time domain.

From this point of view, perceptual encoding is not essentially about *discarding* data, but rather about a *better representation* of data. Another use is for backward compatibility and graceful degradation: in color television, encoding color via a luminance-chrominance transform domain (such as YUV) means that black-and-white sets display the luminance, while ignoring the color information. Another example is chroma subsampling: the use of color spaces such as YIQ, used in NTSC, allow one to reduce the resolution on the components to accord with human perception – humans have highest resolution for black-and-white (luma), lower resolution for mid-spectrum colors like yellow and green, and lowest for red and blues – thus NTSC displays approximately 350 pixels of luma per scanline, 150 pixels of yellow vs. green, and 50 pixels of blue vs. red, which are proportional to human sensitivity to each component.

Information Loss

Lossy compression formats suffer from generation loss: repeatedly compressing and decompressing the file will cause it to progressively lose quality. This is in contrast with lossless data compression, where data will not be lost via the use of such a procedure. Information-theoretical foundations for lossy data compression are provided by rate-distortion theory. Much like the use of probability in optimal coding theory, rate-distortion theory heavily draws on Bayesian estimation and decision theory in order to model perceptual distortion and even aesthetic judgment.

There are two basic lossy compression schemes:

- In *lossy transform codecs*, samples of picture or sound are taken, chopped into small segments, transformed into a new basis space, and quantized. The resulting quantized values are then entropy coded.

- In *lossy predictive codecs*, previous and/or subsequent decoded data is used to predict the current sound sample or image frame. The error between the predicted data and the real data, together with any extra information needed to reproduce the prediction, is then quantized and coded.

In some systems the two techniques are combined, with transform codecs being used to compress the error signals generated by the predictive stage.

Comparison

The advantage of lossy methods over lossless methods is that in some cases a lossy method can produce a much smaller compressed file than any lossless method, while still meeting the requirements of the application. Lossy methods are most often used for compressing sound, images or videos. This is because these types of data are intended for human interpretation where the mind can easily "fill in the blanks" or see past very minor errors or inconsistencies – ideally lossy compression is transparent (imperceptible), which can be verified via an ABX test. Data files using lossy compression are smaller in size and thus cost less to store and to transmit over the Internet, a crucial consideration for streaming video services such as Netflix and streaming audio services such as Spotify.

Transparency

When a user acquires a lossily compressed file, (for example, to reduce download time) the retrieved file can be quite different from the original at the bit level while being indistinguishable to the human ear or eye for most practical purposes. Many compression methods focus on the idiosyncrasies of human physiology, taking into account, for instance, that the human eye can see only certain wavelengths of light. The psychoacoustic model describes how sound can be highly compressed without degrading perceived quality. Flaws caused by lossy compression that are noticeable to the human eye or ear are known as compression artifacts.

Compression Ratio

The compression ratio (that is, the size of the compressed file compared to that of the uncompressed file) of lossy video codecs is nearly always far superior to that of the audio and still-image equivalents.

- Video can be compressed immensely (e.g. 100:1) with little visible quality loss

- Audio can often be compressed at 10:1 with imperceptible loss of quality

- Still images are often lossily compressed at 10:1, as with audio, but the quality loss is more noticeable, especially on closer inspection.

Transcoding and Editing

An important caveat about lossy compression (formally transcoding), is that editing lossily compressed files causes digital generation loss from the re-encoding. This can be avoided by only producing lossy files from (lossless) originals and only editing (copies of) original files, such as images in raw image format instead of JPEG. If data which has been compressed lossily is decoded and compressed losslessly, the size of the result can be comparable with the size of the data before lossy compression, but the data already lost cannot be recovered. When deciding to use lossy conversion without keeping the original, one should remember that format conversion may be needed in the future to achieve compatibility with software or devices (format shifting), or to avoid paying patent royalties for decoding or distribution of compressed files.

Editing of Lossy Files

By modifying the compressed data directly without decoding and re-encoding, some editing of lossily compressed files without degradation of quality is possible. Editing which reduces the file size as if it had been compressed to a greater degree, but without more loss than this, is sometimes also possible.

JPEG

The primary programs for lossless editing of JPEGs are `jpegtran`, and the derived `exiftran` (which also preserves Exif information), and Jpegcrop (which provides a Windows interface).

These allow the image to be

- cropped

- rotated, flipped, and flopped, or

- converted to grayscale (by dropping the chrominance channel).

While unwanted information is destroyed, the quality of the remaining portion is unchanged.

Some other transforms are possible to some extent, such as joining images with the same encoding (composing side by side, as on a grid) or pasting images (such as logos) onto existing images (both via Jpegjoin), or scaling.

Some changes can be made to the compression without re-encoding:

- optimizing the compression (to reduce size without change to the decoded image)

- converting between progressive and non-progressive encoding.

The freeware Windows-only IrfanView has some lossless JPEG operations in its JPG_TRANS-FORM plugin.

Metadata

Metadata, such as ID3 tags, Vorbis comments, or Exif information, can usually be modified or removed without modifying the underlying data.

Downsampling/Compressed Representation Scalability

One may wish to downsample or otherwise decrease the resolution of the represented source signal and the quantity of data used for its compressed representation without re-encoding, as in bitrate peeling, but this functionality is not supported in all designs, as not all codecs encode data in a form that allows less important detail to simply be dropped. Some well-known designs that have this capability include JPEG 2000 for still images and H.264/MPEG-4 AVC based Scalable Video Coding for video. Such schemes have also been standardized for older designs as well, such as JPEG images with progressive encoding, and MPEG-2 and MPEG-4 Part 2 video, although those prior schemes had limited success in terms of adoption into real-world common usage. Without this capacity, which is often the case in practice, to produce a representation with lower resolution or lower fidelity than a given one, one needs to start with the original source signal and encode, or start with a compressed representation and then decompress and re-encode it (transcoding), though the latter tends to cause digital generation loss.

Another approach is to encode the original signal at several different bitrates, and their either choose which to use (as when streaming over the internet – as in RealNetworks' "SureStream"

– or offering varying downloads, as at Apple's iTunes Store), or broadcast several, where the best that is successfully received is used, as in various implementations of hierarchical modulation. Similar techniques are used in mipmaps, pyramid representations, and more sophisticated scale space methods. Some audio formats feature a combination of a lossy format and a lossless correction which when combined reproduce the original signal; the correction can be stripped, leaving a smaller, lossily compressed, file. Such formats include MPEG-4 SLS (Scalable to Lossless), WavPack, OptimFROG DualStream, and DTS-HD Master Audio in lossless (XLL) mode.

Methods

Image

- Cartesian Perceptual Compression, also known as CPC

- DjVu

- Fractal compression

- ICER, used by the Mars Rovers, related to JPEG 2000 in its use of wavelets

- JBIG2 (lossless or lossy compression)

- JPEG

- JPEG 2000, JPEG's successor format that uses wavelets (lossless or lossy compression)

- JPEG XR, another successor of JPEG with support for high dynamic range, wide gamut pixel formats (lossless or lossy compression)

- PGF, Progressive Graphics File (lossless or lossy compression)

- S3TC texture compression for 3D computer graphics hardware

- Wavelet compression

Video

- Motion JPEG

- MPEG-1 Part 2

- MPEG-2 Part 2

- MPEG-4 Part 2

- H.264/MPEG-4 AVC (may also be lossless, even in certain video sections)

- Ogg Theora (noted for its lack of patent restrictions)

- Dirac

- Sorenson video codec

- VC-1
- H.265/HEVC

Audio

- Opus (mostly for real-time applications)

Music

- AAC
- ADPCM
- ATRAC
- Dolby Digital (AC-3)
- MP2
- MP3
- Musepack (based on Musicam)
- Ogg Vorbis (noted for its lack of patent restrictions)
- WMA (Lossless codec available too)

Speech

- Adaptive Multi-Rate (Used in GSM and 3GPP)
- Codec2 (noted for its lack of patent restrictions)
- Speex (noted for its lack of patent restrictions)

Other Data

Researchers have (semi-seriously) performed lossy compression on text by either using a thesaurus to substitute short words for long ones, or generative text techniques, although these sometimes fall into the related category of lossy data conversion.

Lowering Resolution

A general kind of lossy compression is to lower the resolution of an image, as in image scaling, particularly decimation. One may also remove less "lower information" parts of an image, such as by seam carving. Many media transforms, such as Gaussian blur, are, like lossy compression, irreversible: the original signal cannot be reconstructed from the transformed signal. However, in general these will have the same size as the original, and are not a form of compression. Lowering resolution has practical uses, as the NASA New Horizons craft will transmit thumbnails of its encounter with Pluto-Charon before it sends the higher resolution images. Another solution for slow connections is the usage of Image interlacing which progressively defines the image. Thus a partial transmission is enough to preview the final image, in a lower resolution version, without creating a scaled and a full version too.

Lossless Compression

Lossless compression is a class of data compression algorithms that allows the original data to be perfectly reconstructed from the compressed data. By contrast, lossy compression permits reconstruction only of an approximation of the original data, though this usually improves compression rates (and therefore reduces file sizes).

Lossless data compression is used in many applications. For example, it is used in the ZIP file format and in the GNU tool gzip. It is also often used as a component within lossy data compression technologies (e.g. lossless mid/side joint stereo preprocessing by the LAME MP3 encoder and other lossy audio encoders).

Lossless compression is used in cases where it is important that the original and the decompressed data be identical, or where deviations from the original data could be deleterious. Typical examples are executable programs, text documents, and source code. Some image file formats, like PNG or GIF, use only lossless compression, while others like TIFF and MNG may use either lossless or lossy methods. Lossless audio formats are most often used for archiving or production purposes, while smaller lossy audio files are typically used on portable players and in other cases where storage space is limited or exact replication of the audio is unnecessary.

Lossless Compression Techniques

Most lossless compression programs do two things in sequence: the first step generates a *statistical model* for the input data, and the second step uses this model to map input data to bit sequences in such a way that "probable" (e.g. frequently encountered) data will produce shorter output than "improbable" data.

The primary encoding algorithms used to produce bit sequences are Huffman coding (also used by DEFLATE) and arithmetic coding. Arithmetic coding achieves compression rates close to the best possible for a particular statistical model, which is given by the information entropy, whereas Huffman compression is simpler and faster but produces poor results for models that deal with symbol probabilities close to 1.

There are two primary ways of constructing statistical models: in a *static* model, the data is analyzed and a model is constructed, then this model is stored with the compressed data. This approach is simple and modular, but has the disadvantage that the model itself can be expensive to store, and also that it forces using a single model for all data being compressed, and so performs poorly on files that contain heterogeneous data. *Adaptive* models dynamically update the model as the data is compressed. Both the encoder and decoder begin with a trivial model, yielding poor compression of initial data, but as they learn more about the data, performance improves. Most popular types of compression used in practice now use adaptive coders.

Lossless compression methods may be categorized according to the type of data they are designed to compress. While, in principle, any general-purpose lossless compression algorithm (*general-purpose* meaning that they can accept any bitstring) can be used on any type of data, many are unable to achieve significant compression on data that are not of the form for which they were designed to compress. Many of the lossless compression techniques used for text also work reasonably well for indexed images.

Multimedia

These techniques take advantage of the specific characteristics of images such as the common phenomenon of contiguous 2-D areas of similar tones. Every pixel but the first is replaced by the difference to its left neighbor. This leads to small values having a much higher probability than large values. This is often also applied to sound files, and can compress files that contain mostly low frequencies and low volumes. For images, this step can be repeated by taking the difference to the top pixel, and then in videos, the difference to the pixel in the next frame can be taken.

A hierarchical version of this technique takes neighboring pairs of data points, stores their difference and sum, and on a higher level with lower resolution continues with the sums. This is called discrete wavelet transform. JPEG2000 additionally uses data points from other pairs and multiplication factors to mix them into the difference. These factors must be integers, so that the result is an integer under all circumstances. So the values are increased, increasing file size, but hopefully the distribution of values is more peaked.

The adaptive encoding uses the probabilities from the previous sample in sound encoding, from the left and upper pixel in image encoding, and additionally from the previous frame in video encoding. In the wavelet transformation, the probabilities are also passed through the hierarchy.

Historical Legal Issues

Many of these methods are implemented in open-source and proprietary tools, particularly LZW and its variants. Some algorithms are patented in the United States and other countries and their legal usage requires licensing by the patent holder. Because of patents on certain kinds of LZW compression, and in particular licensing practices by patent holder Unisys that many developers considered abusive, some open source proponents encouraged people to avoid using the Graphics Interchange Format (GIF) for compressing still image files in favor of Portable Network Graphics (PNG), which combines the LZ77-based deflate algorithm with a selection of domain-specific prediction filters. However, the patents on LZW expired on June 20, 2003.

Many of the lossless compression techniques used for text also work reasonably well for indexed images, but there are other techniques that do not work for typical text that are useful for some images (particularly simple bitmaps), and other techniques that take advantage of the specific characteristics of images (such as the common phenomenon of contiguous 2-D areas of similar tones, and the fact that color images usually have a preponderance of a limited range of colors out of those representable in the color space).

As mentioned previously, lossless sound compression is a somewhat specialized area. Lossless sound compression algorithms can take advantage of the repeating patterns shown by the wave-like nature of the data – essentially using autoregressive models to predict the "next" value and encoding the (hopefully small) difference between the expected value and the actual data. If the difference between the predicted and the actual data (called the *error*) tends to be small, then certain difference values (like 0, +1, −1 etc. on sample values) become very frequent, which can be exploited by encoding them in few output bits.

It is sometimes beneficial to compress only the differences between two versions of a file (or, in video compression, of successive images within a sequence). This is called delta encoding (from the Greek letter Δ, which in mathematics, denotes a difference), but the term is typically only used if both versions are meaningful outside compression and decompression. For example, while the process of compressing the error in the above-mentioned lossless audio compression scheme could be described as delta encoding from the approximated sound wave to the original sound wave, the approximated version of the sound wave is not meaningful in any other context.

Lossless Compression Methods

By operation of the pigeonhole principle, no lossless compression algorithm can efficiently compress all possible data. For this reason, many different algorithms exist that are designed either with a specific type of input data in mind or with specific assumptions about what kinds of redundancy the uncompressed data are likely to contain.

Some of the most common lossless compression algorithms are listed below.

General Purpose

- Run-length encoding (RLE) – Simple scheme that provides good compression of data containing lots of runs of the same value

- Huffman coding – Pairs well with other algorithms, used by Unix's pack utility

- Prediction by partial matching (PPM) – Optimized for compressing plain text

- bzip2 – Combines Burrows–Wheeler transform with RLE and Huffman coding

- Lempel-Ziv compression (LZ77 and LZ78) – Dictionary-based algorithm that forms the basis for many other algorithms

  o DEFLATE – Combines Lempel-Ziv compression with Huffman coding, used by ZIP, gzip, and PNG images

  o Lempel–Ziv–Markov chain algorithm (LZMA) – Very high compression ratio, used by 7zip and xz

  o Lempel–Ziv–Oberhumer (LZO) – Designed for compression/decompression speed at the expense of compression ratios

  o Lempel–Ziv–Storer–Szymanski (LZSS) – Used by WinRAR in tandem with Huffman coding

  o Lempel–Ziv–Welch (LZW) – Used by GIF images and Unix's compress utility

Audio

- Apple Lossless (ALAC - Apple Lossless Audio Codec)
- Adaptive Transform Acoustic Coding (ATRAC)
- apt-X Lossless
- Audio Lossless Coding (also known as MPEG-4 ALS)
- Direct Stream Transfer (DST)
- Dolby TrueHD
- DTS-HD Master Audio
- Free Lossless Audio Codec (FLAC)
- Meridian Lossless Packing (MLP)
- Monkey's Audio (Monkey's Audio APE)
- MPEG-4 SLS (also known as HD-AAC)
- OptimFROG
- Original Sound Quality (OSQ)
- RealPlayer (RealAudio Lossless)
- Shorten (SHN)
- TTA (True Audio Lossless)
- WavPack (WavPack lossless)
- WMA Lossless (Windows Media Lossless)

Graphics

- PNG – Portable Network Graphics
- TIFF – Tagged Image File Format
- WebP – (high-density lossless or lossy compression of RGB and RGBA images)
- BPG – Better Portable Graphics (lossless/lossy compression based on HEVC)
- FLIF – Free Lossless Image Format
- JPEG-LS – (lossless/near-lossless compression standard)
- TGA - Truevision TGA
- PCX - PiCture eXchange
- JPEG 2000 – (includes lossless compression method, as proven by Sunil Kumar, Prof San Diego State University)

- JPEG XR – formerly *WMPhoto* and *HD Photo*, includes a lossless compression method
- ILBM – (lossless RLE compression of Amiga IFF images)
- JBIG2 – (lossless or lossy compression of B&W images)
- PGF – Progressive Graphics File (lossless or lossy compression)

3D Graphics

- OpenCTM – Lossless compression of 3D triangle meshes

Cryptography

Cryptosystems often compress data (the "plaintext") *before* encryption for added security. When properly implemented, compression greatly increases the unicity distance by removing patterns that might facilitate cryptanalysis. However, many ordinary lossless compression algorithms produce headers, wrappers, tables, or other predictable output that might instead make cryptanalysis easier. Thus, cryptosystems must utilize compression algorithms whose output does not contain these predictable patterns.

Genetics

Genetics compression algorithms are the latest generation of lossless algorithms that compress data (typically sequences of nucleotides) using both conventional compression algorithms and specific algorithms adapted to genetic data. In 2012, a team of scientists from Johns Hopkins University published the first genetic compression algorithm that does not rely on external genetic databases for compression. HAPZIPPER was tailored for HapMap data and achieves over 20-fold compression (95% reduction in file size), providing 2- to 4-fold better compression and in much faster time than the leading general-purpose compression utilities.

Executables

Self-extracting executables contain a compressed application and a decompressor. When executed, the decompressor transparently decompresses and runs the original application. This is especially often used in demo coding, where competitions are held for demos with strict size limits, as small as 1k. This type of compression is not strictly limited to binary executables, but can also be applied to scripts, such as JavaScript.

Lossless Compression Benchmarks

Lossless compression algorithms and their implementations are routinely tested in head-to-head benchmarks. There are a number of better-known compression benchmarks. Some benchmarks cover only the data compression ratio, so winners in these benchmarks may be unsuitable for everyday use due to the slow speed of the top performers. Another drawback of some benchmarks is that their data files are known, so some program writers may optimize their programs for best performance on a particular data set. The winners on these benchmarks often come from the class of context-mixing compression software.

The benchmarks listed in the 5th edition of the *Handbook of Data Compression* (Springer, 2009) are:

- The Maximum Compression benchmark, started in 2003 and updated until November 2011, includes over 150 programs. Maintained by Werner Bergmans, it tests on a variety of data sets, including text, images, and executable code. Two types of results are reported: single file compression (SFC) and multiple file compression (MFC). Not surprisingly, context mixing programs often win here; programs from the PAQ series and WinRK often are in the top. The site also has a list of pointers to other benchmarks.

- UCLC (the ultimate command-line compressors) benchmark by Johan de Bock is another actively maintained benchmark including over 100 programs. The winners in most tests usually are PAQ programs and WinRK, with the exception of lossless audio encoding and grayscale image compression where some specialized algorithms shine.

- Squeeze Chart by Stephan Busch is another frequently updated site.

- The EmilCont benchmarks by Berto Destasio are somewhat outdated having been most recently updated in 2004. A distinctive feature is that the data set is not public, to prevent optimizations targeting it specifically. Nevertheless, the best ratio winners are again the PAQ family, SLIM and WinRK.

- The Archive Comparison Test (ACT) by Jeff Gilchrist included 162 DOS/Windows and 8 Macintosh lossless compression programs, but it was last updated in 2002.

- The Art Of Lossless Data Compression by Alexander Ratushnyak provides a similar test performed in 2003.

Matt Mahoney, in his February 2010 edition of the free booklet *Data Compression Explained*, additionally lists the following:

- The Calgary Corpus dating back to 1987 is no longer widely used due to its small size. Matt Mahoney currently maintains the Calgary Compression Challenge , created and maintained from May 21, 1996 through May 21, 2016 by Leonid A. Broukhis .

- The Large Text Compression Benchmark and the similar Hutter Prize both use a trimmed Wikipedia XML UTF-8 data set.

- The Generic Compression Benchmark, maintained by Mahoney himself, test compression on random data.

- Sami Runsas (author of NanoZip) maintains Compression Ratings, a benchmark similar to Maximum Compression multiple file test, but with minimum speed requirements. It also offers a calculator that allows the user to weight the importance of speed and compression ratio. The top programs here are fairly different due to speed requirement. In January 2010, the top programs were NanoZip followed by FreeArc, CCM, flashzip, and 7-Zip.

- The Monster of Compression benchmark by N. F. Antonio tests compression on 1Gb of public data with a 40-minute time limit. As of Dec. 20, 2009 the top ranked archiver is NanoZip 0.07a and the top ranked single file compressor is ccmx 1.30c, both context mixing.

Compression Ratings publishes a chart summary of the "frontier" in compression ratio and time.

The Compression Analysis Tool is a Windows application that enables end users to benchmark the performance characteristics of streaming implementations of LZF4, DEFLATE, ZLIB, GZIP, BZIP2 and LZMA using their own data. It produces measurements and charts with which users can compare the compression speed, decompression speed and compression ratio of the different compression methods and to examine how the compression level, buffer size and flushing operations affect the results.

The Squash Compression Benchmark uses the Squash library to compare more than 25 compression libraries in many different configurations using numerous different datasets on several different machines, and provides a web interface to help explore the results. There are currently over 50,000 results to compare.

Limitations

Lossless data compression algorithms cannot guarantee compression for all input data sets. In other words, for any lossless data compression algorithm, there will be an input data set that does not get smaller when processed by the algorithm, and for any lossless data compression algorithm that makes at least one file smaller, there will be at least one file that it makes larger. This is easily proven with elementary mathematics using a counting argument, as follows:

- Assume that each file is represented as a string of bits of some arbitrary length.

- Suppose that there is a compression algorithm that transforms every file into an output file that is no longer than the original file, and that at least one file will be compressed into an output file that is shorter than the original file.

- Let M be the least number such that there is a file F with length M bits that compresses to something shorter. Let N be the length (in bits) of the compressed version of F.

- Because $N<M$, every file of length N keeps its size during compression. There are 2^N such files. Together with F, this makes 2^N+1 files that all compress into one of the 2^N files of length N.

- But 2^N is smaller than 2^N+1, so by the pigeonhole principle there must be some file of length N that is simultaneously the output of the compression function on two different inputs. That file cannot be decompressed reliably (which of the two originals should that yield?), which contradicts the assumption that the algorithm was lossless.

- We must therefore conclude that our original hypothesis (that the compression function makes no file longer) is necessarily untrue.

Any lossless compression algorithm that makes some files shorter must necessarily make some files longer, but it is not necessary that those files become *very much* longer. Most practical compression algorithms provide an "escape" facility that can turn off the normal coding for files that would become longer by being encoded. In theory, only a single additional bit is required to tell the decoder that the normal coding has been turned off for the entire input; however, most encoding algorithms use at least one full byte (and typically more than one) for this purpose. For example, DEFLATE compressed files never need to grow by more than 5 bytes per 65,535 bytes of input.

In fact, if we consider files of length N, if all files were equally probable, then for any lossless compression that reduces the size of some file, the expected length of a compressed file (averaged over all possible files of length N) must necessarily be *greater* than N. So if we know nothing about the properties of the data we are compressing, we might as well not compress it at all. A lossless compression algorithm is useful only when we are more likely to compress certain types of files than others; then the algorithm could be designed to compress those types of data better.

Thus, the main lesson from the argument is not that one risks big losses, but merely that one cannot always win. To choose an algorithm always means implicitly to select a *subset* of all files that will become usefully shorter. This is the theoretical reason why we need to have different compression algorithms for different kinds of files: there cannot be any algorithm that is good for all kinds of data.

The "trick" that allows lossless compression algorithms, used on the type of data they were designed for, to consistently compress such files to a shorter form is that the files the algorithms are designed to act on all have some form of easily modeled redundancy that the algorithm is designed to remove, and thus belong to the subset of files that that algorithm can make shorter, whereas other files would not get compressed or even get bigger. Algorithms are generally quite specifically tuned to a particular type of file: for example, lossless audio compression programs do not work well on text files, and vice versa.

In particular, files of random data cannot be consistently compressed by any conceivable lossless data compression algorithm: indeed, this result is used to *define* the concept of randomness in algorithmic complexity theory.

It's provably impossible to create an algorithm that can losslessly compress any data. While there have been many claims through the years of companies achieving "perfect compression" where an arbitrary number N of random bits can always be compressed to $N - 1$ bits, these kinds of claims can be safely discarded without even looking at any further details regarding the purported compression scheme. Such an algorithm contradicts fundamental laws of mathematics because, if it existed, it could be applied repeatedly to losslessly reduce any file to length 0. Allegedly "perfect" compression algorithms are often derisively referred to as "magic" compression algorithms for this reason.

On the other hand, it has also been proven that there is no algorithm to determine whether a file is incompressible in the sense of Kolmogorov complexity. Hence it's possible that any particular file, even if it appears random, may be significantly compressed, even including the size of the decompressor. An example is the digits of the mathematical constant *pi*, which appear random but can be generated by a very small program. However, even though it cannot be determined whether a particular file is incompressible, a simple theorem about incompressible strings shows that over 99% of files of any given length cannot be compressed by more than one byte (including the size of the decompressor).

Mathematical Background

Abstractly, a compression algorithm can be viewed as a function on sequences (normally of octets). Compression is successful if the resulting sequence is shorter than the original sequence (and the instructions for the decompression map). For a compression algorithm to be lossless, the compression map must form an injection from "plain" to "compressed" bit sequences.

The pigeonhole principle prohibits a bijection between the collection of sequences of length N and any subset of the collection of sequences of length $N-1$. Therefore, it is not possible to produce an algorithm that reduces the size of every possible input sequence.

Psychological Background

Most everyday files are relatively 'sparse' in an information entropy sense, and thus, most lossless algorithms a layperson is likely to apply on regular files compress them relatively well. This may, through misapplication of intuition, lead some individuals to conclude that a well-designed compression algorithm can compress *any* input, thus, constituting a *magic compression algorithm*.

Points of Application in Real Compression Theory

Real compression algorithm designers accept that streams of high information entropy cannot be compressed, and accordingly, include facilities for detecting and handling this condition. An obvious way of detection is applying a raw compression algorithm and testing if its output is smaller than its input. Sometimes, detection is made by heuristics; for example, a compression application may consider files whose names end in ".zip", ".arj" or ".lha" uncompressible without any more sophisticated detection. A common way of handling this situation is quoting input, or uncompressible parts of the input in the output, minimizing the compression overhead. For example, the zip data format specifies the 'compression method' of 'Stored' for input files that have been copied into the archive verbatim.

The Million Random Number Challenge

Mark Nelson, in response to claims of magic compression algorithms appearing in comp.compression, has constructed a 415,241 byte binary file of highly entropic content, and issued a public challenge of $100 to anyone to write a program that, together with its input, would be smaller than his provided binary data yet be able to reconstitute it without error.

The FAQ for the comp.compression newsgroup contains a challenge by Mike Goldman offering $5,000 for a program that can compress random data. Patrick Craig took up the challenge, but rather than compressing the data, he split it up into separate files all of which ended in the number 5, which was not stored as part of the file. Omitting this character allowed the resulting files (plus, in accordance with the rules, the size of the program that reassembled them) to be smaller than the original file. However, no actual compression took place, and the information stored in the names of the files was necessary to reassemble them in the correct order in the original file, and this information was not taken into account in the file size comparison. The files themselves are thus not sufficient to reconstitute the original file; the file names are also necessary. Patrick Craig agreed that no meaningful compression had taken place, but argued that the wording of the challenge did not actually require this. A full history of the event, including discussion on whether or not the challenge was technically met, is on Patrick Craig's web site.

Measuring the Quality of Reconstructed Images

The reconstructed images obtained through lossy compression/de-compression schemes are never exactly the same as the original. The simplest measure often employed to measure the quality of such reconstructed images is *Mean Square Error (MSE)*. For an M x N original image array $f(i,j)$, where i and j are the row and column indices, ($i=0,1,......,M-1$; $j=0,1,......,N-1$), if $f'(i,j)$ is the reconstructed image array of the same size, the *MSE* is given by

$$MSE = \frac{1}{MN} \sum_{i=0}^{M-1} \sum_{j=0}^{N-1} \left[f(i,j) - f'(i,j) \right]^2$$

The mean squared error essentially measures the noise in the reconstruction. The reconstruction quality is also measured with Signal-to-Noise Ratio (SNR) and the Peak Signal-to-Noise Ratio (PSNR). In the former, the noise power is measured with respect to the actual signal power, whereas in the latter, the noise power is measured with respect to the peak signal power, considering the intensities in the range of 0-255. These measures are given by

$$SNR = 20 \log_{10} \frac{\sum_{i=0}^{M-1} \sum_{j=0}^{N-1} \left[f(i,j) \right]^2}{\sum_{i=0}^{M-1} \sum_{j=0}^{N-1} \left[f(i,j) - f'(i,j) \right]^2}$$

$$PSNR = 20 \log_{10} \frac{255^2 MN}{\sum_{i=0}^{M-1} \sum_{j=0}^{N-1} \left[f(i,j) - f'(i,j) \right]^2}.$$

Both these measures are expressed in the units of decibels (dB). It may however be noted that these measures often do not correspond well to the perceptual quality, but in absence of any perceptual measure, which is essentially subjective in nature, one can use these measures to judge the quality of reconstruction.

Elements of Image Compression System

Due to the high degree of statistical (spatial) and psychovisual redundancies present in a natural image, it can be compressed without significant degradation of the visual quality. A typical image compression system consists of the following elements –

(a) Transformer,   (b) quantizer and   (c) coder.

An image compression system is often referred to in the literature as image encoder.

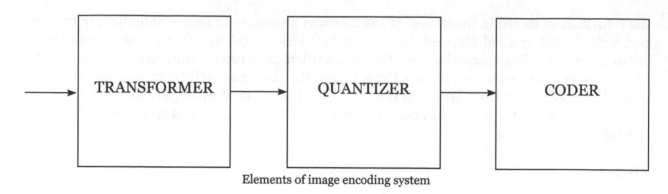

Elements of image encoding system

The roles of these blocks are explained below.

Transformer

This block transforms the original input data into a form that is more amenable to compression. The transformation can be local, involving pixels in the neighbourhood or global, involving the full image or a block of pixels. Global transformation techniques use Discrete Fourier Transforms (DFT), Discrete Cosine Transforms (DCT), Karhunen-Love Transforms (KLT), Discrete Wavelet Transforms (DWT) etc, which we are going to discuss in the subsequent lessons. The transformer block transforms the original spatial domain signal into another spatial domain signal of reduced dynamic range, as is done in DPCM or into the transform domain, where only a few coefficients contain bulk of the energy and efficient compression is possible. Please note that this block in itself does not perform any compression and is lossless.

Quantizer

The quantizer follows the transformer block in image compression systems and generates a limited number of symbols that can be used in the representation of the transformed signal. It is a many-to-one mapping which is irreversible. Quantizers are of two basic types-

(i)   Scalar quantization – refers to element-by-element quantization of data

(ii)   Vector quantization - refers to quantization of a block at a time. Quantization exploits psychovisual redundancy and achieves significant bit reduction. It is the only block in image compression system, which is lossy.

Coder

Coders assign a code word, a binary bit-stream, to each symbol at the output of the quantizer. The coder may employ

(i)   Fixed-length coding (FLC), which have codeword length fixed, irrespective of the probabilities of occurrence of quantized symbols or,

(ii)   Variable length coding (VLC), also known as entropy coding, assigns code words in such a way as to minimize the average length of the binary representation of the symbols. This is achieved by assigning shorter code words to the more probable symbols.

Source Entropy

Generation of information is generally modeled as a random process that has probability associated with it. If P(E) is the probability of an event, its information content I(E), also known as self information is measured as

$$I(E) = log\frac{1}{P(E)} \quad \text{(A)}$$

If P(E)=1, that is, the event always occurs (like saying "The sun rises in the east"), then we obtain from above that I(E)=0, which means that there is no information associated with it. The base of the logarithm expresses the unit of information and if the base is 2, the unit is bits. For other values m of the base, the information is expressed as m-ary units. Unless otherwise mentioned, we shall be using the base-2 system to measure information content.

Now, suppose that we have an alphabet of n symbols $\{a_i \mid i = 1,2,......,n\}$ having probabilities of occurrences $P(a_1), P(a_2),......, P(a_n)$. If k is the number of source outputs generated, which is considered to be sufficiently large, then the average number of occurrences of symbol a_i is $kP(a_i)$ obtained from k outputs is given by

$$-k\sum_{i=1}^{n} P(a_i)\log P(a_i)$$

and the average information per source output for the source z is given by

$$H(z) = -\sum_{i=1}^{n} P(a_i)\log P(a_i) \quad \text{(B)}$$

The above quantity is defined as the *entropy* of the source and measures the uncertainty of the source. The relationship between uncertainty and entropy can be illustrated by a simple example of two symbols a_1 and a_2 having probabilities $P(a_1)$ and $P(a_2)$ respectively. Since, the summation of probabilities is equal to 1, $P(a_2) = 1 - P(a_1)$ and using equation (B), we obtain

$$H(z) = -P(a_1)\log P(a_1) - (1 - P(a_1))\log(1 - P(a_1)) \quad \text{(C)}$$

If we plot H(z) versus $P(a_1)$, we obtain the graph shown in the figure.

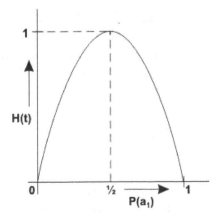

It is interesting to note that the entropy is equal to zero for $P(a_1)=0$ and $P(a_1)=1$. These correspond to the cases where at least one of the two symbols is certain to be present. $H(z)$ assumes maximum value of 1-bit for $P(a_1)=1/2$. This corresponds to the most uncertain case, where both the symbols are equally probable.

Example: Measurement of source entropy

If the probabilities of the source symbols are known, the *source entropy* can be measured using equation above. Say, we have five symbols the a_1, a_2,...,a_5 following probabilities:

$$P(a_1) = 0.2, \, P(a_2) = 0.1, \, P(a_3) = 0.05, \, P(a_4) = 0.6, \, P(a_5) = 0.05$$

Using equation above, the source entropy is given by

$$H(z) = -0.2 \log 0.2 - 0.1 \log 0.1 - 0.05 \log 0.05 - 0.6 \log 0.6 - 0.05 \log 0.05 \text{ bits}$$

$$= 1.67 \text{ bits}$$

Shannon's Source Coding Theorem

In information theory, Shannon's source coding theorem (or noiseless coding theorem) establishes the limits to possible data compression, and the operational meaning of the Shannon entropy.

The source coding theorem shows that (in the limit, as the length of a stream of independent and identically-distributed random variable (i.i.d.) data tends to infinity) it is impossible to compress the data such that the code rate (average number of bits per symbol) is less than the Shannon entropy of the source, without it being virtually certain that information will be lost. However it is possible to get the code rate arbitrarily close to the Shannon entropy, with negligible probability of loss.

The source coding theorem for symbol codes places an upper and a lower bound on the minimal possible expected length of codewords as a function of the entropy of the input word (which is viewed as a random variable) and of the size of the target alphabet.

Statements

Source coding is a mapping from (a sequence of) symbols from an information source to a sequence of alphabet symbols (usually bits) such that the source symbols can be exactly recovered from the binary bits (lossless source coding) or recovered within some distortion (lossy source coding). This is the concept behind data compression.

Source Coding Theorem

In information theory, the source coding theorem (Shannon 1948) informally states that (MacKay 2003,Chapter 5):

N i.i.d. random variables each with entropy $H(X)$ can be compressed into more than $NH(X)$ bits with negligible risk of information loss, as $N \to \infty$; but conversely, if they are compressed into fewer than $NH(X)$ bits it is virtually certain that information will be lost.

Source Coding Theorem for Symbol Codes

Let Σ_1, Σ_2 denote two finite alphabets and let Σ_1^* and Σ_2^* denote the set of all finite words from those alphabets (respectively).

Suppose that X is a random variable taking values in Σ_1 and let f be a uniquely decodable code from Σ_1^* to Σ_2^* where $|\Sigma_2| = a$. Let S denote the random variable given by the word length $f(X)$.

If f is optimal in the sense that it has the minimal expected word length for X, then (Shannon 1948):

$$\frac{H(X)}{\log_2 a} \leq \mathbb{E}S < \frac{H(X)}{\log_2 a} + 1$$

Proof: Source Coding Theorem

Given X is an i.i.d. source, its time series $X_1, ..., X_n$ is i.i.d. with entropy $H(X)$ in the discrete-valued case and differential entropy in the continuous-valued case. The Source coding theorem states that for any $\varepsilon > 0$ for any rate larger than the entropy of the source, there is large enough n and an encoder that takes n i.i.d. repetition of the source, $X^{1:n}$, and maps it to $n(H(X) + \varepsilon)$ binary bits such that the source symbols $X^{1:n}$ are recoverable from the binary bits with probability at least $1 - \varepsilon$.

Proof of Achievability. Fix some $\varepsilon > 0$, and let

$$p(x_1, ..., x_n) = \Pr\left[X_1 = x_1, \cdots, X_n = x_n\right].$$

The typical set, A_n^ε, is defined as follows:

$$A_n^\varepsilon = \{(x_1, \cdots, x_n) : \left|-\frac{1}{n}\log p(x_1, \cdots, x_n) - H_n(X)\right| < \varepsilon\}.$$

The Asymptotic Equipartition Property (AEP) shows that for large enough n, the probability that a sequence generated by the source lies in the typical set, A_n^ε, as defined approaches one. In particular, for sufficiently large n, $P((X_1, X_2, \cdots, X_n) \in A_n^\varepsilon)$ can be made arbitrarily close to 1, and specifically, greater than $1 - \varepsilon$.

The definition of typical sets implies that those sequences that lie in the typical set satisfy:

$$2^{-n(H(X)+\varepsilon)} \leq p\left(x_1, \cdots, x_n\right) \leq 2^{-n(H(X)-\varepsilon)}$$

Note that:

- The probability of a sequence $(X_1, X_2, \cdots X_n)$ being drawn from A_n^ε is greater than $1 - \varepsilon$.

- $\left|A_n^\varepsilon\right| \leq 2^{n(H(X)+\varepsilon)}$, which follows from the left hand side (lower bound) for $p(x_1, x_2, \cdots x_n)$.

- $\left|A_n^\varepsilon\right| \geq (1-\varepsilon)2^{n(H(X)-\varepsilon)}$, which follows from upper bound for $p(x_1, x_2, \cdots x_n)$ and the lower bound on the total probability of the whole set A_n^ε.

Since $\left|A_n^\varepsilon\right| \leq 2^{n(H(X)+\varepsilon)}$, $n.(H(X)+\varepsilon)$ bits are enough to point to any string in this set.

The encoding algorithm: The encoder checks if the input sequence lies within the typical set; if yes, it outputs the index of the input sequence within the typical set; if not, the encoder outputs an arbitrary $n(H(X)+\varepsilon)$ digit number. As long as the input sequence lies within the typical set (with probability at least $1-\varepsilon$), the encoder doesn't make any error. So, the probability of error of the encoder is bounded above by ε.

Proof of Converse. The converse is proved by showing that any set of size smaller than A_n^ε (in the sense of exponent) would cover a set of probability bounded away from 1.

Proof: Source Coding Theorem for Symbol Codes

For $1 \leq i \leq n$ let s_i denote the word length of each possible x_i. Define $q_i = a^{-s_i}/C$, where C is chosen so that $q_1 + ... + q_n = 1$. Then

$$H(X) = -\sum_{i=1}^{n} p_i \log_2 p_i$$

$$\leq -\sum_{i=1}^{n} p_i \log_2 q_i$$

$$= -\sum_{i=1}^{n} p_i \log_2 a^{-s_i} + \sum_{i=1}^{n} p_i \log_2 C$$

$$= -\sum_{i=1}^{n} p_i \log_2 a^{-s_i} + \log_2 C$$

$$\leq -\sum_{i=1}^{n} -s_i p_i \log_2 a$$

$$\leq \mathbb{E}S \log_2 a$$

where the second line follows from Gibbs' inequality and the fifth line follows from Kraft's inequality:

$$C = \sum_{i=1}^{n} a^{-s_i} \leq 1$$

so $\log C \leq 0$.

For the second inequality we may set

$$s_i = \lceil -\log_a p_i \rceil$$

so that

$$-\log_a p_i \leq s_i < -\log_a p_i + 1$$

and so

$$a^{-s_i} \leq p_i$$

and

$$\sum a^{-s_i} \leq \sum p_i = 1$$

and so by Kraft's inequality there exists a prefix-free code having those word lengths. Thus the minimal S satisfies

$$
\begin{aligned}
\mathbb{E}S &= \sum p_i s_i \\
&< \sum p_i \left(-\log_a p_i + 1\right) \\
&= \sum -p_i \frac{\log_2 p_i}{\log_2 a} + 1 \\
&= \frac{H(X)}{\log_2 a} + 1
\end{aligned}
$$

Extension to Non-stationary Independent Sources

Fixed Rate Lossless Source Coding for Discrete Time Non-stationary Independent Sources

Define typical set A_n^ε as:

$$
A_n^\varepsilon = \{x_1^n : \left|-\frac{1}{n}\log p\left(X_1, \cdots, X_n\right) - \overline{H}_n(X)\right| < \varepsilon\}.
$$

Then, for given $\delta > 0$, for n large enough, $\Pr(A_n^\varepsilon) > 1 - \delta$. Now we just encode the sequences in the typical set, and usual methods in source coding show that the cardinality of this set is smaller than $2^{n(\overline{H}_n(X)+\varepsilon)}$. Thus, on an average, $\overline{H}_n(X) + \varepsilon$ bits suffice for encoding with probability greater than $1 - \delta$, where ε and δ can be made arbitrarily small, by making n larger.

Huffman Coding

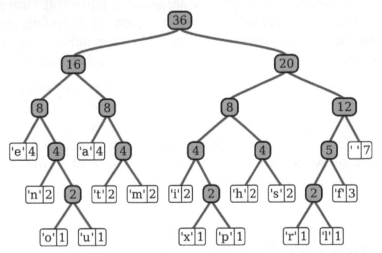

Huffman tree generated from the exact frequencies of the text "this is an example of a huffman tree". The frequencies and codes of each character are below. Encoding the sentence with this code requires 135 bits, as opposed to 288 (or 180) bits if 36 characters of 8 (or 5) bits were used. (This assumes that the code tree structure is known to the decoder and thus does not need to be counted as part of the transmitted information.)

Char	Freq	Code
space	7	111
a	4	010
e	4	000
f	3	1101
h	2	1010
i	2	1000
m	2	0111
n	2	0010
s	2	1011
t	2	0110
l	1	11001
o	1	00110
p	1	10011
r	1	11000
u	1	00111
x	1	10010

In computer science and information theory, a Huffman code is a particular type of optimal prefix code that is commonly used for lossless data compression. The process of finding and/or using such a code proceeds by means of Huffman coding, an algorithm developed by David A. Huffman while he was a Sc.D. student at MIT, and published in the 1952 paper "A Method for the Construction of Minimum-Redundancy Codes".

The output from Huffman's algorithm can be viewed as a variable-length code table for encoding a source symbol (such as a character in a file). The algorithm derives this table from the estimated probability or frequency of occurrence (*weight*) for each possible value of the source symbol. As in other entropy encoding methods, more common symbols are generally represented using fewer bits than less common symbols. Huffman's method can be efficiently implemented, finding a code in time linear to the number of input weights if these weights are sorted. However, although optimal among methods encoding symbols separately, Huffman coding is not always optimal among all compression methods.

Specifically, Huffman coding is optimal only if the probabilities of symbols are natural powers of 1/2. This is usually not the case. As an example, a symbol of probability 0.99 carries only $\log_2(1/0.99) \approx 0.014$ bits of information, but Huffman coding encodes each symbol separately and therefore the minimum length for each symbol is 1 bit. This sub-optimality is repaired in arithmetic coding and recent faster Asymmetric Numeral Systems family of entropy codings.

History

In 1951, David A. Huffman and his MIT information theory classmates were given the choice of a term paper or a final exam. The professor, Robert M. Fano, assigned a term paper on the problem of finding the most efficient binary code. Huffman, unable to prove any codes were the most efficient, was about to give up and start studying for the final when he hit upon the idea of using a frequency-sorted binary tree and quickly proved this method the most efficient.

In doing so, Huffman outdid Fano, who had worked with information theory inventor Claude Shannon to develop a similar code. By building the tree from the bottom up instead of the top down, Huffman avoided the major flaw of the suboptimal Shannon-Fano coding.

Terminology

Huffman coding uses a specific method for choosing the representation for each symbol, resulting in a prefix code (sometimes called "prefix-free codes", that is, the bit string representing some particular symbol is never a prefix of the bit string representing any other symbol). Huffman coding is such a widespread method for creating prefix codes that the term "Huffman code" is widely used as a synonym for "prefix code" even when such a code is not produced by Huffman's algorithm.

Problem Definition

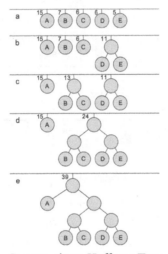

Constructing a Huffman Tree

Informal Description

Given

A set of symbols and their weights (usually proportional to probabilities).

Find

A prefix-free binary code (a set of codewords) with minimum expected codeword length (equivalently, a tree with minimum weighted path length from the root).

Formalized Description

Input

Alphabet $A = \{a_1, a_2, \cdots, a_n\}$, which is the symbol alphabet of size n.

Set $W = \{w_1, w_2, \cdots, w_n\}$, which is the set of the (positive) symbol weights (usually proportional to probabilities), i.e. $w_i = \text{weight}(a_i), 1 \le i \le n.$.

Output

Code $C(A,W) = (c_1, c_2, \cdots, c_n)$, which is the tuple of (binary) codewords, where c_i is the codeword for $a_i, 1 \le i \le n.$

Goal

Let $L(C) = \sum_{i=1}^{n} w_i \times \text{length}(c_i)$ be the weighted path length of code C. Condition: $L(C) \le L(T)$ for any code $T(A,W)$.

Example

We give an example of the result of Huffman coding for a code with five characters and given weights. We will not verify that it minimizes L over all codes, but we will compute L and compare it to the Shannon entropy H of the given set of weights; the result is nearly optimal.

Input (A, W)	Symbol (a_i)	a	b	c	d	e	**Sum**
	Weights (w_i)	0.10	0.15	0.30	0.16	0.29	= 1
Output C	Codewords (c_i)	010	011	11	00	10	
	Codeword length (in bits) (l_i)	3	3	2	2	2	
	Contribution to weighted path length ($l_i w_i$)	0.30	0.45	0.60	0.32	0.58	$L(C) = 2.25$
Optimality	Probability budget (2^{-l_i})	1/8	1/8	1/4	1/4	1/4	= 1.00
	Information content (in bits) ($-\log_2 w_i$) ≈	3.32	2.74	1.74	2.64	1.79	
	Contribution to entropy ($-w_i \log_2 w_i$)	0.332	0.411	0.521	0.423	0.518	$H(A) = 2.205$

For any code that is *biunique*, meaning that the code is *uniquely decodeable*, the sum of the probability budgets across all symbols is always less than or equal to one. In this example, the sum is strictly equal to one; as a result, the code is termed a *complete* code. If this is not the case, you can always derive an equivalent code by adding extra symbols (with associated null probabilities), to make the code complete while keeping it *biunique*.

As defined by Shannon (1948), the information content h (in bits) of each symbol a_i with non-null probability is

$$h(a_i) = \log_2 \frac{1}{w_i}.$$

The entropy H (in bits) is the weighted sum, across all symbols a_i with non-zero probability w_i, of the information content of each symbol:

$$H(A) = \sum_{w_i>0} w_i h(a_i) = \sum_{w_i>0} w_i \log_2 \frac{1}{w_i} = -\sum_{w_i>0} w_i \log_2 w_i.$$

(Note: A symbol with zero probability has zero contribution to the entropy, since $\lim_{w\to 0^+} w\log_2 w = 0$ So for simplicity, symbols with zero probability can be left out of the formula above.)

As a consequence of Shannon's source coding theorem, the entropy is a measure of the smallest codeword length that is theoretically possible for the given alphabet with associated weights. In this example, the weighted average codeword length is 2.25 bits per symbol, only slightly larger than the calculated entropy of 2.205 bits per symbol. So not only is this code optimal in the sense that no other feasible code performs better, but it is very close to the theoretical limit established by Shannon.

In general, a Huffman code need not be unique. Thus the set of Huffman codes for a given probability distribution is a non-empty subset of the codes minimizing $L(C)$ for that probability distribution. (However, for each minimizing codeword length assignment, there exists at least one Huffman code with those lengths.)

Basic Technique

Compression

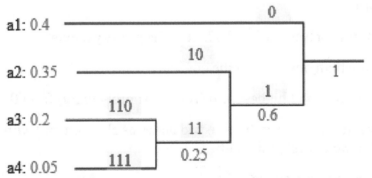

A source generates 4 different symbols $\{a_1, a_2, a_3, a_4\}$ with probability $\{0.4; 0.35; 0.2; 0.05\}$. A binary tree is generated from left to right taking the two least probable symbols and putting them together to form another equivalent symbol having a probability that equals the sum of the two symbols. The process is repeated until there is just one symbol. The tree can then be read backwards, from right to left, assigning different bits to different branches. The final Huffman code is:

Symbol	Code
a1	0
a2	10
a3	110
a4	111

The standard way to represent a signal made of 4 symbols is by using 2 bits/symbol, but the entropy of the source is 1.74 bits/symbol. If this Huffman code is used to represent the signal, then the average length is lowered to 1.85 bits/symbol; it is still far from the theoretical limit because the probabilities of the symbols are different from negative powers of two.

The technique works by creating a binary tree of nodes. These can be stored in a regular array, the size of which depends on the number of symbols, n. A node can be either a leaf node or an internal node. Initially, all nodes are leaf nodes, which contain the symbol itself, the weight (frequency of appearance) of the symbol and optionally, a link to a parent node which makes it easy to read the code (in reverse) starting from a leaf node. Internal nodes contain a weight, links to two child nodes and an optional link to a parent node. As a common convention, bit '0' represents following the left child and bit '1' represents following the right child. A finished tree has up to n leaf nodes and $n-1$ internal nodes. A Huffman tree that omits unused symbols produces the most optimal code lengths.

The process begins with the leaf nodes containing the probabilities of the symbol they represent. Then, the process takes the two nodes with smallest probability, and creates a new internal node having these two nodes has children. The weight of the new node is set to the sum of the weight of the children. We then apply the process again, on the new internal node and on the remaining nodes (i.e., we exclude the two leaf nodes), we repeat this process until only one node remains, which is the root of the Huffman tree.

The simplest construction algorithm uses a priority queue where the node with lowest probability is given highest priority:

1. Create a leaf node for each symbol and add it to the priority queue.

2. While there is more than one node in the queue:

    •   Remove the two nodes of highest priority (lowest probability) from the queue

    •   Create a new internal node with these two nodes as children and with probability equal to the sum of the two nodes' probabilities.

    •   Add the new node to the queue.

3. The remaining node is the root node and the tree is complete.

Since efficient priority queue data structures require O(log n) time per insertion, and a tree with n leaves has $2n-1$ nodes, this algorithm operates in O(n log n) time, where n is the number of symbols.

If the symbols are sorted by probability, there is a linear-time (O(n)) method to create a Huffman tree using two queues, the first one containing the initial weights (along with pointers to the associated leaves), and combined weights (along with pointers to the trees) being put in the back of the second queue. This assures that the lowest weight is always kept at the front of one of the two queues:

1. Start with as many leaves as there are symbols.

2. Enqueue all leaf nodes into the first queue (by probability in increasing order so that the least likely item is in the head of the queue).

3. While there is more than one node in the queues:

- Dequeue the two nodes with the lowest weight by examining the fronts of both queues.

- Create a new internal node, with the two just-removed nodes as children (either node can be either child) and the sum of their weights as the new weight.

- Enqueue the new node into the rear of the second queue.

4. The remaining node is the root node; the tree has now been generated.

Although linear-time given sorted input, in the general case of arbitrary input, using this algorithm requires pre-sorting. Thus, since sorting takes $O(n \log n)$ time in the general case, both methods have the same overall complexity.

In many cases, time complexity is not very important in the choice of algorithm here, since n here is the number of symbols in the alphabet, which is typically a very small number (compared to the length of the message to be encoded); whereas complexity analysis concerns the behavior when n grows to be very large.

It is generally beneficial to minimize the variance of codeword length. For example, a communication buffer receiving Huffman-encoded data may need to be larger to deal with especially long symbols if the tree is especially unbalanced. To minimize variance, simply break ties between queues by choosing the item in the first queue. This modification will retain the mathematical optimality of the Huffman coding while both minimizing variance and minimizing the length of the longest character code.

Decompression

Generally speaking, the process of decompression is simply a matter of translating the stream of prefix codes to individual byte values, usually by traversing the Huffman tree node by node as each bit is read from the input stream (reaching a leaf node necessarily terminates the search for that particular byte value). Before this can take place, however, the Huffman tree must be somehow reconstructed. In the simplest case, where character frequencies are fairly predictable, the tree can be preconstructed (and even statistically adjusted on each compression cycle) and thus reused every time, at the expense of at least some measure of compression efficiency. Otherwise, the information to reconstruct the tree must be sent a priori. A naive approach might be to prepend the frequency count of each character to the compression stream. Unfortunately, the overhead in such a case could amount to several kilobytes, so this method has little practical use. If the data is compressed using canonical encoding, the compression model can be precisely reconstructed with just $B2^B$ bits of information (where B is the number of bits per symbol). Another method is to simply prepend the Huffman tree, bit by bit, to the output stream. For example, assuming that the value of 0 represents a parent node and 1 a leaf node, whenever the latter is encountered the tree building routine simply reads the next 8 bits to determine the character value of that particular leaf. The process continues recursively until the last leaf node is reached; at that point, the Huffman tree will thus be faithfully reconstructed. The overhead using such a method ranges from roughly 2 to 320 bytes (assuming an 8-bit alphabet). Many other techniques are possible as well. In any case, since the compressed data can include unused "trailing bits" the decompressor must be able to determine when to stop producing output.

This can be accomplished by either transmitting the length of the decompressed data along with the compression model or by defining a special code symbol to signify the end of input (the latter method can adversely affect code length optimality, however).

Main Properties

The probabilities used can be generic ones for the application domain that are based on average experience, or they can be the actual frequencies found in the text being compressed. This requires that a frequency table must be stored with the compressed text.

Optimality

Although Huffman's original algorithm is optimal for a symbol-by-symbol coding (i.e., a stream of unrelated symbols) with a known input probability distribution, it is not optimal when the symbol-by-symbol restriction is dropped, or when the probability mass functions are unknown. Also, if symbols are not independent and identically distributed, a single code may be insufficient for optimality. Other methods such as arithmetic coding and LZW coding often have better compression capability: Both of these methods can combine an arbitrary number of symbols for more efficient coding, and generally adapt to the actual input statistics, useful when input probabilities are not precisely known or vary significantly within the stream. However, these methods have higher computational complexity. Also, both arithmetic coding and LZW were historically a subject of some concern over patent issues. However, as of mid-2010, the most commonly used techniques for these alternatives to Huffman coding have passed into the public domain as the early patents have expired.

However, Huffman coding still has advantages: it can be used adaptively, accommodating unknown, changing, or context-dependent probabilities. In the case of known independent and identically distributed random variables, combining symbols ("blocking") reduces inefficiency in a way that approaches optimality as the number of symbols combined increases. Huffman coding is optimal when each input symbol is a known independent and identically distributed random variable having a probability that is the inverse of a power of two.

Prefix codes tend to have inefficiency on small alphabets, where probabilities often fall between these optimal points. The worst case for Huffman coding can happen when the probability of a symbol exceeds $2^{-1} = 0.5$, making the upper limit of inefficiency unbounded. These situations often respond well to a form of blocking called run-length encoding; for the simple case of Bernoulli processes, Golomb coding is a probably optimal run-length code.

For a set of symbols with a uniform probability distribution and a number of members which is a power of two, Huffman coding is equivalent to simple binary block encoding, e.g., ASCII coding. This reflects the fact that compression is not possible with such an input.

Variations

Many variations of Huffman coding exist, some of which use a Huffman-like algorithm, and others of which find optimal prefix codes (while, for example, putting different restrictions on the output). Note that, in the latter case, the method need not be Huffman-like, and, indeed, need not even be polynomial time.

n-ary Huffman coding

The *n*-ary Huffman algorithm uses the {0, 1, ... , *n* − 1} alphabet to encode message and build an *n*-ary tree. This approach was considered by Huffman in his original paper. The same algorithm applies as for binary (*n* equals 2) codes, except that the *n* least probable symbols are taken together, instead of just the 2 least probable. Note that for *n* greater than 2, not all sets of source words can properly form an *n*-ary tree for Huffman coding. In these cases, additional 0-probability place holders must be added. This is because the tree must form an *n* to 1 contractor; for binary coding, this is a 2 to 1 contractor, and any sized set can form such a contractor. If the number of source words is congruent to 1 modulo *n*-1, then the set of source words will form a proper Huffman tree.

Adaptive Huffman Coding

A variation called adaptive Huffman coding involves calculating the probabilities dynamically based on recent actual frequencies in the sequence of source symbols, and changing the coding tree structure to match the updated probability estimates. It is used rarely in practice, since the cost of updating the tree makes it slower than optimized adaptive arithmetic coding, which is more flexible and has better compression.

Huffman Template Algorithm

Most often, the weights used in implementations of Huffman coding represent numeric probabilities, but the algorithm given above does not require this; it requires only that the weights form a totally ordered commutative monoid, meaning a way to order weights and to add them. The Huffman template algorithm enables one to use any kind of weights (costs, frequencies, pairs of weights, non-numerical weights) and one of many combining methods (not just addition). Such algorithms can solve other minimization problems, such as minimizing $\max_i[w_i + \text{length}(c_i)]$, a problem first applied to circuit design.

Length-limited Huffman Coding/Minimum Variance Huffman Coding

Length-limited Huffman coding is a variant where the goal is still to achieve a minimum weighted path length, but there is an additional restriction that the length of each codeword must be less than a given constant. The package-merge algorithm solves this problem with a simple greedy approach very similar to that used by Huffman's algorithm. Its time complexity is $O(nL)$, where L is the maximum length of a codeword. No algorithm is known to solve this problem in linear or linearithmic time, unlike the presorted and unsorted conventional Huffman problems, respectively.

Huffman Coding with Unequal Letter Costs

In the standard Huffman coding problem, it is assumed that each symbol in the set that the code words are constructed from has an equal cost to transmit: a code word whose length is N digits will always have a cost of N, no matter how many of those digits are 0s, how many are 1s, etc. When working under this assumption, minimizing the total cost of the message and minimizing the total number of digits are the same thing.

Huffman coding with unequal letter costs is the generalization without this assumption: the letters of the encoding alphabet may have non-uniform lengths, due to characteristics of the transmission medium. An example is the encoding alphabet of Morse code, where a 'dash' takes longer to send than a 'dot', and therefore the cost of a dash in transmission time is higher. The goal is still to minimize the weighted average codeword length, but it is no longer sufficient just to minimize the number of symbols used by the message. No algorithm is known to solve this in the same manner or with the same efficiency as conventional Huffman coding, though it has been solved by Karp whose solution has been refined for the case of integer costs by Golin.

Optimal Alphabetic Binary Trees (Hu–Tucker Coding)

In the standard Huffman coding problem, it is assumed that any codeword can correspond to any input symbol. In the alphabetic version, the alphabetic order of inputs and outputs must be identical. Thus, for example, $A = \{a,b,c\}$ could not be assigned code $H(A,C) = \{00,1,01\}$, but instead should be assigned either $H(A,C) = \{00,01,1\}$ or $H(A,C) = \{0,10,11\}$.. This is also known as the Hu–Tucker problem, after T. C. Hu and Alan Tucker, the authors of the paper presenting the first linearithmic solution to this optimal binary alphabetic problem, which has some similarities to Huffman algorithm, but is not a variation of this algorithm. These optimal alphabetic binary trees are often used as binary search trees.

The Canonical Huffman Code

If weights corresponding to the alphabetically ordered inputs are in numerical order, the Huffman code has the same lengths as the optimal alphabetic code, which can be found from calculating these lengths, rendering Hu–Tucker coding unnecessary. The code resulting from numerically (re-)ordered input is sometimes called the *canonical Huffman code* and is often the code used in practice, due to ease of encoding/decoding. The technique for finding this code is sometimes called Huffman-Shannon-Fano coding, since it is optimal like Huffman coding, but alphabetic in weight probability, like Shannon-Fano coding. The Huffman-Shannon-Fano code corresponding to the example is $\{000,001,01,10,11\}$, which, having the same codeword lengths as the original solution, is also optimal. But in *canonical Huffman code*, the result is $\{110, 111,00,01,10\}$.

Relationship with tANS Coding - Generalization to Include Fractional Bits

Huffman coding approximates informational content of symbols to a natural number of bits (approximates probabilities with powers of 1/2). It turns out its decoder can be seen as a special case of tabled variant of Asymmetric Numeral Systems entropy coding (tANS), used for example in Facebook Zstandard compressor, which takes fractional bits into considerations to improve the compression ratio. Their common decoding step can be implemented as:

```
t = decodingTable[x];

x = t.newX + readBits(t.nbBits);   //state transition

writeSymbol(t.symbol);     //decoded symbol
```

where `x` is a natural number acting as a bit buffer, which for Huffman coding contains the maximal number of bits used per symbol (D being depth of the prefix tree). Some number of its oldest bits determine the symbol to decode, the remaining bits have to be shifted to the oldest position of x, and its youngest positions are refilled with bits from the bitstream. Finally, for Huffman coding we have `decodingTable[x].newX = (x << nbBits) & mask`, where `mask=2^D-1` allows to extract D bits.

The tANS coding also uses the above decoding step, but instead of just shifting the remaining unused bits, they are modified accordingly to the remaining fractional number of bits by a proper choice of `decodingTable[x].newX` table. Its specific choice is determined by assigning a symbol to every possible value of x, such that the number of symbol appearances are proportional to the assumed probability distribution. While tANS has a freedom of choosing a specific assignment, it becomes Huffman decoder if every symbol is assigned a range of length being a power of 2, for example "aaaabcdd" assignment for a->0, b->100, c->101, d->11 prefix code, which is optimal for Pr(a)=4/8, Pr(b)=1/8, Pr(c)=1/8, Pr(d)=2/8 probability distribution. In contrast, tANS could also use e.g. "abdacdac" assignment, which would provide a better compression ratio for Pr(a)=3/8, Pr(b)=1/8, Pr(c)=2/8, Pr(d)=2/8 probability distribution.

Applications

Arithmetic coding can be viewed as a generalization of Huffman coding, in the sense that they produce the same output when every symbol has a probability of the form $1/2^k$; in particular it tends to offer significantly better compression for small alphabet sizes. Huffman coding nevertheless remains in wide use because of its simplicity, high speed, and lack of patent coverage. Intuitively, arithmetic coding can offer better compression than Huffman coding because its "code words" can have effectively non-integer bit lengths, whereas code words in Huffman coding can only have an integer number of bits. Therefore, there is an inefficiency in Huffman coding where a code word of length k only optimally matches a symbol of probability $1/2^k$ and other probabilities are not represented as optimally; whereas the code word length in arithmetic coding can be made to exactly match the true probability of the symbol.

In 2013 faster alternative to Arithmetic coding was proposed, capable of using fractional number of bits to store codewords with Asymmetric Numeral Systems (ANS). This variant is used in Facebook's Zstandard (2016) and in Apple's LZFSE (2015).

Huffman coding today is often used as a "back-end" to some other compression methods. DEFLATE (PKZIP's algorithm) and multimedia codecs such as JPEG and MP3 have a front-end model and quantization followed by Huffman coding (or variable-length prefix-free codes with a similar structure, although perhaps not necessarily designed by using Huffman's algorithm).

Assigning Binary Huffman Codes

We shall now discuss how Huffman codes are assigned to a set of source symbols of known probability. If the probabilities are not known *a priori,* it should be estimated from a sufficiently large set of samples. The code assignment is based on a series of source reductions and we shall illustrate this with reference to the example. The steps are as follows:

Step-1: Arrange the symbols in the decreasing order of their probabilities.

Symbol	Probability
a_4	0.6
a_1	0.2
a_2	0.1

a_3	0.05
a_5	0.05

Step-2: Combine the lowest probability symbols into a single compound symbol that replaces them in the next source reduction.

Symbol	Probability
a_4	$P(a_4)=0.6$
a_1	$P(a_1)=0.2$
a_2	$P(a_2)=0.1$
$a_3 \vee a_5$	$P(a_3)+P(a_5)=0.1$

In this example, a_3 and a_5 are combined into a compound symbol of probability 0.1.

Step-3: Continue the source reductions of *Step-2*, until we are left with only two symbols.

Symbol	Probability
a_4	$P(a_4)=0.6$
a_1	$P(a_1)=0.2$
$a_2 \vee (a_3 \vee a_5)$	$P(a_2)+P(a_3)+P(a_5)=0.2$

Symbol	Probability
a_4	$P(a_4)=0.6$
$a_1 \vee (a_2 \vee (a_3 \vee a_5))$	$P(a_1)+P(a_2)+P(a_3)+P(a_5)=0.4$

The second symbol in this table indicates a compound symbol of probability 0.4. We are now in a position to assign codes to the symbols.

Step-4: Assign codes "0" and "1" to the last two symbols.

Symbol	Probability	Assigned Code
a_4	0.6	0
a_1	0.2	10
a_2	0.1	110
$a_3 \vee a_5$	0.1	111

In this case, "0" is assigned to the symbol a_4 and "1" is assigned to the compound symbol $a_1 \vee (a_2 \vee (a_3 \vee a_5))$. All the elements within this compound symbol will therefore have a prefix "1".

Step-5: Work backwards along the table to assign the codes to the elements of the compound symbols. Continue till codes are assigned to all the elementary symbols.

Symbol	Probability	Assigned Code
a_4	0.6	0
$a_1 \vee (a_2 \vee (a_3 \vee a_5))$	0.4	1

"11" is therefore going to be the prefix of a_2, a_3 and a_5, since this is the code assigned to the compound symbol of these three.

This completes the Huffman code assignment pertaining to this example. From this table, it is evident that shortest code word (length=1) is assigned to the most probable symbol a_4 and the longest code words (length=4) are assigned to the two least probable symbols a_3 and a_5. Also, each symbol has a unique code and no code word is a prefix of code word for another symbol. The coding has therefore fulfilled the basic requirements of Huffman coding.

Symbol	Probability	Assigned Code
a_4	0.6	0
a_1	0.2	10
$a_2 \, V(a_3 V a_5)$	0.2	11

For this example, we can compute the average code word length. If $L(a_i)$ is the codeword length of symbol a_i, then the average codeword length is given by

Symbol	Probability	Assigned Code
a_4	0.6	0
a_1	0.2	10
a_2	0.1	110
a_3	0.05	1110
a_5	0.05	1111

$$L(z) = \sum_{i=1}^{n} L(a_i) P(a_i)$$
$$= 0.6 \times 1 + 0.2 \times 2 + 0.1 \times 3 + 2 \times 0.05 \times 4$$
$$= 1.7 \, \text{bits}$$

The coding efficiency is given by

$$\eta = \frac{H(z)}{L(z)} = 0.982$$

Encoding a String of Symbols using Huffman Codes

After obtaining the Huffman codes for each symbol, it is easy to construct the encoded bit stream for a string of symbols. For example, if we have to encode a string of symbols $a_4 \, a_3 \, a_5 \, a_4 \, a_1 a_4 \, a_2$, we shall start from the left, taking one symbol at a time. The code corresponding to the first symbol a_4 is 0, the second symbol a_3 has a code 1110 and so on. Proceeding as above, we obtain the encoded bit stream as 0111011110100110.

In this example, 16 bits were used to encode the string of 7 symbols. A straight binary encoding of

7 symbols, chosen from an alphabet of 5 symbols would have required 21 bits (3 bits/symbol) and this encoding scheme therefore demonstrates substantial compression.

Decoding a Huffman Coded Bit Stream

Since no codeword is a prefix of another codeword, Huffman codes are uniquely decodable. The decoding process is straightforward and can be summarized below:

Step-1: Examine the leftmost bit in the bit stream. If this corresponds to the codeword of an elementary symbol, add that symbol to the list of decoded symbols, remove the examined bit from the bit stream and go back to step-1 until all the bits in the bit stream are considered. Else, follow step-2.

Step-2: Append the next bit from the left to the already examined bit(s) and examine if the group of bits correspond to the codeword of an elementary symbol. If yes, add that symbol to the list of decoded symbols, remove the examined bits from the bit stream and go back to step-1 until all the bits in the bit stream are considered. Else, repeat step-2 by appending more bits.

In the encoded bit stream example, if we receive the bit stream 0111011110100110 and follow the steps described above, we shall first decode a_4 ("0"), then a_3 ("1110"), followed by a_5 ("1111"), a_4 ("0"), a_1 ("10"), a4 ("0") and a_2 ("110"). This is exactly what we had encoded.

In this chapter, we have discussed Huffman Coding, which is one of the very popular lossless Variable Length Coding (VLC) schemes, named after the scientist who proposed it. The details of the coding scheme can be read from his original paper.

We have discussed how Huffman codes can be constructed from the probabilities of the symbols. The symbol probabilities can be obtained by making a relative frequency of occurrences of the symbols and these essentially make a first order estimate of the source entropy. Better source entropy estimates can be obtained if we examine the relative frequency of occurrences of a group of symbols, say by considering two consecutive symbols at a time. With reference to images, we can form pairs of gray level values, considering two consecutive pixels at a time and thus form a second order estimate of the source entropy. In this case, Huffman codes will be assigned to the pair of symbols, instead of individual symbols. Although third, fourth and even higher order estimates would make better approximations of the source entropy, the convergence will be slow and excessive computations are involved.

We have also seen that Huffman coding assignment is based on successive source reductions. For an n-symbol source, (n-2) source reductions must be performed. When n is large, like in the case of gray level values of the images for which n=256, we require 254 steps of reduction, which is excessively high. In such cases, Huffman coding is done only for few symbols of higher probability and for the remaining, a suitable prefix code, followed by a fixed length code is adopted. This scheme is referred to as truncated Huffman coding. It is somewhat less optimal as compared to Huffman Coding, but code assignment is much easier.

There are other variants of Huffman Coding. In one of the variants, the source symbols, arranged in order of decreasing probabilities are divided into a few blocks. Special shift up and/or shift down symbols are used to identify each block and symbols within the block are assigned Huffman codes. This encoding scheme is referred to as Shift Huffman Coding. The shift symbol is the most probable symbol and is assigned the shortest code word.

Arithmetic Coding

Arithmetic coding is a form of entropy encoding used in lossless data compression. Normally, a string of characters such as the words "hello there" is represented using a fixed number of bits per character, as in the ASCII code. When a string is converted to arithmetic encoding, frequently used characters will be stored with fewer bits and not-so-frequently occurring characters will be stored with more bits, resulting in fewer bits used in total. Arithmetic coding differs from other forms of entropy encoding, such as Huffman coding, in that rather than separating the input into component symbols and replacing each with a code, arithmetic coding encodes the entire message into a single number, an arbitrary-precision fraction n where [0.0 ≤ n < 1.0). It represents the current information as a range, defined by two numbers. Recent Asymmetric Numeral Systems family of entropy coders allows for faster implementations thanks to directly operating on a single natural number representing the current information.

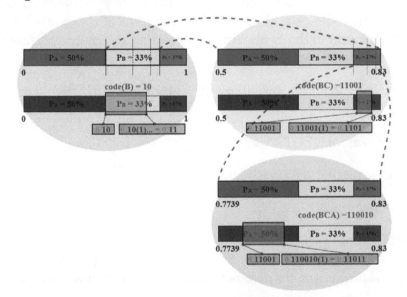

An arithmetic coding example assuming a fixed probability distribution of three Symbols "A", "B", and "C". Probability of "A" is 50%, probability of "B" is 33% and probability of "C" is 17%. Furthermore we assume that the recursion depth is known in each step. In step one we code "B" which is inside the interval [0.5, 0.83): The binary number "0.10x" is the shortest code that represents an Interval that is entirely inside [0.5, 0.83). "x" means an arbitrary bit sequence. There are two extreme cases: the smallest x stands for zero which represents the left side of the represented interval. Then the left side of the interval is dec(0.10) = 0.5. At the other extreme, x stands for a finite sequence of ones which has the upper limit dec(0.11) = 0.75 Therefore "0.10x" represents the interval [0.5, 0.75) which is inside [0.5, 0.83) Now we can leave out the "0." part since all intervals begin with "0." and we can ignore the "x" part because no matter what bit-sequence it represents, we will stay inside [0.5, 0.75).

Implementation Details and Examples

Equal Probabilities

In the simplest case, the probability of each symbol occurring is equal. For example, consider a set of three symbols, A, B, and C, each equally likely to occur. Simple block encoding would require 2 bits per symbol, which is wasteful: one of the bit variations is never used. That is to say, A=00, B=01, and C=10, but 11 is unused.

A more efficient solution is to represent a sequence of these three symbols as a rational number in base 3 where each digit represents a symbol. For example, the sequence "ABBCAB" could become 0.011201_3 (in arithmetic coding the numbers are between 0 and 1). The next step is to encode this ternary number using a fixed-point binary number of sufficient precision to recover it, such as 0.0010110010_2 — this is only 10 bits; 2 bits are saved in comparison with naïve block encoding. This is feasible for long sequences because there are efficient, in-place algorithms for converting the base of arbitrarily precise numbers.

To decode the value, knowing the original string had length 6, one can simply convert back to base 3, round to 6 digits, and recover the string.

Defining a Model

In general, arithmetic coders can produce near-optimal output for any given set of symbols and probabilities (the optimal value is $-\log_2 P$ bits for each symbol of probability P). Compression algorithms that use arithmetic coding start by determining a model of the data – basically a prediction of what patterns will be found in the symbols of the message. The more accurate this prediction is, the closer to optimal the output will be.

Example: a simple, static model for describing the output of a particular monitoring instrument over time might be:

- 60% chance of symbol NEUTRAL

- 20% chance of symbol POSITIVE

- 10% chance of symbol NEGATIVE

- 10% chance of symbol END-OF-DATA. *(The presence of this symbol means that the stream will be 'internally terminated', as is fairly common in data compression; when this symbol appears in the data stream, the decoder will know that the entire stream has been decoded.)*

Models can also handle alphabets other than the simple four-symbol set chosen for this example. More sophisticated models are also possible: *higher-order* modelling changes its estimation of the current probability of a symbol based on the symbols that precede it (the *context*), so that in a model for English text, for example, the percentage chance of "u" would be much higher when it follows a "Q" or a "q". Models can even be *adaptive*, so that they continually change their prediction of the data based on what the stream actually contains. The decoder must have the same model as the encoder.

Encoding and Decoding: Overview

In general, each step of the encoding process, except for the very last, is the same; the encoder has basically just three pieces of data to consider:

- The next symbol that needs to be encoded

- The current interval (at the very start of the encoding process, the interval is set to [0,1], but that will change)

- The probabilities the model assigns to each of the various symbols that are possible at this stage (as mentioned earlier, higher-order or adaptive models mean that these probabilities are not necessarily the same in each step.)

The encoder divides the current interval into sub-intervals, each representing a fraction of the current interval proportional to the probability of that symbol in the current context. Whichever interval corresponds to the actual symbol that is next to be encoded becomes the interval used in the next step.

Example: for the four-symbol model above:

- the interval for NEUTRAL would be [0, 0.6)

- the interval for POSITIVE would be [0.6, 0.8)

- the interval for NEGATIVE would be [0.8, 0.9)

- the interval for END-OF-DATA would be [0.9, 1).

When all symbols have been encoded, the resulting interval unambiguously identifies the sequence of symbols that produced it. Anyone who has the same final interval and model that is being used can reconstruct the symbol sequence that must have entered the encoder to result in that final interval.

It is not necessary to transmit the final interval, however; it is only necessary to transmit *one fraction* that lies within that interval. In particular, it is only necessary to transmit enough digits (in whatever base) of the fraction so that all fractions that begin with those digits fall into the final interval; this will guarantee that the resulting code is a prefix code.

Encoding and Decoding: Example

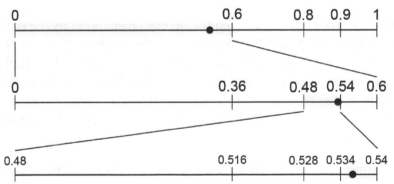

A diagram showing decoding of 0.538 (the circular point) in the example model. The region is divided into subregions proportional to symbol frequencies, then the subregion containing the point is successively subdivided in the same way.

Consider the process for decoding a message encoded with the given four-symbol model. The message is encoded in the fraction 0.538 (using decimal for clarity, instead of binary; also assuming that there are only as many digits as needed to decode the message.)

The process starts with the same interval used by the encoder: [0,1), and using the same model, dividing it into the same four sub-intervals that the encoder must have. The fraction 0.538 falls into the sub-interval for NEUTRAL, [0, 0.6); this indicates that the first symbol the encoder read must have been NEUTRAL, so this is the first symbol of the message.

Next divide the interval [0, 0.6) into sub-intervals:

- the interval for NEUTRAL would be [0, 0.36), *60% of [0, 0.6)*.

- the interval for POSITIVE would be [0.36, 0.48), *20% of [0, 0.6)*.

- the interval for NEGATIVE would be [0.48, 0.54), *10% of [0, 0.6)*.

- the interval for END-OF-DATA would be [0.54, 0.6), *10% of [0, 0.6)*.

Since .538 is within the interval [0.48, 0.54), the second symbol of the message must have been NEGATIVE.

Again divide our current interval into sub-intervals:

- the interval for NEUTRAL would be [0.48, 0.516).

- the interval for POSITIVE would be [0.516, 0.528).

- the interval for NEGATIVE would be [0.528, 0.534).

- the interval for END-OF-DATA would be [0.534, 0.540).

Now 0.538 falls within the interval of the END-OF-DATA symbol; therefore, this must be the next symbol. Since it is also the internal termination symbol, it means the decoding is complete. If the stream is not internally terminated, there needs to be some other way to indicate where the stream stops. Otherwise, the decoding process could continue forever, mistakenly reading more symbols from the fraction than were in fact encoded into it.

Sources of Inefficiency

The message 0.538 in the previous example could have been encoded by the equally short fractions 0.534, 0.535, 0.536, 0.537 or 0.539. This suggests that the use of decimal instead of binary introduced some inefficiency. This is correct; the information content of a three-digit decimal is approximately 9.966 bits; the same message could have been encoded in the binary fraction 0.10001010 (equivalent to 0.5390625 decimal) at a cost of only 8 bits. (The final zero must be specified in the binary fraction, or else the message would be ambiguous without external information such as compressed stream size.)

This 8 bit output is larger than the information content, or entropy of the message, which is

$$\sum - \log_2(p_i) = -\log_2(0.6) - \log_2(0.1) - \log_2(0.1) = 7.381 \text{ bits}$$

But an integer number of bits must be used, so an encoder for this message would use at least 8 bits, on average, which is achieved by the coding method, resulting in a message 8.4% larger than the minimum. This inefficiency of at most 1 bit becomes less significant as the message size grows.

Moreover, the claimed symbol probabilities were [0.6, 0.2, 0.1, 0.1), but the actual frequencies in this example are [0.33, 0, 0.33, 0.33). If the intervals are readjusted for these frequencies, the entropy of the message would be 4.755 bits and the same NEUTRAL NEGATIVE ENDOFDATA message could be encoded as intervals [0, 1/3); [1/9, 2/9); [5/27, 6/27); and a binary interval of

[0.00101111011, 0.00111000111). This is also an example of how statistical coding methods like arithmetic encoding can produce an output message that is larger than the input message, especially if the probability model is off.

Adaptive Arithmetic Coding

One advantage of arithmetic coding over other similar methods of data compression is the convenience of adaptation. *Adaptation* is the changing of the frequency (or probability) tables while processing the data. The decoded data matches the original data as long as the frequency table in decoding is replaced in the same way and in the same step as in encoding. The synchronization is, usually, based on a combination of symbols occurring during the encoding and decoding process.

Precision and Renormalization

The above explanations of arithmetic coding contain some simplification. In particular, they are written as if the encoder first calculated the fractions representing the endpoints of the interval in full, using infinite precision, and only converted the fraction to its final form at the end of encoding. Rather than try to simulate infinite precision, most arithmetic coders instead operate at a fixed limit of precision which they know the decoder will be able to match, and round the calculated fractions to their nearest equivalents at that precision. An example shows how this would work if the model called for the interval [0,1) to be divided into thirds, and this was approximated with 8 bit precision. Note that since now the precision is known, so are the binary ranges we'll be able to use.

Sym-bol	Probability (expressed as fraction)	Interval reduced to eight-bit precision (as fractions)	Interval reduced to eight-bit precision (in binary)	Range in binary
A	1/3	[0, 85/256)	[0.00000000, 0.01010101)	00000000 – 01010100
B	1/3	[85/256, 171/256)	[0.01010101, 0.10101011)	01010101 – 10101010
C	1/3	[171/256, 1)	[0.10101011, 1.00000000)	10101011 – 11111111

A process called *renormalization* keeps the finite precision from becoming a limit on the total number of symbols that can be encoded. Whenever the range is reduced to the point where all values in the range share certain beginning digits, those digits are sent to the output. For however many digits of precision the computer *can* handle, it is now handling fewer than that, so the existing digits are shifted left, and at the right, new digits are added to expand the range as widely as possible. Note that this result occurs in two of the three cases from our previous example.

Symbol	Probability	Range	Digits that can be sent to output	Range after renormalization
A	1/3	00000000 – 01010100	0	00000000 – 10101001
B	1/3	01010101 – 10101010	None	01010101 – 10101010
C	1/3	10101011 – 11111111	1	01010110 – 11111111

Arithmetic Coding as a Generalized Change of Radix

Recall that in the case where the symbols had equal probabilities, arithmetic coding could be implemented by a simple change of base, or radix. In general, arithmetic (and range) coding may be interpreted as a generalized change of radix. For example, we may look at any sequence of symbols:

DABDDB

as a number in a certain base presuming that the involved symbols form an ordered set and each symbol in the ordered set denotes a sequential integer $A = 0$, $B = 1$, $C = 2$, $D = 3$, and so on. This results in the following frequencies and cumulative frequencies:

Symbol	Frequency of occurrence	Cumulative frequency
A	1	0
B	2	1
D	3	3

The *cumulative frequency* is the total of all frequencies below it in a frequency distribution (a running total of frequencies).

In a positional numeral system the radix, or base, is numerically equal to a number of different symbols used to express the number. For example, in the decimal system the number of symbols is 10, namely 0, 1, 2, 3, 4, 5, 6, 7, 8, and 9. The radix is used to express any finite integer in a presumed multiplier in polynomial form. For example, the number 457 is actually $4 \times 10^2 + 5 \times 10^1 + 7 \times 10^0$, where base 10 is presumed but not shown explicitly.

Initially, we will convert DABDDB into a base-6 numeral, because 6 is the length of the string. The string is first mapped into the digit string 301331, which then maps to an integer by the polynomial:

$$6^5 \times 3 + 6^4 \times 0 + 6^3 \times 1 + 6^2 \times 3 + 6^1 \times 3 + 6^0 \times 1 = 23671$$

The result 23671 has a length of 15 bits, which is not very close to the theoretical limit (the entropy of the message), which is approximately 9 bits.

To encode a message with a length closer to the theoretical limit imposed by information theory we need to slightly generalize the classic formula for changing the radix. We will compute lower and upper bounds L and U and choose a number between them. For the computation of L we multiply each term in the above expression by the product of the frequencies of all previously occurred symbols:

$$
\begin{aligned}
L = {} & (6^5 \times 3) + \\
& 3 \times (6^4 \times 0) + \\
& (3 \times 1) \times (6^3 \times 1) + \\
& (3 \times 1 \times 2) \times (6^2 \times 3) + \\
& (3 \times 1 \times 2 \times 3) \times (6^1 \times 3) + \\
& (3 \times 1 \times 2 \times 3 \times 3) \times (6^0 \times 1) \\
= {} & 25002
\end{aligned}
$$

The difference between this polynomial and the polynomial above is that each term is multiplied by the product of the frequencies of all previously occurring symbols. More generally, L may be computed as:

$$L = \sum_{i=1}^{n} n^{n-i} C_i \prod_{k=1}^{i-1} f_k$$

where C_i are the cumulative frequencies and f_k are the frequencies of occurrences. Indexes denote the position of the symbol in a message. In the special case where all frequencies f_k are 1, this is the change-of-base formula.

The upper bound U will be L plus the product of all frequencies; in this case $U = L + (3 \times 1 \times 2 \times 3 \times 3 \times 2) = 25002 + 108 = 25110$. In general, U is given by:

$$U = L + \prod$$

Now we can choose any number from the interval [L, U) to represent the message; one convenient choice is the value with the longest possible trail of zeroes, 25100, since it allows us to achieve compression by representing the result as 251×10^2. The zeroes can also be truncated, giving 251, if the length of the message is stored separately. Longer messages will tend to have longer trails of zeroes.

To decode the integer 25100, the polynomial computation can be reversed as shown in the table below. At each stage the current symbol is identified, then the corresponding term is subtracted from the result.

Remainder	Identification	Identified symbol	Corrected remainder
25100	$25100 / 6^5 = 3$	D	$(25100 - 6^5 \times 3) / 3 = 590$
590	$590 / 6^4 = 0$	A	$(590 - 6^4 \times 0) / 1 = 590$
590	$590 / 6^3 = 2$	B	$(590 - 6^3 \times 1) / 2 = 187$
187	$187 / 6^2 = 5$	D	$(187 - 6^2 \times 3) / 3 = 26$
26	$26 / 6^1 = 4$	D	$(26 - 6^1 \times 3) / 3 = 2$
2	$2 / 6^0 = 2$	B	

During decoding we take the floor after dividing by the corresponding power of 6. The result is then matched against the cumulative intervals and the appropriate symbol is selected from look up table. When the symbol is identified the result is corrected. The process is continued for the known length of the message or while the remaining result is positive. The only difference compared to the classical change-of-base is that there may be a range of values associated with each symbol. In this example, A is always 0, B is either 1 or 2, and D is any of 3, 4, 5. This is in exact accordance with our intervals that are determined by the frequencies. When all intervals are equal to 1 we have a special case of the classic base change.

Theoretical Limit of Compressed Message

The lower bound L never exceeds n^n, where n is the size of the message, and so can be represented in $\log_2(n^n) = n \log_2(n)$ bits. After the computation of the upper bound U and the reduction of the message by selecting a number from the interval $[L, U)$ with the longest trail of zeros we can presume that this length can be reduced by $\log_2\left(\prod_{k=1}^{n} f_k\right)$ bits. Since each frequency in a product occurs exactly same number of times as the value of this frequency, we can use the size of the alphabet A for the computation of the product

$$\prod_{k=1}^{n} f_k = \prod_{k=1}^{A} f_k^{f_k}$$

Applying $\log_2$ for the estimated number of bits in the message, the final message (not counting a logarithmic overhead for the message length and frequency tables) will match the number of bits given by entropy, which for long messages is very close to optimal:

$$n \log_2(n) - \sum_{i=1}^{A} f_i \log_2(f_i)$$

p-adic Interpretation of Arithmetic Coding Algorithm

Arithmetic coding being expressed in terms of real numbers looks very natural and is easy to understand. It is nothing but a sequence of semi intervals each lies inside the previous one. But here is a problem – one has to use infinite precision real numbers to implement this algorithm and there is no such a thing like effective infinite precision real arithmetic. This problem was always considered as a technical one. Solution is simple - just use integers instead. There is a canonical implementation, first written in C [Witten], which was later reproduced in other languages, but no analysis of what happens to the algorithm after moving it from the real numbers to integer numbers was published. In fact, the integer variant of the algorithm looks very artificial and contains some magic rules: E1, E2 and E3. Though these rules work quite well the question remains – do they have natural mathematical explanation?

The p-adic numbers provides clear interpretation of the algorithm. In fact, all the intermediate data and the result can be seen as p-adic integers with p=2. The modified algorithm operates on p-adic semi intervals in the same way, as the original works with real semi intervals. For example the magic rules E1, E2 mean that the current p-adic semi interval lies completely in a p-adic ball. In this case the p-adic ball can be pushed out and p-adic semi interval rescaled. From this point of view Huffman algorithm is just a specific variant of arithmetic coding when semi intervals are always p-adic balls.

The algorithm can be extended to arbitrary p. All E1, E2, and E3 rules work in this case too. More information on p-adic variant of arithmetic coding can be found in [Rodionov, Volkov 2007, 2010].

Connections with Other Compression Methods
Huffman Coding

There is great similarity between arithmetic coding and Huffman coding – in fact, it has been shown that Huffman is just a specialized case of arithmetic coding – but because arithmetic coding translates the entire message into one number represented in base b, rather than translating each symbol of the message into a series of digits in base b, it will sometimes approach optimal entropy encoding much more closely than Huffman can.

In fact, a Huffman code corresponds closely to an arithmetic code where each of the frequencies is rounded to a nearby power of ½ — for this reason, Huffman deals relatively poorly with distributions where symbols have frequencies far from a power of ½, such as 0.75 or 0.375. This includes most distributions where there are either a small number of symbols (such as just the bits 0 and 1) or where one or two symbols dominate the rest.

For an alphabet {a, b, c} with equal probabilities of 1/3, Huffman coding may produce the following code:

- a → 0: 50%

- b → 10: 25%

- c → 11: 25%

This code has an expected $(2 + 2 + 1)/3 \approx 1.667$ bits per symbol for Huffman coding, an inefficiency of 5 percent compared to $\log_2 3 \approx 1.585$ bits per symbol for arithmetic coding.

For an alphabet {0, 1} with probabilities 0.625 and 0.375, Huffman encoding treats them as though they had 0.5 probability each, assigning 1 bit to each value, which does not achieve any compression over naive block encoding. Arithmetic coding approaches the optimal compression ratio of

$$1 - [-0.625\log_2(0.625) + -0.375\log_2(0.375)] \approx 4.6\%.$$

When the symbol 0 has a high probability of 0.95, the difference is much greater:

$$1 - [-0.95\log_2(0.95) + -0.05\log_2(0.05)] \approx 71.4\%.$$

One simple way to address this weakness is to concatenate symbols to form a new alphabet in which each symbol represents a sequence of symbols in the original alphabet. In the above example, grouping sequences of three symbols before encoding would produce new "super-symbols" with the following frequencies:

- 000: 85.7%

- 001, 010, 100: 4.5% each

- 011, 101, 110: 0.24% each

- 111: 0.0125%

With this grouping, Huffman coding averages 1.3 bits for every three symbols, or 0.433 bits per symbol, compared with one bit per symbol in the original encoding.

US Patents

A variety of specific techniques for arithmetic coding have historically been covered by US patents, although various well-known methods have since passed into the public domain as the patents have expired. Techniques covered by patents may be essential for implementing the algorithms for arithmetic coding that are specified in some formal international standards. When this is the case, such patents are generally available for licensing under what is called "reasonable and non-discriminatory" (RAND) licensing terms (at least as a matter of standards-committee policy). In some well-known instances, (including some involving IBM patents that have since expired), such licenses were available for free, and in other instances, licensing fees have been required. The availability of licenses under RAND terms does not necessarily satisfy everyone who might want to use the technology, as what may seem "reasonable" for a company preparing a proprietary commercial software product may seem much less reasonable for a free software or open source project.

At least one significant compression software program, bzip2, deliberately discontinued the use of arithmetic coding in favor of Huffman coding due to the perceived patent situation at the time. Also, encoders and decoders of the JPEG file format, which has options for both Huffman encoding and arithmetic coding, typically only support the Huffman encoding option, which was originally because of patent concerns; the result is that nearly all JPEG images in use today use Huffman encoding although JPEG's arithmetic coding patents have expired due to the age of the JPEG standard (the design of which was approximately completed by 1990). There are some archivers like PackJPG, that can losslessly convert Huffman encoded files to ones with arithmetic coding (with custom file name .pjg), showing up to 25% size saving.

Some US patents relating to arithmetic coding are listed below.

- U.S. Patent 4,122,440 — (IBM) Filed 4 March 1977, Granted 24 October 1978 (Now expired)

- U.S. Patent 4,286,256 — (IBM) Granted 25 August 1981 (Now expired)

- U.S. Patent 4,467,317 — (IBM) Granted 21 August 1984 (Now expired)

- U.S. Patent 4,652,856 — (IBM) Granted 4 February 1986 (Now expired)

- U.S. Patent 4,891,643 — (IBM) Filed 15 September 1986, granted 2 January 1990 (Now expired)

- U.S. Patent 4,905,297 — (IBM) Filed 18 November 1988, granted 27 February 1990 (Now expired)

- U.S. Patent 4,933,883 — (IBM) Filed 3 May 1988, granted 12 June 1990 (Now expired)

- U.S. Patent 4,935,882 — (IBM) Filed 20 July 1988, granted 19 June 1990 (Now expired)

- U.S. Patent 4,989,000 — Filed 19 June 1989, granted 29 January 1991 (Now expired)

- U.S. Patent 5,099,440 — (IBM) Filed 5 January 1990, granted 24 March 1992 (Now expired)

- U.S. Patent 5,272,478 — (Ricoh) Filed 17 August 1992, granted 21 December 1993 (Now expired)

Note: This list is not exhaustive. The Dirac codec uses arithmetic coding and is not patent pending.

Patents on arithmetic coding may exist in other jurisdictions.

Benchmarks and Other Technical Characteristics

Every programmatic implementation of arithmetic encoding has a different compression ratio and performance. While compression ratios vary only a little (usually under 1%), the code execution time can vary by a factor of 10. Choosing the right encoder from a list of publicly available encoders is not a simple task because performance and compression ratio depend also on the type of data, particularly on the size of the alphabet (number of different symbols). One of two particular encoders may have better performance for small alphabets while the other may show better performance for large alphabets. Most encoders have limitations on the size of the alphabet and many of them are specialized for alphabets of exactly two symbols (0 and 1).

Basic Principles of Arithmetic Coding

Like *Huffman coding*, this too is a Variable Length Coding (VLC) scheme requiring *a priori* knowledge of the symbol probabilities. The basic principles of *arithmetic coding* are as follows:

a) Unlike *Huffman coding*, which assigns variable length codes to a fixed group symbols (usually of length one), *arithmetic coding* assigns variable length codes to a variable group of symbols.

b) All the symbols in a message are considered together to assign a single arithmetic code word.

c) There is no one-to-one correspondence between the symbol and its corresponding code word.

d) The code word itself defines a real number within the half-open interval [0,1) and as more symbols are added, the interval is divided into smaller and smaller subintervals, based on the probabilities of the added symbols.

Algorithm for Arithmetic Coding

The steps of the encoding algorithm are as follows:

Step-1: Consider a range of real numbers in [0,1). Subdivide this range into a number of sub-ranges that is equal to the total number of symbols in the source alphabet. Each sub-range spans a real value equal to the probability of the source symbol.

Step-2: Consider a source message and take its first symbol. Find to which sub- range does this source symbol belongs.

Step-3: Subdivide this sub-range into a number of next level sub-ranges, according to the probability of the source symbols.

Step-4: Now parse the next symbol in the given source message and determine the next-level sub-range to which it belongs.

Step-5: Repeat step-3 and step-4 until all the symbols in the source message are parsed. The message may be encoded using any real value in the last sub-range so formed. The final message symbol is reserved as a special end-of-symbol message indicator.

Decoding an Arithmetic-Coded Bit Stream

The decoding process of arithmetic coded bit stream is very straightforward. We should follow these steps:

Step-1: Identify the message bit stream. Convert this to the real decimal number and determine its position within the subintervals identified at the beginning of encoding process. The corresponding symbol is the first one in the message.

In this example, the message bit stream corresponds to decimal number 506 i.e., 0.506 in the real valued interval [0,1). This corresponds to the subinterval [0.4, 0.7) of a_2 in *step-1* of encoding. The first symbol is therefore a_2.

Step-2: Consider the expanded subinterval of the previous decoded symbol and map the real number within this to determine the next subinterval and obtain the next decoded symbol. Repeat this step until the end-of-message indicator is parsed.

In this example, following *step-1* and *step-2,* we obtain the complete sequence
$$a_2 a_1 a_3 a_4 a_1 a_2.$$

Coding Efficiency Limitations of Arithmetic-Coded Bit Stream

Although we may expect coding efficiency close to unity for *arithmetic coding*, its performance falls short of the Shannon's noiseless coding theorem bounds, due to the following limitations:

a) Every message ends with a special end-of-message symbol. This adds to an overhead in encoding and optimal performance can only be reached for very long messages.

b) Finite precision arithmetic also restricts the coding performance. This problem has been addressed by Langdon and Rissanen through the introduction of a scaling and rounding strategy.

LZ77 and LZ78

LZ77 and LZ78 are the two lossless data compression algorithms published in papers by Abraham Lempel and Jacob Ziv in 1977 and 1978. They are also known as LZ1 and LZ2 respectively. These two algorithms form the basis for many variations including LZW, LZSS, LZMA and others. Besides their academic influence, these algorithms formed the basis of several ubiquitous compression schemes, including GIF and the DEFLATE algorithm used in PNG.

They are both theoretically dictionary coders. LZ77 maintains a *sliding window* during compression. This was later shown to be equivalent to the *explicit dictionary* constructed by LZ78—however, they are only equivalent when the entire data is intended to be decompressed. LZ78 decompression allows random access to the input as long as the entire dictionary is available while LZ77 decompression must always start at the beginning of the input.

The algorithms were named an IEEE Milestone in 2004.

Theoretical Efficiency

In the second of the two papers that introduced these algorithms they are analyzed as encoders defined by finite-state machines. A measure analogous to information entropy is developed for individual sequences (as opposed to probabilistic ensembles). This measure gives a bound on the data compression ratio that can be achieved. It is then shown that there exist finite lossless encoders for every sequence that achieve this bound as the length of the sequence grows to infinity. In this sense an algorithm based on this scheme produces asymptotically optimal encodings.

LZ77

LZ77 algorithms achieve compression by replacing repeated occurrences of data with references to a single copy of that data existing earlier in the uncompressed data stream. A match is encoded by a pair of numbers called a *length-distance pair*, which is equivalent to the statement "each of the next *length* characters is equal to the characters exactly *distance* characters behind it in the uncompressed stream". (The "distance" is sometimes called the "offset" instead.)

To spot matches, the encoder must keep track of some amount of the most recent data, such as the last 2 kB, 4 kB, or 32 kB. The structure in which this data is held is called a *sliding window*, which is why LZ77 is sometimes called *sliding window compression*. The encoder needs to keep this data to look for matches, and the decoder needs to keep this data to interpret the matches the encoder refers to. The larger the sliding window is, the longer back the encoder may search for creating references.

It is not only acceptable but frequently useful to allow length-distance pairs to specify a length that actually exceeds the distance. As a copy command, this is puzzling: "Go back *four* characters and copy *ten* characters from that position into the current position". How can ten characters be copied over when only four of them are actually in the buffer? Tackling one byte at a time, there is no problem serving this request, because as a byte is copied over, it may be fed again as input to the copy command. When the copy-from position makes it to the initial destination position, it is consequently fed data that was pasted from the *beginning* of the copy-from position. The operation is thus equivalent to the statement "copy the data you were given and repetitively paste it until it fits". As this type of pair repeats a single copy of data multiple times, it can be used to incorporate a flexible and easy form of run-length encoding.

Another way to see things is as follows: While encoding, for the search pointer to continue finding matched pairs past the end of the search window, all characters from the first match at offset D and forward to the end of the search window must have matched input, and these are the (previously seen) characters that comprise a single run unit of length L_R, which must equal D. Then as the search pointer proceeds past the search window and forward, as far as the run pattern repeats in the input, the search and input pointers will be in sync and match characters until the run pattern is interrupted. Then L characters have been matched in total, L>D, and the code is [D,L,c].

Upon decoding [D,L,c], again, D=L_R. When the first L_R characters are read to the output, this corresponds to a single run unit appended to the output buffer. At this point, the read pointer could be thought of as only needing to return int(L/L_R) + (1 if L mod L_R does not equal 0) times to the start of that single buffered run unit, read L_R characters (or maybe fewer on the last return), and repeat until a total of L characters are read. But mirroring the encoding process, since the pattern is repetitive, the read pointer need only trail in sync with the write pointer by a fixed distance equal to the run length L_R until L characters have been copied to output in total.

Considering the above, especially if the compression of data runs is expected to predominate, the window search should begin at the end of the window and proceed backwards, since run patterns, if they exist, will be found first and allow the search to terminate, absolutely if the current maximum matching sequence length is met, or judiciously, if a sufficient length is met, and finally for the simple possibility that the data is more recent and may correlate better with the next input.

Pseudocode

The pseudocode is a reproduction of the LZ77 compression algorithm sliding window.

```
begin
      fill view from input
      while (view is not empty) do
      begin
            find longest prefix p of view starting in coded part
            i := position of p in window
            j := length of p
            X := first char after p in view
            output(i,j,X)
            add j+1 chars
      end
end
```

Implementations

Even though all LZ77 algorithms work by definition on the same basic principle, they can vary widely in how they encode their compressed data to vary the numerical ranges of a length-distance pair, alter the number of bits consumed for a length-distance pair, and distinguish their length-distance pairs from *literals* (raw data encoded as itself, rather than as part of a length-distance pair). A few examples:

- The algorithm illustrated in Lempel and Ziv's original 1977 paper outputs all its data three values at a time: the length and distance of the longest match found in the buffer, and the literal which followed that match. If two successive characters in the input stream could be encoded only as literals, the length of the length-distance pair would be 0.

- LZSS improves on LZ77 by using a 1 bit flag to indicate whether the next chunk of data is a literal or a length-distance pair, and using literals if a length-distance pair would be longer.

- In the PalmDoc format, a length-distance pair is always encoded by a two-byte sequence. Of the 16 bits that make up these two bytes, 11 bits go to encoding the distance, 3 go to encoding the length, and the remaining two are used to make sure the decoder can identify the first byte as the beginning of such a two-byte sequence.

- In the implementation used for many games by Electronic Arts, the size in bytes of a length-distance pair can be specified inside the first byte of the length-distance pair itself; depending on if the first byte begins with a 0, 10, 110, or 111 (when read in big-endian bit orientation), the length of the entire length-distance pair can be 1 to 4 bytes large.

- As of 2008, the most popular LZ77 based compression method is DEFLATE; it combines LZ77 with Huffman coding. Literals, lengths, and a symbol to indicate the end of the current block of data are all placed together into one alphabet. Distances can be safely placed into a separate alphabet; because a distance only occurs just after a length, it cannot be mistaken for another kind of symbol or vice versa.

LZ78

LZ78 algorithms achieve compression by replacing repeated occurrences of data with references to a dictionary that is built based on the input data stream. Each dictionary entry is of the form dictionary[...] = {index, character}, where *index* is the index to a previous dictionary entry, and character is appended to the string represented by dictionary[index]. For example, "abc" would be stored (in reverse order) as follows: dictionary[k] = {j, 'c'}, dictionary[j] = {i, 'b'}, dictionary[i] = {0, 'a'}, where an index of 0 specifies the first character of a string. The algorithm initializes *last matching index* = 0 and *next available index* = 1. For each character of the input stream, the dictionary is searched for a match: {last matching index, character}. If a match is found, then *last matching index* is set to the index of the matching entry, and nothing is output. If a match is not found, then a new dictionary entry is created: dictionary[next available index] = {last matching index, character}, and the algorithm outputs *last matching index*, followed by *character*, then resets *last matching index* = 0 and increments *next available index*. Once the dictionary is full, no more entries are added. When the end of the input stream is reached, the algorithm outputs *last matching index*. Note that strings are stored in the dictionary in reverse order, which an LZ78 decoder will have to deal with.

LZW is an LZ78-based algorithm that uses a dictionary pre-initialized with all possible characters (symbols), (or emulation of a pre-initialized dictionary). The main improvement of LZW is that when a match is not found, the current input stream character is assumed to be the first character of an existing string in the dictionary (since the dictionary is initialized with all possible characters), so only the *last matching index* is output (which may be the pre-initialized dictionary index corresponding to the previous (or the initial) input character).

BTLZ is an LZ78 based algorithm that was developed for use in real time communications systems (originally modems) and standardized by CCITT/ITU as V.42bis. When the TRIE structured dictionary is full, a simple re-use/recovery algorithm is used to ensure that the dictionary can keep adapting to changing data. A counter cycles through the dictionary. When a new entry is needed, the counter steps through the dictionary until a leaf node is found (a node with no dependents). This is deleted and the space re-used for the new entry. This is simpler to implement than LRU or LFU and achieves equivalent performance.

Basic Principles of Lempel-Ziv Coding

We now consider yet another popular lossless compression scheme, which is originally called *Lempel-Ziv coding,* and also referred to as *Lempel-Ziv-Welch (LZW)* coding, following the modifications of Welch for image compression. This coding scheme has been adopted in a variety of imaging file formats, such as the *graphic interchange format* (GIF), *tagged image file format* (TIFF) and the *portable document format* (PDF). The basic principles of this encoding scheme are:

a) It assigns a fixed length codeword to a variable length of symbols.

b) Unlike *Huffman coding* and *arithmetic coding*, this coding scheme does not require *a priori* knowledge of the probabilities of the source symbols.

c) The coding is based on a "dictionary" or "codebook" containing the source symbols to be encoded. The coding starts with an initial dictionary, which is enlarged with the arrival of new symbol sequences.

d) There is no need to transmit the dictionary from the encoder to the decoder. A Lempel-Ziv decoder builds an identical dictionary during the decoding process.

Encoding a Sequence of Symbols using Lempel-Ziv Coding

The encoding process will now be illustrated for one line of image having the following intensity values in sequence:

$$32 \quad 32 \quad 34 \quad 32 \quad 34 \quad 32 \quad 32 \quad 33 \quad 32 \quad 32 \quad 32 \quad 34$$

This indicates a near uniform intensity line strip with a little perturbation, that is commonly encountered in practical images.

To begin the encoding process, we consider a dictionary of size 256 locations (numbered 0 to 255) that contain entries corresponding to each pixel intensity value in the range 0-255. When we encounter the first pixel of intensity 32, we do not encode it and wait for the second pixel to arrive. When the next pixel intensity of 32 is encountered, we encode the first pixel as 32, corresponding to its dictionary location number, but at the same time, we make a new entry to the dictionary at the location number 256 to include the newly detected sequence 32- 32 (a short form of writing 32 followed by 32), so that next time we encounter this sequence 32-32, we are going to encode as 256, instead of two consecutive code words of 32. The arrival of the third pixel of intensity 34 makes a new sequence entry 32-34 at the location number 257 and the previous pixel (the second one) will be encoded as 32. The fourth pixel of intensity 32 will add another code entry at location number 258 to include the sequence 34-32 and the third pixel will be encoded as 34. The arrival of fifth pixel of intensity 34 will find a matching sequence of 32-34 at location number 257. We do not encode any pixel now and wait for the arrival of the sixth pixel of intensity 32. The previously found matching sequence of 32-34 will be encoded as 257. With the arrival of the sixth pixel, we also recognize the sequence 34-32 and add a triplet of sequence 32-34-32 to the dictionary. We can now follow the rest of the coding process illustrated in the table.

It is to be noted that the encoding process of the pixel intensities and the sequence of pixel intensities will require 9 bits, as long as the dictionary size is restricted to 2^9 (=512) locations. There is considerable bit savings when the pixel sequences find matching with a dictionary entry. For example, encoding the sequence 32-34 requires only 9-bits, as compared to 16-bits, which would have been required to independently encode the two pixels. Longer matching sequences (triplets and higher) results in substantial bit savings. In fact, it will be more and more efficient to encode larger file sizes. However, the size of the dictionary is a very crucial parameter. If it is too small, we are going to have less frequent matches and consequently less compression. On the other hand, too large a dictionary size would lead to increased bit consumption in encoding unmatched sequence of pixels.

Currently Recognized Sequence	Pixel being processed	Encoded Output	Dictionary Location (Code word)	Dictionary Entry
	32			
32	32	32	256	32-32
32	34	32	257	32-34
34	32	34	258	34-32
32	34			
32-34	32	257	259	32-34-32
32	32			
32-32	33	256	260	32-33
33	32	33	261	33-32
32	32			
32-32	32	256	262	32-32-32
32	34			
32-34		257		

Lempel-Ziv coding example

Decoding a Lempel-Ziv Encoded Sequence

Decoding of Lempel-Ziv encoded sequence is quite straightforward. If we follow the example shown in the above table, we find that the encoded sequence of symbols will be 32 32 34 257 256 33 256 257

Like the encoder, the decoder also starts with the initial dictionary entries of 0- 255 only. When the decoder receives this sequence at the input, it first receives 32, which can be directly decoded as a pixel of intensity of 32. Next received symbol, as well as the next pixel is also 32. However, the dictionary now makes a new entry of 32-32 sequence at the location 256. Next received symbol, as well as the next pixel is 34. The dictionary now enters the sequence 32-34 at the location 257. Having made this entry, when the next received symbol is 257, the decoder detects two consecutive pixels 32, followed by 34. The next received symbol is 256, i.e., 32 followed by 32. The reader should verify that this way we decode the sequence of pixels as 32 32 34 32 34 32 32 33 32 32 32 34 which is the original sequence.

Lossless Coding Schemes for Binary Images

We first note that any integer value s in the interval $[0, 2^n - 1]$ can be represented by a polynomial of base-2, as follows:

$$s = a_{n-1} 2^{n-1} + a_{n-2} 2^{n-2} + \ldots\ldots\ldots a_1 2^1 + a_0 2^0$$

where, $a_{n-1}, a_{n-2}, \ldots a_0$ are the n binary coefficients associated with the corresponding powers of 2. This basically converts the integer s into the binary number representation $a_{n-1}, a_{n-2}, \ldots a_0$ with a_{n-1} as the most significant bit and a_0 as the least significant bits. Following this, all the pixel values having intensities in the range [0, 255] of an image array can be converted into its 8-bit binary representation. If we now consider an array containing only the ith bit of every pixel $(i = 0, 1, \ldots, 7)$ we get the ith bit plane image.

Let us consider a simple 4x4 array, whose elements are integers in the range 0-15 . The corresponding 4-bit binary representations are indicated within the parenthesis, s shown below:

13(1101)	12(1100)	13(1101)	9(1001)
15(1111)	13(1101)	11(1011)	10(1010)
14(1110)	11(1011)	12(1100)	9(1001)
11(1011)	12(1100)	14(1110)	7(0111)

The corresponding 4 bit planes are shown below:

1	1	1	1	1	1	1	0	0	0	0	0	1	0	1	1
1	1	1	1	1	1	0	0	1	0	1	1	1	1	1	0
1	1	1	1	1	0	1	0	1	1	0	0	0	1	0	1
1	1	1	0	0	1	1	1	1	0	1	1	1	0	0	1

| Bit-plane-3(MSB) | Bit-plane-2 | Bit-plane-1 | Bit-plane-0(LSB) |

Run-length Coding of Bit-plane Images

In one-dimensional run-length coding schemes for binary images, runs of continuous 1s or 0s in every row of an image are encoded together, resulting in substantial bit savings. Either, it is to be indicated whether the row begins with a run of 1s or 0s, or the encoding of a row compulsorily begins with 1s, where the count could be zero, if it begins with 0s.

Run-length encoding may be illustrated with the following example of a row of an image:

00011010001111001011111111111111101110000000001000011111110000000001

Let us say, we adopt the second scheme, to begin with runs of 1s. Hence, the first run count in the given binary sequence is 0. Then we have a run of three 0s. Hence, the next count is 3. Proceeding in this manner, the reader may verify that the given binary sequence gets encoded to:

0,3,2,1,1,3,5,2,1,1,15,1,3,9,1,4,7,7,1

Every run count values for 1s and 0s are associated with some probabilities, which may be determined through some statistical observations. It is therefore possible to estimate the entropies H_o and H_1 for the runs of 0s and 1s respectively. If L_0 and L_1 are the average values of run-lengths for 0s and 1s, the run-length entropy of the image is expressed as

$$H_R = \frac{H_0 + H_1}{L_0 + L_1}$$

We may apply some *variable length coding* to encode the run values.

Although, run-length coding is essentially a compression technique for binary images, it can be applied to gray-scale images in an indirect way by first decomposing the gray-scale image to bit-plane images and then applying run- length coding on each of the bit-plane images.

What we have just described is one-dimensional run-length coding. Two dimensional extension of run-length coding, using *relative address coding* (RAC) have also been reported in the literature.

Lossless Predictive Coding

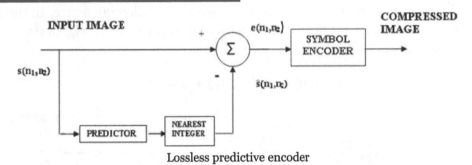

Lossless predictive encoder

Figure above shows the block diagram of the lossless predictive encoder. Here, the current pixel $s(n_1, n_2)$ is predicted as $\hat{s}(n_1, n_2)$ using a linear combination of previously received pixels, which are spatial neighbors of the current pixel. The error in prediction, given by

$$e(n_1, n_2) = s(n_1, n_2) - \hat{s}(n_1, n_2)$$

is encoded using any of the lossless compression schemes discussed so far. Since the predictor can only consider the pixels received so far, the prediction is based the set of pixels $\{s(n_1, n_2 - i) \mid i = 1, 2, \ldots, n_2\}$ from the current row and the set of pixels $\{s(n_1 - i, j) \mid i = 1, 2, \ldots, n_1 ; j = 0, 1, \ldots, N_2 - 1\}$ from the previous row, where N_2 is the number of columns. In practice, we normally consider the closest past neighbors of $s(n_1, n_2)$ and obtain the predicted value $\hat{s}(n_1, n_2)$ as a linear combination of these pixels, illustrated in the figure below and mathematically expressed as:

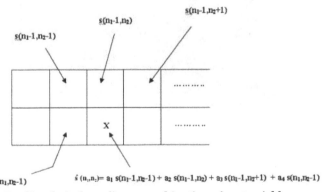

Predicted pixel as a linear combination of past neighbours

$$\hat{s}(n_1, n_2) = a_1 s(n_1-1, n_2-1) + a_2 s(n_1-1, n_2) + a_3 s(n_1-1, n_2+1) + a_4 s(n_1, n_2-1)$$

where a_1, a_2, a_3, a_4 are the coefficients associated with the respective neighboring pixels, such that $a_1 + a_2 + a_3 + a_4 = 1$. In the simplest case of $a_1 = a_2 = a_3 = 0$, we have $a_4 = 1$ and $\hat{s}(n_1, n_2) = s(n_1, n_2 - 1)$, which realizes a previous pixel predictor.

Equation above describes a *linear predictive coding*. The first pixel $s(0,0)$ of an image does not have any previously received neighbor and will be encoded directly without any prediction (in other words $\hat{s}(n_1, n_2) = 0$). In absence of any quantization, the error encoding is lossless. Although, the pixel intensities are always expressed in integers, the predicted intensities computed using equation above and consequently the error intensity computed through equation earlier may have fractional components and mathematical rounding operation will be necessary. However, the rounding operation does not create any loss, since fractional intensity change can never be perceived.

The corresponding lossless predictive decoder is shown in the following figure. In the decoder, the same prediction mechanism is replicated. It receives the encoded error signal $e(n_1, n_2)$ and reconstructs the current pixel $s(n_1, n_2)$ using

$$s(n_1, n_2) = \hat{s}(n_1, n_2) + e(n_1, n_2)$$

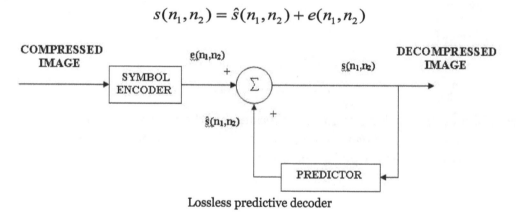

Lossless predictive decoder

Example of Predictive Coding

As an illustrative example, we are now going to apply linear predictive coding on an image.

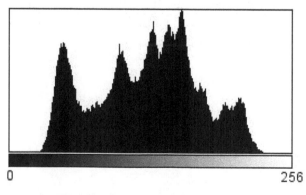

Count: 262144   Min: 25
Mean: 124.047   Max: 245
StdDev: 47.856   Mode: 155 (2742)
Histogram of original image

The corresponding histogram of image intensities is shown in the figure. For a large number of samples, the histogram approximates the probability density function (pdf) of the intensity and the probability P_i of the intensity level i $(i = 0,1,\cdots,255)$ is given by $P_i = \dfrac{n_i}{N}$, where n_i is the number of pixels having intensity value i and N is the total pixel count. We can now apply equation (B) to measure the entropy of the original image and it is found to be (calculate the value). Now, we apply the closest past neighbor prediction, given in equation (4) to obtain a predicted image $\hat{s}(n_1, n_2)$. Subtracting the predicted image from the original, we obtain the error image.

Since the error values can be positive or negative, we have added an offset of intensity value 127 on all the pixels to display the negative intensity values as well. It is clearly seen that the error image has very little intensity variations and its histogram is shown in the figure below.

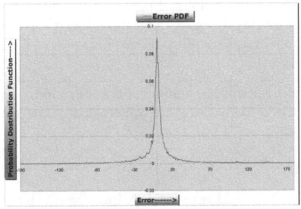

Histogram of error image

The histogram is peaked about 127 and by calculating the entropy on the error image, we obtain (calculate the value). The error image entropy being much lower than that of the original image, Shannon's theorem on noiseless coding suggests that it is possible to achieve considerable bit reduction, if we apply one of the entropy coding schemes, like *Arithmetic Coding* and *Huffman Coding* to encode the error image.

Quantization (Image Processing)

Quantization, involved in image processing, is a lossy compression technique achieved by compressing a range of values to a single quantum value. When the number of discrete symbols in a given stream is reduced, the stream becomes more compressible. For example, reducing the number of colors required to represent a digital image makes it possible to reduce its file size. Specific applications include DCT data quantization in JPEG and DWT data quantization in JPEG 2000.

Color Quantization

Color quantization reduces the number of colors used in an image; this is important for displaying images on devices that support a limited number of colors and for efficiently compressing certain kinds of images. Most bitmap editors and many operating systems have built-in support for color quantization. Popular modern color quantization algorithms include the nearest color algorithm (for fixed palettes), the median cut algorithm, and an algorithm based on octrees.

It is common to combine color quantization with dithering to create an impression of a larger number of colors and eliminate banding artifacts.

Frequency Quantization for Image Compression

The human eye is fairly good at seeing small differences in brightness over a relatively large area, but not so good at distinguishing the exact strength of a high frequency (rapidly varying) brightness variation. This fact allows one to reduce the amount of information required by ignoring the high frequency components. This is done by simply dividing each component in the frequency domain by a constant for that component, and then rounding to the nearest integer. This is the main lossy operation in the whole process. As a result of this, it is typically the case that many of the higher frequency components are rounded to zero, and many of the rest become small positive or negative numbers.

As human vision is also more sensitive to luminance than chrominance, further compression can be obtained by working in a non-RGB color space which separates the two (e.g., YCbCr), and quantizing the channels separately.

Quantization Matrices

A typical video codec works by breaking the picture into discrete blocks (8×8 pixels in the case of MPEG). These blocks can then be subjected to discrete cosine transform (DCT) to calculate the frequency components, both horizontally and vertically. The resulting block (the same size as the original block) is then pre-multiplied by the quantisation scale code and divided element-wise by the quantization matrix, and rounding each resultant element. The quantization matrix is designed to provide more resolution to more perceivable frequency components over less perceivable components (usually lower frequencies over high frequencies) in addition to transforming as many components to 0, which can be encoded with greatest efficiency. Many video encoders (such as DivX, Xvid, and 3ivx) and compression standards (such as MPEG-2 and H.264/AVC) allow custom matrices to be used. The extent of the reduction may be varied by changing the quantizer scale code, taking up much less bandwidth than a full quantizer matrix.

This is an example of DCT coefficient matrix:

$$\begin{bmatrix} -415 & -33 & -58 & 35 & 58 & -51 & -15 & -12 \\ 5 & -34 & 49 & 18 & 27 & 1 & -5 & 3 \\ -46 & 14 & 80 & -35 & -50 & 19 & 7 & -18 \\ -53 & 21 & 34 & -20 & 2 & 34 & 36 & 12 \\ 9 & -2 & 9 & -5 & -32 & -15 & 45 & 37 \\ -8 & 15 & -16 & 7 & -8 & 11 & 4 & 7 \\ 19 & -28 & -2 & -26 & -2 & 7 & -44 & -21 \\ 18 & 25 & -12 & -44 & 35 & 48 & -37 & -3 \end{bmatrix}$$

A common quantization matrix is:

$$\begin{bmatrix} 16 & 11 & 10 & 16 & 24 & 40 & 51 & 61 \\ 12 & 12 & 14 & 19 & 26 & 58 & 60 & 55 \\ 14 & 13 & 16 & 24 & 40 & 57 & 69 & 56 \\ 14 & 17 & 22 & 29 & 51 & 87 & 80 & 62 \\ 18 & 22 & 37 & 56 & 68 & 109 & 103 & 77 \\ 24 & 35 & 55 & 64 & 81 & 104 & 113 & 92 \\ 49 & 64 & 78 & 87 & 103 & 121 & 120 & 101 \\ 72 & 92 & 95 & 98 & 112 & 100 & 103 & 99 \end{bmatrix}$$

Dividing the DCT coefficient matrix element-wise with this quantization matrix, and rounding to integers results in:

$$\begin{bmatrix} -26 & -3 & -6 & 2 & 2 & -1 & 0 & 0 \\ 0 & -3 & 4 & 1 & 1 & 0 & 0 & 0 \\ -3 & 1 & 5 & -1 & -1 & 0 & 0 & 0 \\ -4 & 1 & 2 & -1 & 0 & 0 & 0 & 0 \\ 1 & 0 & 0 & 0 & 0 & 0 & 0 & 0 \\ 0 & 0 & 0 & 0 & 0 & 0 & 0 & 0 \\ 0 & 0 & 0 & 0 & 0 & 0 & 0 & 0 \\ 0 & 0 & 0 & 0 & 0 & 0 & 0 & 0 \end{bmatrix}$$

For example, using −415 (the DC coefficient) and rounding to the nearest integer

$$\text{round}\left(\frac{-415}{16}\right) = \text{round}(-25.9375) = -26$$

Typically this process will result in matrices with values primarily in the upper left (low frequency) corner. By using a zig-zag ordering to group the non-zero entries and run length encoding, the quantized matrix can be much more efficiently stored than the non-quantized version.

Quantization is of two basic types – (a) *scalar quantization* and (b) *vector quantization*.

In *scalar quantization*, each sample is quantized independently. A scalar quantizer $Q(.)$ is a function that maps a continuous-valued variable s having a probability density function $p(s)$ into a discrete set of reconstruction levels r_i $(i = 1, 2, \ldots, L)$ by applying a set of the decision levels d_i $(i = 1, 2, \ldots, L)$, applied on the continuous-valued samples s, such that

$$Q(s) = r_i \quad f s \in (d_{i-1}, d_i], \qquad i = 1, 2, \ldots, L \ldots$$

where, L is the number of output level. In words, we can say that the output of the quantizer is the reconstruction level r_i if the value of the sample lies within the range $(d_{i-1}, d_i]$.

In vector quantization, each of the samples is not quantized. Instead, a set of continuous-valued samples, expressed collectively as a vector is represented by a limited number of vector states. In this chapter, we shall restrict our discussions to scalar quantization. In particular, we shall concentrate on the scalar quantizer design, i.e., how to design d_i and r_i in earlier equation.

The performance of a quantizer is determined by its distortion measure. Let $\dot{s} = Q(s)$ be the quantized variable. Then, $\varepsilon = s - \dot{s}$ is the quantization error and the distortion D is measured in terms of the expectation of the square of the quantization error (i.e., the mean-square error) and is given by $D = E[(s - \dot{s})^2]$ We should design d_i and r_i so that the distortion D is minimized.

There are two different approaches to the optimal quantizer design –

(a) Minimize $D = E[(s - \dot{s})^2]$ with respect to d_i and r_i $(i = 1, 2, \dots, L)$ subject to the constraint that L, the number of output states in the quantizer is fixed These quantizers perform non-uniform quantization in general and are known as *Lloyd-Max quantizers*.

(b) Minimize $D = E[(s - \dot{s})^2]$ with respect to d_i and r_i $(i = 1, 2, \dots, L)$ subject to the constraint that the source entropy $H(s) = C$ is a constant and the number of output states L may vary. These quantizers are called *entropy- constrained quantizers*.

In case of *fixed-length coding*, the rate R for quantizers with L states is given by $\lfloor \log_2 R \rfloor$ while $R > H(\dot{s})$ in case of *variable-length coding*. Thus, *Lloyd-Max while quantizers* are more suited for use with *fixed-length coding*, while *entropy- constrained quantizers* are more suitable for use with *variable-length coding*.

Design of Lloyd-Max Quantizers

The design of Lloyd-Max quantizers requires the minimization of

$$D = E[(s - r_i)^2] = \sum_{i=1}^{L} \int_{d_{i-1}}^{d_i} (s - r_i)^2 p(s) ds$$

Setting the partial derivatives of D with respect to d_i and i_r $(i = 1, 2, \dots, L)$ to zero and solving, we obtain the necessary conditions for minimization as

$$r_i = \frac{\int_{d_{i-1}}^{d_i} s p(s) ds}{\int_{d_{i-1}}^{d_i} p(s) ds}, \qquad 1 \le i \le L$$

$$d_i = \frac{r_i + r_{i+1}}{2}, \qquad 1 \le i \le L.$$

Mathematically, the decision and the reconstruction levels are solutions to the above set of nonlinear equations. In general, closed form solutions to equations above do not exist and they need to be solved by numerical techniques. Using numerical techniques, these equations could be solved in an iterative way by first assuming an initial set of values for the decision levels $\{d_i\}$. For simplicity, one can start with decision levels corresponding to uniform quantization, where decision levels are equally spaced. Based on the initial set of decision levels, the reconstruction levels can be computed using above equation if the pdf of the input variable to the quantizer is known. These reconstruction levels are used in earlier equation to obtain the updated values of $\{d_i\}$.

Solutions of earlier equations are iteratively repeated until a convergence in the decision and reconstruction levels are achieved. In most of the cases, the convergence is achieved quite fast for a wide range of initial values.

Uniform and Non-uniform Quantization

Lloyd-Max quantizers described above perform *non-uniform quantization* if the *pdf* of the input variable is not uniform. This is expected, since we should perform *finer quantization* (that is, the decision levels more closely packed and consequently more number of reconstruction levels) wherever the *pdf* is large and *coarser quantization* (that is, decision levels widely spaced apart and hence, less number of reconstruction levels), wherever *pdf* is low. In contrast, the reconstruction levels are equally spaced in *uniform quantization*, i.e.

$$r_{i+1} - r_i = \theta \qquad 1 \le i \le L - 1,$$

where θ is a constant, that is defined as the *quantization step-size*.

In case, the *pdf* of the input variable s is uniform in the interval $[A, B]$, i.e.,

$$p(s) = \begin{cases} \dfrac{1}{B - A} & A \le s \le B \\ 0 & otherwise \end{cases}$$

the design of Lloyd-Max quantizer leads to a uniform quantizer, where

$$\theta = \frac{B - A}{L}$$

$$d_i = A + i\theta \qquad 0 \le i \le L$$

$$r_i = d_{i-1} + \frac{\theta}{2} \qquad 1 \le i \le L$$

If the *pdf* exhibits even symmetric properties about its mean, e.g., Gaussian and Laplacian distributions, then the decision and the reconstruction levels have some symmetry relations for both uniform and non-uniform quantizers, as shown in the figures or some typical quantizer characteristics (reconstruction vels vs. input variable s) for L even and odd respectively.

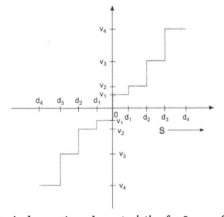

Typical quantizer characteristics for L even (=8)

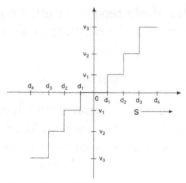

Typical quantizer characteristics for L odd (=7)

When *pdf* is even symmetric about its mean, the quantizer is to be designed for only $L/2$ levels or $(L-1)/2$ levels, depending upon whether L is even or odd, respectively.

Rate-Distortion Function and Source Coding Theorem

Shannon's Coding Theorem on noiseless channels considers the channel, as well as the encoding process to be lossless. With the introduction of quantizers, the encoding process becomes lossy, even if the channel remains as lossless. In most cases of lossy compressions, a limit is generally specified on the maximum tolerable distortion D from fidelity consideration. The question that arises is "Given a distortion measure D, how to obtain the smallest possible rate?" The answer is provided by a branch of information theory that is known as the *rate- distortion theory*. The corresponding function that relates the smallest possible rate to the distortion, is called the *rate-distortion function R(D)*. A typical nature of *rate-distortion function* is shown in the figure.

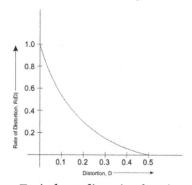

Typical rate distortion function

At no distortion (D=0), i.e. for lossless encoding, the corresponding rate R(0) is equal to the entropy, as per Shannon's coding theorem on noiseless channels. Rate-distortion functions can be computed analytically for simple sources and distortion measures. Computer algorithms exist to compute R(D) when analytical methods fail or are impractical. In terms of the rate-distortion function, the source coding theorem is presented below.

Source Coding Theorem

There exists a mapping from the source symbols to codewords such that for a given distortion D, R(D) bits/symbol are sufficient to enable source reconstruction with an average distortion arbitrarily close to D. The actual bits R is given by $R \geq R(D)$

Color Quantization

An example image in 24-bit RGB color

The same image reduced to a palette of 16 colors specifically chosen to best represent the image;
the selected palette is shown by the squares above

In computer graphics, color quantization or color image quantization is a process that reduces the number of distinct colors used in an image, usually with the intention that the new image should be as visually similar as possible to the original image. Computer algorithms to perform color quantization on bitmaps have been studied since the 1970s. Color quantization is critical for displaying images with many colors on devices that can only display a limited number of colors, usually due to memory limitations, and enables efficient compression of certain types of images.

The name "color quantization" is primarily used in computer graphics research literature; in applications, terms such as *optimized palette generation*, *optimal palette generation*, or *decreasing color depth* are used. Some of these are misleading, as the palettes generated by standard algorithms are not necessarily the best possible.

Algorithms

Most standard techniques treat color quantization as a problem of clustering points in three-dimensional space, where the points represent colors found in the original image and the three axes represent the three color channels. Almost any three-dimensional clustering algorithm can be applied to color quantization, and vice versa. After the clusters are located, typically the points in each cluster are averaged to obtain the representative color that all colors in that cluster are mapped to. The three color channels are usually red, green, and blue, but another popular choice is the Lab color space, in which Euclidean distance is more consistent with perceptual difference.

The most popular algorithm by far for color quantization, invented by Paul Heckbert in 1979, is the median cut algorithm. Many variations on this scheme are in use. Before this time, most color quantization was done using the *population algorithm* or *population method*, which essentially constructs a histogram of equal-sized ranges and assigns colors to the ranges containing the most points. A more modern popular method is clustering using octrees, first conceived by Gervautz and Purgathofer and improved by Xerox PARC researcher Dan Bloomberg.

A small photograph that has had its blue channel removed. This means all of its pixel colors lie in a two-dimensional plane in the color cube.

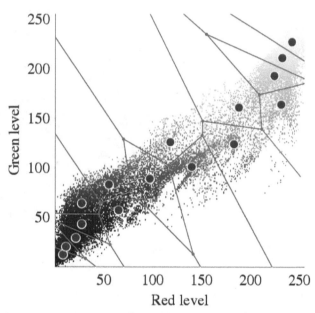

The color space of the photograph to the left, along with a 16-color optimized palette produced by Photoshop. The Voronoi regions of each palette entry are shown.

If the palette is fixed, as is often the case in real-time color quantization systems such as those used in operating systems, color quantization is usually done using the "straight-line distance" or "nearest color" algorithm, which simply takes each color in the original image and finds the closest palette entry, where distance is determined by the distance between the two corresponding points in three-dimensional space. In other words, if the colors are (r_1, g_1, b_1) and (r_2, g_2, b_2), we want to minimize the Euclidean distance:

$$\sqrt{(r_1 - r_2)^2 + (g_1 - g_2)^2 + (b_1 - b_2)^2}.$$

This effectively decomposes the color cube into a Voronoi diagram, where the palette entries are the points and a cell contains all colors mapping to a single palette entry. There are efficient algorithms from computational geometry for computing Voronoi diagrams and determining which region a given point falls in; in practice, indexed palettes are so small that these are usually overkill.

A colorful image reduced to 4 colors using spatial color quantization.

Color quantization is frequently combined with dithering, which can eliminate unpleasant arti-facts such as banding that appear when quantizing smooth gradients and give the appearance of a larger number of colors. Some modern schemes for color quantization attempt to combine palette selection with dithering in one stage, rather than perform them independently.

A number of other much less frequently used methods have been invented that use entirely differ-ent approaches. The Local K-means algorithm, conceived by Oleg Verevka in 1995, is designed for use in windowing systems where a core set of "reserved colors" is fixed for use by the system and many images with different color schemes might be displayed simultaneously. It is a post-cluster-ing scheme that makes an initial guess at the palette and then iteratively refines it.

The high-quality but slow *NeuQuant* algorithm reduces images to 256 colors by training a Kohonen neural network "which self-organises through learning to match the distribution of colours in an input image. Taking the position in RGB-space of each neuron gives a high-quality colour map in which adjacent colours are similar." It is particularly advantageous for images with gradients.

Finally, one of the most promising methods is *spatial color quantization*, conceived by Puzicha, Held, Ketterer, Buhmann, and Fellner of the University of Bonn, which combines dithering with palette generation and a simplified model of human perception to produce visually impressive results even for very small numbers of colors. It does not treat palette selection strictly as a clustering problem, in that the colors of nearby pixels in the original image also affect the color of a pixel.

In the early days of color quantization, the k-means clustering algorithm was deemed unsuitable because of its high computational requirements and sensitivity to initialization. In 2011, M. Emre Celebi reinvestigated the performance of k-means as a color quantizer . He demonstrated that an efficient implementation of k-means outperforms a large number of color quantization methods.

History and Applications

In the early days of PCs, it was common for video adapters to support only 2, 4, 16, or (eventually) 256 colors due to video memory limitations; they preferred to dedicate the video memory to having more pixels (higher resolution) rather than more colors. Color quantization helped to justify this tradeoff by making it possible to display many high color images in 16- and 256-color modes with limited visual degradation. Many operating systems automatically perform quantization and dithering when viewing high color images in a 256 color video mode, which was important when video devices limited to 256 color modes were dominant. Modern computers can now display millions of colors at once, far more than can be distinguished by the human eye, limiting this application primarily to mobile devices and legacy hardware.

Nowadays, color quantization is mainly used in GIF and PNG images. GIF, for a long time the most popular lossless and animated bitmap format on the World Wide Web, only supports up to 256 colors, necessitating quantization for many images. Some early web browsers constrained images to use a specific palette known as the web colors, leading to severe degradation in quality compared to optimized palettes. PNG images support 24-bit color, but can often be made much smaller in filesize without much visual degradation by application of color quantization, since PNG files use fewer bits per pixel for palettized images.

The infinite number of colors available through the lens of a camera is impossible to display on a computer screen; thus converting any photograph to a digital representation necessarily involves some quantization. Practically speaking, 24-bit color is sufficiently rich to represent almost all colors perceivable by humans with sufficiently small error as to be visually identical (if presented faithfully), within the available color space. However, the digitization of color, either in a camera detector or on a screen, necessarily limits the available color space. Consequently there are many colors that may be impossible to reproduce, regardless of how many bits are used to represent the color. For example, it is impossible in typical RGB color spaces (common on computer monitors) to reproduce the full range of green colors that the human eye is capable of perceiving.

With the few colors available on early computers, different quantization algorithms produced very different-looking output images. As a result, a lot of time was spent on writing sophisticated algorithms to be more lifelike.

Editor Support

Many bitmap graphics editors contain built-in support for color quantization, and will automatically perform it when converting an image with many colors to an image format with fewer colors.

Most of these implementations allow the user to set exactly the number of desired colors. Examples of such support include:

- Photoshop's *Mode→Indexed Color* function supplies a number of quantization algorithms ranging from the fixed Windows system and Web palettes to the proprietary Local and Global algorithms for generating palettes suited to a particular image or images.

- Paint Shop Pro, in its *Colors→Decrease Color Depth* dialog, supplies three standard color quantization algorithms: median cut, octree, and the fixed standard "web safe" palette.

- The GIMP's *Generate Optimal Palette with 256 Colours* option is known to use the median cut algorithm. There has been some discussion in the developer community of adding support for spatial color quantization.

Color quantization is also used to create posterization effects, although posterization has the slightly different goal of minimizing the number of colors used within the same color space, and typically uses a fixed palette.

Some vector graphics editors also utilize color quantization, especially for raster-to-vector techniques that create tracings of bitmap images with the help of edge detection.

- Inkscape's *Path→Trace Bitmap: Multiple Scans: Color* function uses octree quantization to create color traces.

Lossy Predictive Coding

Like lossless predictive coding schemes, the basic principle of lossy predictive coding is also the prediction of current sample, based on the past samples, usually picked up from the neighborhood of the current pixels for images. The error in prediction, given by

$$e(n) = s(n) - \hat{s}(n)$$

is quantized and further compressed through one of the lossless compression schemes. Figure (A) shows the block diagram of the lossy predictive coding encoder and figure (B) shows the corresponding decoder to generate the reconstructed sample. At the decoder, the quantized error signal $\dot{e}(n)$ is added to the predicted sample $\hat{s}(n)$ to generate the reconstructed sample $\dot{s}(n)$, which is not equal to the original sample $s(n)$ because of the introduction of the quantizer. The reconstructed sample is given by

$$\dot{s}(n) = \dot{e}(n) + \hat{s}(n)$$

The reconstructed sample (and a set of past reconstructed samples) is used to generate the next predicted sample. Identical predictors should exist at both encoder and the decoder to prevent error accumulation and hence, the encoder should also derive the reconstructed sample, in accordance with equation above. The encoder thus contains a feedback path to derive the predicted sample, as shown in the figure (A).

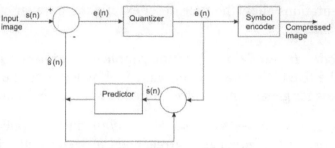

(A) Lossy predictive coding scheme

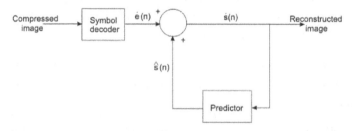

(B) Decoder for lossy predictive coding

Pulse-code Modulation

Pulse-code modulation (PCM) is a method used to digitally represent sampled analog signals. It is the standard form of digital audio in computers, compact discs, digital telephony and other digital audio applications. In a PCM stream, the amplitude of the analog signal is sampled regularly at uniform intervals, and each sample is quantized to the nearest value within a range of digital steps.

Linear pulse-code modulation (LPCM) is a specific type of PCM where the quantization levels are linearly uniform. This is in contrast to PCM encodings where quantization levels vary as a function of amplitude (as with the A-law algorithm or the μ-law algorithm). Though PCM is a more general term, it is often used to describe data encoded as LPCM.

A PCM stream has two basic properties that determine the stream's fidelity to the original analog signal: the sampling rate, which is the number of times per second that samples are taken; and the bit depth, which determines the number of possible digital values that can be used to represent each sample.

History

Early electrical communications started to sample signals in order to interlace samples from multiple telegraphy sources and to convey them over a single telegraph cable. The American inventor Moses G. Farmer conveyed telegraph time-division multiplexing (TDM) as early as 1853. Electrical engineer W. M. Miner, in 1903, used an electro-mechanical commutator for time-division multiplexing multiple telegraph signals; he also applied this technology to telephony. He obtained intelligible speech from channels sampled at a rate above 3500–4300 Hz; lower rates proved unsatisfactory. This was TDM, but pulse-amplitude modulation (PAM) rather than PCM.

In 1920 the Bartlane cable picture transmission system, named after its inventors Harry G. Bartholomew and Maynard D. McFarlane, used telegraph signaling of characters punched in paper tape to send samples of images quantized to 5 levels; whether this is considered PCM or not depends on how one interprets "pulse code", but it involved transmission of quantized samples.

In 1926, Paul M. Rainey of Western Electric patented a facsimile machine which transmitted its signal using 5-bit PCM, encoded by an opto-mechanical analog-to-digital converter. The machine did not go into production.

British engineer Alec Reeves, unaware of previous work, conceived the use of PCM for voice communication in 1937 while working for International Telephone and Telegraph in France. He described the theory and advantages, but no practical application resulted. Reeves filed for a French patent in 1938, and his US patent was granted in 1943. By this time Reeves had started working at the Telecommunications Research Establishment (TRE).

The first transmission of speech by digital techniques, the SIGSALY encryption equipment, conveyed high-level Allied communications during World War II. In 1943 the Bell Labs researchers who designed the SIGSALY system became aware of the use of PCM binary coding as already proposed by Alec Reeves. In 1949 for the Canadian Navy's DATAR system, Ferranti Canada built a working PCM radio system that was able to transmit digitized radar data over long distances.

PCM in the late 1940s and early 1950s used a cathode-ray coding tube with a plate electrode having encoding perforations. As in an oscilloscope, the beam was swept horizontally at the sample rate while the vertical deflection was controlled by the input analog signal, causing the beam to pass through higher or lower portions of the perforated plate. The plate collected or passed the beam, producing current variations in binary code, one bit at a time. Rather than natural binary, the grid of Goodall's later tube was perforated to produce a glitch-free Gray code, and produced all bits simultaneously by using a fan beam instead of a scanning beam.

In the United States, the National Inventors Hall of Fame has honored Bernard M. Oliver and Claude Shannon as the inventors of PCM, as described in "Communication System Employing Pulse Code Modulation", U.S. Patent 2,801,281 filed in 1946 and 1952, granted in 1956. Another patent by the same title was filed by John R. Pierce in 1945, and issued in 1948: U.S. Patent 2,437,707. The three of them published "The Philosophy of PCM" in 1948.

Implementations

PCM is the method of encoding generally used for uncompressed audio, although there are other methods such as pulse-density modulation (used also on Super Audio CD).

- The 4ESS switch introduced time-division switching into the US telephone system in 1976, based on medium scale integrated circuit technology.

- LPCM is used for the lossless encoding of audio data in the Compact disc Red Book standard (informally also known as *Audio CD*), introduced in 1982.

- AES3 (specified in 1985, upon which S/PDIF is based) is a particular format using LPCM.

- On PCs, PCM and LPCM often refer to the format used in WAV (defined in 1991) and AIFF audio container formats (defined in 1988). LPCM data may also be stored in other formats such as AU, raw audio format (header-less file) and various multimedia container formats.

- LPCM has been defined as a part of the DVD (since 1995) and Blu-ray (since 2006) standards. It is also defined as a part of various digital video and audio storage formats (e.g. DV since 1995, AVCHD since 2006).

- LPCM is used by HDMI (defined in 2002), a single-cable digital audio/video connector interface for transmitting uncompressed digital data.

- RF64 container format (defined in 2007) uses LPCM and also allows non-PCM bitstream storage: various compression formats contained in the RF64 file as data bursts (Dolby E, Dolby AC3, DTS, MPEG-1/MPEG-2 Audio) can be "disguised" as PCM linear.

Modulation

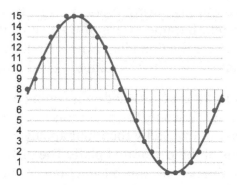

Sampling and quantization of a signal (red) for 4-bit LPCM

In the diagram, a sine wave (red curve) is sampled and quantized for PCM. The sine wave is sampled at regular intervals, shown as vertical lines. For each sample, one of the available values (on the y-axis) is chosen by some algorithm. This produces a fully discrete representation of the input signal (blue points) that can be easily encoded as digital data for storage or manipulation. For the sine wave example at right, we can verify that the quantized values at the sampling moments are 8, 9, 11, 13, 14, 15, 15, 15, 14, etc. Encoding these values as binary numbers would result in the following set of nibbles: 1000 ($2^3 \times 1 + 2^2 \times 0 + 2^1 \times 0 + 2^0 \times 0 = 8+0+0+0 = 8$), 1001, 1011, 1101, 1110, 1111, 1111, 1111, 1110, etc. These digital values could then be further processed or analyzed by a digital signal processor. Several PCM streams could also be multiplexed into a larger aggregate data stream, generally for transmission of multiple streams over a single physical link. One technique is called time-division multiplexing (TDM) and is widely used, notably in the modern public telephone system.

The PCM process is commonly implemented on a single integrated circuit generally referred to as an analog-to-digital converter (ADC).

Demodulation

To recover the original signal from the sampled data, a "demodulator" can apply the procedure of modulation in reverse. After each sampling period, the demodulator reads the next value and shifts the output signal to the new value. As a result of these transitions, the signal has a significant amount of high-frequency energy caused by aliasing. To remove these undesirable frequencies and leave the original signal, the demodulator passes the signal through analog filters that suppress energy outside the expected frequency range (greater than the Nyquist frequency $f_s/2$). The sampling theorem shows PCM devices can operate without introducing distortions within their designed frequency bands if they provide a sampling frequency twice that of the input signal. For example, in telephony, the usable voice frequency band ranges from approximately 300 Hz to 3400 Hz. Therefore, per the Nyquist–Shannon sampling theorem, the sampling frequency (8 kHz) must be at least twice the voice frequency (4 kHz) for effective reconstruction of the voice signal.

The electronics involved in producing an accurate analog signal from the discrete data are similar to those used for generating the digital signal. These devices are Digital-to-analog converters (DACs). They produce a voltage or current (depending on type) that represents the value presented on their digital inputs. This output would then generally be filtered and amplified for use.

Standard Sampling Precision and Rates

Common sample depths for LPCM are 8, 16, 20 or 24 bits per sample.

LPCM encodes a single sound channel. Support for multichannel audio depends on file format and relies on interweaving or synchronization of LPCM streams. While two channels (stereo) is the most common format, some can support up to 8 audio channels (7.1 surround).

Common sampling frequencies are 48 kHz as used with DVD format videos, or 44.1 kHz as used in Compact discs. Sampling frequencies of 96 kHz or 192 kHz can be used on some newer equipment, with the higher value equating to 6.144 megabit per second for two channels at 16-bit per sample value, but the benefits have been debated. The bitrate limit for LPCM audio on DVD-Video is also 6.144 Mbit/s, allowing 8 channels (7.1 surround) × 48 kHz × 16-bit per sample = 6,144 kbit/s.

There is a L32 bit PCM, and there are many sound cards that support it.

Limitations

There are potential sources of impairment implicit in any PCM system:

- Choosing a discrete value that is near but not exactly at the analog signal level for each sample leads to quantization error.

- Between samples no measurement of the signal is made; the sampling theorem guarantees non-ambiguous representation and recovery of the signal only if it has no energy at frequency $f_s/2$ or higher (one half the sampling frequency, known as the Nyquist frequency); higher frequencies will generally not be correctly represented or recovered.

- As samples are dependent on *time*, an accurate clock is required for accurate reproduction. If either the encoding or decoding clock is not stable, its frequency drift will directly affect the output quality of the device.

Digitization as Part of the PCM Process

In conventional PCM, the analog signal may be processed (e.g., by amplitude compression) before being digitized. Once the signal is digitized, the PCM signal is usually subjected to further processing (e.g., digital data compression).

PCM with linear quantization is known as Linear PCM (LPCM).

Some forms of PCM combine signal processing with coding. Older versions of these systems applied the processing in the analog domain as part of the analog-to-digital process; newer implementations do so in the digital domain. These simple techniques have been largely rendered obsolete by modern transform-based audio compression techniques.

- DPCM encodes the PCM values as differences between the current and the predicted value. An algorithm predicts the next sample based on the previous samples, and the encoder stores only the difference between this prediction and the actual value. If the prediction is reasonable, fewer bits can be used to represent the same information. For audio, this type of encoding reduces the number of bits required per sample by about 25% compared to PCM.

- Adaptive DPCM (ADPCM) is a variant of DPCM that varies the size of the quantization step, to allow further reduction of the required bandwidth for a given signal-to-noise ratio.

- Delta modulation is a form of DPCM which uses one bit per sample.

In telephony, a standard audio signal for a single phone call is encoded as 8,000 analog samples per second, of 8 bits each, giving a 64 kbit/s digital signal known as DS0. The default signal compression encoding on a DS0 is either µ-law (mu-law) PCM (North America and Japan) or A-law PCM (Europe and most of the rest of the world). These are logarithmic compression systems where a 12 or 13-bit linear PCM sample number is mapped into an 8-bit value. This system is described by international standard G.711. An alternative proposal for a floating point representation, with 5-bit mantissa and 3-bit exponent, was abandoned.

Where circuit costs are high and loss of voice quality is acceptable, it sometimes makes sense to compress the voice signal even further. An ADPCM algorithm is used to map a series of 8-bit µ-law or A-law PCM samples into a series of 4-bit ADPCM samples. In this way, the capacity of the line is doubled. The technique is detailed in the G.726 standard.

Later it was found that even further compression was possible and additional standards were published. Some of these international standards describe systems and ideas which are covered by privately owned patents and thus use of these standards requires payments to the patent holders.

Some ADPCM techniques are used in Voice over IP communications.

Encoding for Serial Transmission

PCM can be either return-to-zero (RZ) or non-return-to-zero (NRZ). For a NRZ system to be synchronized using in-band information, there must not be long sequences of identical symbols, such as ones or zeroes. For binary PCM systems, the density of 1-symbols is called *ones-density*.

Ones-density is often controlled using precoding techniques such as Run Length Limited encoding, where the PCM code is expanded into a slightly longer code with a guaranteed bound on ones-density before modulation into the channel. In other cases, extra framing bits are added into the stream which guarantee at least occasional symbol transitions.

Another technique used to control ones-density is the use of a scrambler polynomial on the raw data which will tend to turn the raw data stream into a stream that looks pseudo-random, but where the raw stream can be recovered exactly by reversing the effect of the polynomial. In this case, long runs of zeroes or ones are still possible on the output, but are considered unlikely enough to be within normal engineering tolerance.

In other cases, the long term DC value of the modulated signal is important, as building up a DC offset will tend to bias detector circuits out of their operating range. In this case special measures are taken to keep a count of the cumulative DC offset, and to modify the codes if necessary to make the DC offset always tend back to zero.

Many of these codes are bipolar codes, where the pulses can be positive, negative or absent. In the typical alternate mark inversion code, non-zero pulses alternate between being positive and negative. These rules may be violated to generate special symbols used for framing or other special purposes.

Nomenclature

The word *pulse* in the term *pulse-code modulation* refers to the "pulses" to be found in the transmission line. This perhaps is a natural consequence of this technique having evolved alongside two analog methods, pulse width modulation and pulse position modulation, in which the information to be encoded is represented by discrete signal pulses of varying width or position, respectively. In this respect, PCM bears little resemblance to these other forms of signal encoding, except that all can be used in time division multiplexing, and the numbers of the PCM codes are represented as electrical pulses. The device that performs the coding and decoding function in a telephone, or other, circuit is called a codec.

Delta Modulation

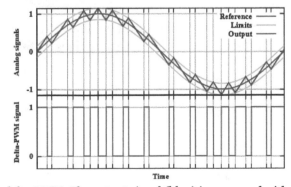

Principle of the delta PWM. The output signal (blue) is compared with the limits (green).
The limits (green) correspond to the reference signal (red), offset by a given value.
Every time the output signal reaches one of the limits, the PWM signal changes state.

A delta modulation (DM or Δ-modulation) is an analog-to-digital and digital-to-analog signal conversion technique used for transmission of voice information where quality is not of primary importance. DM is the simplest form of differential pulse-code modulation (DPCM) where the difference between successive samples are encoded into n-bit data streams. In delta modulation, the transmitted data are reduced to a 1-bit data stream. Its main features are:

- The analog signal is approximated with a series of segments.

- Each segment of the approximated signal is compared of successive bits is determined by this comparison.

- Only the change of information is sent, that is, only an increase or decrease of the signal amplitude from the previous sample is sent whereas a no-change condition causes the modulated signal to remain at the same 0 or 1 state of the previous sample.

To achieve high signal-to-noise ratio, delta modulation must use oversampling techniques, that is, the analog signal is sampled at a rate several times higher than the Nyquist rate.

Derived forms of delta modulation are continuously variable slope delta modulation, delta-sigma modulation, and differential modulation. Differential pulse-code modulation is the superset of DM.

Principle

Rather than quantizing the absolute value of the input analog waveform, delta modulation quantizes the difference between the current and the previous step, as shown in the block diagram in figure.

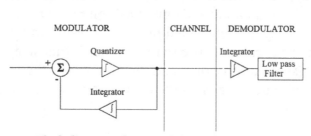

Block diagram of a Δ-modulator/demodulator

The modulator is made by a quantizer which converts the difference between the input signal and the average of the previous steps. In its simplest form, the quantizer can be realized with a comparator referenced to 0 (two levels quantizer), whose output is *1* or *0* if the input signal is positive or negative. It is also a bit-quantizer as it quantizes only a bit at a time. The demodulator is simply an integrator (like the one in the feedback loop) whose output rises or falls with each 1 or 0 received. The integrator itself constitutes a low-pass filter.

Transfer Characteristics

The transfer characteristics of a delta modulated system follows a signum function, as it quantizes only two levels and also one-bit at a time.

The two sources of noise in delta modulation are "slope overload", when step size is too small to track the original waveform, and "granularity", when step size is too large. But a 1971 study shows that slope overload is less objectionable compared to granularity than one might expect based solely on SNR measures.

Output Signal Power

In delta modulation there is a restriction on the amplitude of the input signal, because if the transmitted signal has a large derivative (abrupt changes) then the modulated signal can not follow the input signal and slope overload occurs. E.g. if the input signal is

$$m(t) = A\cos(\omega t) \,,$$

the modulated signal (derivative of the input signal) which is transmitted by the modulator is

$$|\dot{m}(t)|_{max} = \omega A,$$

whereas the condition to avoid slope overload is

$$|\dot{m}(t)|_{max} = \omega A < \sigma f_s.$$

So the maximum amplitude of the input signal can be

$$A_{max} = \frac{\sigma f_s}{\omega},$$

where f_s is the sampling frequency and ω is the frequency of the input signal and σ is step size in quantization. So A_{max} is the maximum amplitude that DM can transmit without causing the slope overload and the power of transmitted signal depends on the maximum amplitude.

Bit-rate

If the communication channel is of limited bandwidth, there is the possibility of interference in either DM or PCM. Hence, 'DM' and 'PCM' operate at same bit-rate which is equal to N times the sampling frequency.

Adaptive Delta Modulation

Adaptive delta modulation (ADM) was first published by Dr. John E. Abate (AT&T Bell Laboratories Fellow) in his doctoral thesis at NJ Institute Of Technology in 1968. ADM was later selected as the standard for all NASA communications between mission control and space-craft.

Adaptive delta modulation or [continuously (CVSD) is a modification of DM in which the step size is not fixed. Rather, when several consecutive bits have the same direction value, the encoder and decoder assume that slope overload is occurring, and the step size becomes progressively larger.

Otherwise, the step size becomes gradually smaller over time. ADM reduces slope error, at the expense of increasing quantizing error.This error can be reduced by using a low-pass filter. ADM provides robust performance in the presence of bit errors meaning error detection and correction are not typically used in an ADM radio design, this allows fortive-delta-modulation.

Applications

Contemporary applications of Delta Modulation includes, but is not limited to, recreating legacy synthesizer waveforms. With the increasing availability of FPGAs and game-related ASICs, sample rates are easily controlled so as to avoid slope overload and granularity issues. For example, the C64DTV used a 32 MHz sample rate, providing ample dynamic range to recreate the SID output to acceptable levels.

SBS Application 24 kbps Delta Modulation

Delta Modulation was used by Satellite Business Systems or SBS for its voice ports to provide long distance phone service to large domestic corporations with a significant inter-corporation communications need (such as IBM). This system was in service throughout the 1980s. The voice ports used digitally implemented 24 kbit/s delta modulation with Voice Activity Compression (VAC) and echo suppressors to control the half second echo path through the satellite. They performed formal listening tests to verify the 24 kbit/s delta modulator achieved full voice quality with no discernible degradation as compared to a high quality phone line or the standard 64 kbit/s μ-law companded PCM. This provided an eight to three improvement in satellite channel capacity. IBM developed the Satellite Communications Controller and the voice port functions.

The original proposal in 1974, used a state-of-the-art 24 kbit/s delta modulator with a single integrator and a Shindler Compander modified for gain error recovery. This proved to have less than full phone line speech quality. In 1977, one engineer with two assistants in the IBM Research Triangle Park, NC laboratory was assigned to improve the quality.

The final implementation replaced the integrator with a Predictor implemented with a two pole complex pair low-pass filter designed to approximate the long term average speech spectrum. The theory was that ideally the integrator should be a predictor designed to match the signal spectrum. A nearly perfect Shindler Compander replaced the modified version. It was found the modified compander resulted in a less than perfect step size at most signal levels and the fast gain error recovery increased the noise as determined by actual listening tests as compared to simple signal to noise measurements. The final compander achieved a very mild gain error recovery due to the natural truncation rounding error caused by twelve bit arithmetic.

The complete function of delta modulation, VAC and Echo Control for six ports was implemented in a single digital integrated circuit chip with twelve bit arithmetic. A single digital-to-analog converter (DAC) was shared by all six ports providing voltage compare functions for the modulators and feeding sample and hold circuits for the demodulator outputs. A single card held the chip, DAC and all the analog circuits for the phone line interface including transformers.

Differential Pulse-code Modulation

Differential pulse-code modulation (DPCM) is a signal encoder that uses the baseline of pulse-code modulation (PCM) but adds some functionalities based on the prediction of the samples of the signal. The input can be an analog signal or a digital signal.

If the input is a continuous-time analog signal, it needs to be sampled first so that a discrete-time signal is the input to the DPCM encoder.

- Option 1: take the values of two consecutive samples; if they are analog samples, quantize them; calculate the difference between the first one and the next; the output is the difference, and it can be further entropy coded.

- Option 2: instead of taking a difference relative to a previous input sample, take the difference relative to the output of a local model of the decoder process; in this option, the difference can be quantized, which allows a good way to incorporate a controlled loss in the encoding.

Applying one of these two processes, short-term redundancy (positive correlation of nearby values) of the signal is eliminated; compression ratios on the order of 2 to 4 can be achieved if differences are subsequently entropy coded, because the entropy of the difference signal is much smaller than that of the original discrete signal treated as independent samples.

DPCM was invented by C. Chapin Cutler at Bell Labs in 1950; his patent includes both methods.

Option 1: Difference between Two Consecutive Quantized Samples

The encoder performs the function of differentiation; a quantizer precedes the differencing of adjacent quantized samples; the decoder is an accumulator, which if correctly initialized exactly recovers the quantized signal.

Option 2: Analysis by Synthesis

The incorporation of the decoder inside the encoder allows quantization of the differences, including nonlinear quantization, in the encoder, as long as an approximate inverse quantizer is used appropriately in the receiver. When the quantizer is uniform, the decoder regenerates the differences implicitly, as in this simple diagram that Cutler showed:

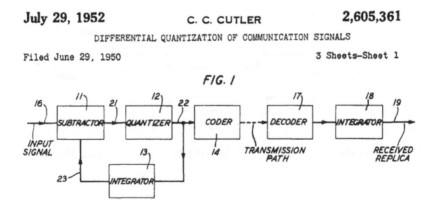

Adaptive Differential Pulse-code Modulation

Adaptive differential pulse-code modulation (ADPCM) is a variant of differential pulse-code modulation (DPCM) that varies the size of the quantization step, to allow further reduction of the required data bandwidth for a given signal-to-noise ratio.

Typically, the adaptation to signal statistics in ADPCM consists simply of an adaptive scale factor before quantizing the difference in the DPCM encoder.

ADPCM was developed in the early 1970s at Bell Labs for voice coding, by P. Cummiskey, N. S. Jayant and James L. Flanagan.

In Telephony

In telephony, a standard audio signal for a single phone call is encoded as 8000 analog samples per second, of 8 bits each, giving a 64 kbit/s digital signal known as DS0. The default signal compression encoding on a DS0 is either μ-law (mu-law) PCM (North America and Japan) or A-law PCM (Europe and most of the rest of the world). These are logarithmic compression systems where a 13 or 14 bit linear PCM sample number is mapped into an 8 bit value. This system is described by international standard G.711. Where circuit costs are high and loss of voice quality is acceptable, it sometimes makes sense to compress the voice signal even further. An ADPCM algorithm is used to map a series of 8 bit μ-law (or a-law) PCM samples into a series of 4 bit ADPCM samples. In this way, the capacity of the line is doubled. The technique is detailed in the G.726 standard.

Some ADPCM techniques are used in Voice over IP communications. ADPCM was also used by Interactive Multimedia Association for development of legacy audio codec known as ADPCM DVI, IMA ADPCM or DVI4, in the early 1990s.

Split-band or Subband ADPCM

G.722 is an ITU-T standard wideband speech codec operating at 48, 56 and 64 kbit/s, based on subband coding with two channels and ADPCM coding of each. Before the digitization process, it catches the analog signal and divides it in frequency bands with QMF filters (quadrature mirror filters) to get two subbands of the signal. When the ADPCM bitstream of each subband is obtained, the results are multiplexed and the next step is storage or transmission of the data. The decoder has to perform the reverse process, that is, demultiplex and decode each subband of the bitstream and recombine them.

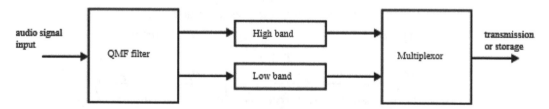

Referring to the coding process, in some applications as voice coding, the subband that includes the voice is coded with more bits than the others. It is a way to reduce the file size.

Software

The Windows Sound System supported ADPCM in .wav files. The corresponding FFmpeg audio codecs are adpcm-ms and adpcm-ima-wav.

Optimal Predictor Design

We consider the linear predictor that we had used to predict the Current pixel value $s(n_1, n_2)$ and reproduce below the general fourth-order prediction equation stated in equation given of the topic Lossless Predictive Coding:

$$\hat{s}(n_1, n_2) = a_1 s(n_1 - 1, n_2 - 1) + a_2 s(n_1 - 1, n_2) + a_3 s(n_1 - 1, n_2 + 1) + a_4 s(n_1, n_2 - 1)$$

where a_1, a_2, a_3, a_4 are the coefficients of prediction. The problem is to design a_1, a_2, a_3, a_4 such that the prediction error is optimal in linear minimum mean square error (LMMSE) sense. The mean squared error (MSE) in DPCM is given by

$$D = E[(s - \dot{s})^T (s - \dot{s})]$$

where s is a vector containing lexicographically ordered pixel intensities in the original and $\dot{s}$ is the corresponding vector for the reconstructed image. Neglecting the quantization error, $\hat{s} = \dot{s}$ where $\hat{s}$ is the vector for the predicted image. Using earlier equation, it is possible to solve for the coefficient vector $a = (a_1 \quad a_2 \quad a_3 \quad a_4)^T$ from the equation

$$\phi = \varphi a$$

where φ is defined as the autocorrelation matrix

$$\varphi = \begin{bmatrix} R(0,0) & R(0,1) & R(0,2) & R(1,0) \\ R(0,-1) & R(0,0) & R(0,1) & R(1,-1) \\ R(0,-2) & R(0,-1) & R(0,0) & R(1,-2) \\ R(-1,0) & R(-1,1) & R(-1,2) & R(0,0) \end{bmatrix}.$$

and ϕ is the vector $[R(1,1) \ R(1,0) \ R(1,-1) \ R(0,1)]^T$.

The autocorrelation values $R(i \ j)$ are given by

$$R(i,j) = E[s(n_1, n_2)s(n_1 - i, n_2 - j)]$$

and these can be measured from the image as

$$R(i,j) = \frac{1}{N} \sum_{n_1 n_2} s(n_1 n_2) s(n_1 - i, n_2 - j)$$

where N is the number of pixels in the image.

The φ matrix defined in earlier equation is mostly invertible and the solution of a is given by

$$a = \varphi^{-1}\phi$$

The solution of a provides optimal prediction in terms of LMMSE, but not in terms of entropy.

Quantization of Prediction Error

The prediction error in DPCM is scalar quantized to K bits/sample, where K must be less than 8 in monochrome images to achieve compression. It is empirically shown that the prediction error in typical images can be modeled by Laplacian distribution with variance σ^2. Since, this distribution is heavily peaked about zero, a non-uniform Lloyd-Max quantization is employed in order to achieve the best image quality. For Laplacian distribution with unit variance, quantizer design is shown for 2,4 and 8 reconstruction levels. For $\sigma^2 \neq 1$, the decision and thereconstruction levels are accordingly scaled.

Transform Coding

Transform coding is a type of data compression for "natural" data like audio signals or photographic images. The transformation is typically lossless (perfectly reversible) on their own but are used to enable better (more targeted) quantization, which then results in a lower quality copy of the original input (lossy compression).

In transform coding, knowledge of the application is used to choose information to discard, thereby lowering its bandwidth. The remaining information can then be compressed via a variety of methods. When the output is decoded, the result may not be identical to the original input, but is expected to be close enough for the purpose of the application.

Colour Television

NTSC

One of the most successful transform encoding system is typically not referred to as such—the example being NTSC color television. After an extensive series of studies in the 1950s, Alda Bedford showed that the human eye has high resolution only for black and white, somewhat less for "mid-range" colors like yellows and greens, and much less for colors on the end of the spectrum, reds and blues.

Using this knowledge allowed RCA to develop a system in which they discarded most of the blue signal after it comes from the camera, keeping most of the green and only some of the red; this is chroma subsampling in the YIQ color space.

The result is a signal with considerably less content, one that would fit within existing 6 MHz black-and-white signals as a phase modulated differential signal. The average TV displays the equivalent of 350 pixels on a line, but the TV signal contains enough information for only about 50 pixels of blue and perhaps 150 of red. This is not apparent to the viewer in most cases, as the eye makes little use of the "missing" information anyway.

PAL and SECAM

The PAL and SECAM systems use nearly identical or very similar methods to transmit colour. In any case both systems are subsampled.

Digital

The term is much more commonly used in digital media and in digital signal processing. The common JPEG image format is an example of a transform coding, one that examines small blocks of the image and transforms them to the frequency domain for more efficient quantization (lossy) and data compression. MPEG modifies this across frames in a motion image, further reducing the size compared to a series of JPEGs. A widely used transform in this regard is the Discrete Cosine Transform (DCT), developed in 1974 by N. Ahmed, T. Natarajan and K. R. Rao; Citation 1 in Discrete cosine transform. The DCT is sometimes referred to as "DCT-II" in the context of a family of discrete cosine transforms; e.g., Discrete cosine transform. MPEG audio compression analyzes the transformed data according to a psychoacoustic model that describes the human ear's sensitivity to parts of the signal, similar to the TV model.

The basic process of digitizing an analog signal is a kind of transform coding that uses sampling in one or more domains as its transform.

Principles of Transform Coding

The basic principle of transform coding is to map the pixel values into a set of linear transform coefficients, which are subsequently quantized and encoded. By applying an inverse transformation on the decoded transform coefficients, it is possible to reconstruct the image with some loss. It must be noted that the loss is not due to the process of transformation and inverse transformation, but due to quantization alone. Since the details of an image and hence it's spatial frequency content vary from one local region to the other, it leads to a better coding efficiency if we apply the transformation on local areas of the image, rather than applying global transformation on the entire image. Such local transformations require manageable size of the hardware, which can be replicated for parallel processing. For transform coding, the first and foremost step is to subdivide the image into non-overlapping blocks of fixed size. Without loss of generality, we can consider a square image of size N x N pixels and divide it into n^2 number of blocks, each of size (N/n) x (N/n), where n<<N and is a factor of N.

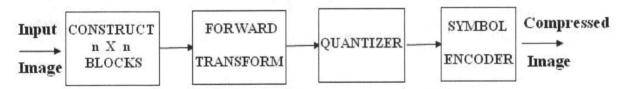

Block Diagram of Transform Coding System Encoder.

Figure above shows the block diagram of a transform coding system and figure below shows the corresponding decoder. Although transformation does not directly achieve any compression, it prepares the input signal to compression in the transformed domain.

Block Diagram of Transform Coding System Decoder

A transformation must necessarily fulfill the following properties –

(i)   The coefficients in the transformed space should be de-correlated.

(ii)   Only a limited number of transform coefficients should carry most of the signal energy (in other words, the transformation should possess *energy compaction* capabilities) and most of the coefficients should carry insignificant energy. Only then the quantization process can coarsely quantize those coefficients to achieve compression, without much of perceptible degradation.

A number of transformation techniques, such as Discrete Fourier Transforms (DFT), Discrete Cosine Transforms (DCT), Discrete Wavelet Transforms (DWT), K-L Transforms (KLT), Discrete Haar Transforms, and Discrete Hadamard Transforms etc. exist that fulfill the above properties, although their energy packing capabilities vary. In terms of energy packing, KLT is optimal and we are going to study KLT in the latter part of this chapter.

Generalized Forward and Inverse Transforms

Several transformation techniques are available, but the choice of the technique depends on the amount of reconstruction error that can be available and the computational resources available.

Let us consider an image block of size n x n whose pixel intensities are represented by $s(n_1, n_2)$ $(n_1, n_2 = 0, 1, ..., n-1)$ where n_1 and n_2 are the row and the column indices of the array. Its general expression for transformation is given by

$$S k_1, k_2) = \sum_{n_1=0}^{n-1} \sum_{n_2=0}^{n-1} s(n_1, n_2) g(n_1, n_2, k_1, k_2) \quad k_1, k_2 = 0, 1, ..., n-1 \quad (1)$$

where $S(k_1, k_2)$ $(k_1, k_2 = 0, 1, ..., n-1)$ represents the transform coefficients of the block with k_1 and k_2 as the row and the column indices in the transformed array and $g(n_1, n_2, k_1, k_2)$ is the transformation kernel that maps the input image pixels into the transform coefficients. Given the transform coefficients $S(k_1, k_2)$, the input image $s(n_1, n_2)$ may be obtained as

$$s(n_1, n_2) = \sum_{k_1=0}^{n-1} \sum_{k_2=0}^{n-1} S(k_1, k_2) h(n_1, n_2, k_1, k_2) \quad n_1, n_2 = 0, 1, ...n-1. \quad (2)$$

In the above equation, $h(n_1, n_2, k_1, k_2)$ represents the inverse transformation kernel.

Separable Kernel

A transformation kernel is said to be separable if it can be expressed as a product of two kernels along the row and the column, i.e.

$$g(n_1, n_2, k_1, k_2) = g_1(n_1, k_1) g_2(n_2, k_2) \quad (3)$$

where $g_1(.)$ and $g_2(.)$ represent the transformation kernels along the row and the column directions respectively. By a similar way, the inverse transformation kernel too can be separable. Separable transforms are easier to implement in hardware, since the transformation can first be applied along the rows (or the columns) and then along the columns (or the rows).

Symmetric Kernel

A separable transform is symmetric, if the kernels along the row and the column have the identical function, i.e. if

$$g(n_1, n_2, k_1, k_2) = g_1(n_1, k_1) g_1(n_2, k_2) \quad (4)$$

Most of the transformations that we deal with have separable, symmetric kernels. For example, the forward and the inverse transformation kernels of Discrete Fourier Transform (DFT) for n x n image block is given by

$$g(n_1,n_2,k_1,k_2) = \frac{1}{n^2}\exp\left[-j\frac{2\pi(n_1k_1+n_2k_2)}{n}\right] \tag{5}$$

and

$$h(n_1,n_2,k_1,k_2) = \exp\left[j\frac{\ddot{u}\pi\ n_1k_1+n_2k_2}{n}\right] \tag{6}$$

are separable and symmetric. The students can easily derive the row and the column transformation kernels by expressing the kernel of equation (5) as a product of two kernels. This is left as an exercise.

Basis Images

Equation (2) relates the pixel intensities of the image block on an element by element basis to the transformation coefficients $S(k_1,k_2)$ $(k_1,k_2=0,1,....,n-1)$ and there are n^2 number of similar equations, defined for each pixel element. These equations can be combined and written in the matrix form

$$s = \sum_{k_1=0}^{n-1}\sum_{k_2=0}^{n-1} S(k_1,k_2)H_{k_1k_2} \tag{7}$$

where s is an $n \times n$ matrix containing the pixels of $s(n_1,n_2)$ and

$$H_{k_1k_2} = \begin{bmatrix} h(0,0,k_1,k_2) & h(0,1,k_1,k_2) & \cdots & \cdots & h(0,n-1,k_1,k_2) \\ h(1,0,k_1,k_2) & \vdots & \cdots & \cdots & \vdots \\ \vdots & \vdots & \cdots & \cdots & \vdots \\ \vdots & \vdots & \cdots & \cdots & \vdots \\ h(n-1,0,k_1,k_2) & h(n-1,1,k_1,k_2) & \cdots & \cdots & h(n-1,n-1,k_1,k_2) \end{bmatrix} \tag{8}$$

$H_{k_1k_2}$ is an $n \times n$ matrix defined for (k_1,k_2). The image block s can therefore be realized by a weighted summation of n^2 images, each of size $n \times n$, defined by equation (8) and the weights are provided by the transform coefficients $S(k_1,k_2)$. The matrix $H_{k_1k_2}$ is known as a basis image corresponding to (k_1,k_2). There are n^2 such basis images, each of size $n \times n$, corresponding to each (k_1,k_2).

Covariance Matrix

Since transforms are applied on a block-by-block basis, each block of an image may be treated as a random field. A block may be represented by a n^2 - dimensional random variable vector x, whose elements are composed by the lexicographic ordering of pixel intensity values. We define a vector b, such that

$$b = x - E[x]. \tag{9}$$

where, $E[.]$ is the expectation operator. The expectation of x can be obtained from the mean of the random variable x over all the blocks present in the image. Thus,

$$b = x - \mu. \qquad (10)$$

where,

$$\mu = \frac{1}{N_B} \sum_{\forall i} x_i. \qquad (11)$$

i is the block index and N_B is the total number of blocks. The covariance matrix R_b computed over blocks of size $n \times n$ is defined by

$$R_b = E\left[(x-\mu)(x-\mu)^T\right] = E\left[bb^T\right] \qquad (12)$$

where, as before, the expectation is calculated by averaging over all the blocks. Since b is an n^2 -dimensional vector, its outer product realizes an $n^2 \times n^2$– dimensional matrix, which is the size of R_b. The matrix R_b is real and symmetric and it is possible to find a set of n^2 orthonormal eigenvectors.

Let e_i and λ_i, $i = 1,2,...,n^2$ be the eigenvectors and the corresponding eigenvalues, arranged in non-increasing order, such that $\lambda_j \geq \lambda_{j+1}$ for $j = 1,2,....,n^2 - 1$.

By the basic definition of eigenvectors,

$$R_b e_j = \lambda_j e_j. \qquad (13)$$

Pre-multiplying both the sides of equation (13) by e_j^T and noting that $e_j^T e_j = 1$ for orthonormal eigenvectors, it follows that

$$e_j^T R_b e_j = \lambda_j. \qquad (14)$$

We now compose a matrix Γ of dimension $n^2 \times n^2$, whose rows are formed from the eigenvectors of R_b, ordered such that the first row of Γ is the eigenvector corresponding to the largest eigenvalue and the last row is the eigenvector corresponding to the smallest eigenvalue. Considering all the eigenvectors, we can write equation (14) in matrix form as

$$\Gamma R_b \Gamma^T = \Lambda \qquad (15)$$

where, Λ is a diagonal matrix of ordered eigenvalues, defined as

$$\Lambda = \begin{bmatrix} \lambda_1 & 0 & 0 & \cdots & 0 \\ 0 & \lambda_2 & 0 & \cdots & 0 \\ \vdots & \vdots & \vdots & \cdots & \vdots \\ \vdots & \vdots & \vdots & \cdots & \vdots \\ 0 & 0 & \cdots & \cdots & \lambda_{n^2} \end{bmatrix} \qquad (16)$$

Pre-multiplying equation (15) by Γ^T, post-multiplying by Γ and noting the orthonormal properties of matrix Γ, i.e., $\Gamma^T = \Gamma^{-1}$, we obtain

$$R_b = \Gamma^T \Lambda \Gamma \qquad (17)$$

K-L Transforms

If we use the matrix Γ to map the block of n^2-dimensional vector b into a transformed block of n^2-dimensional vector y, defined by

$$y = \Gamma b \tag{18}$$

the transformation is called *Karhunen-Loeve transforms (KLT)*.

The covariance matrix R_y of the y's is given by

$$\begin{aligned} R_y &= E\left[yy^T\right] \\ &= E\left[(\Gamma b)(\Gamma b)^T\right] \\ &= \Gamma E\left[bb^T\right]\Gamma^T \\ &= \Gamma R_b \Gamma^T \end{aligned} \tag{19}$$

The pre-multiplication of R_b by Γ and post-multiplication by Γ^T diagonalizes R_b into a diagonal matrix Λ of eigenvectors and the matrix R_y can be written as

$$R_y = \Lambda \tag{20}$$

The covariance matrix R_y has the same eigenvectors and eigenvalues as that of R_b, but its off-diagonal elements are zero, which signifies that the elements of the transform-domain vectors y are uncorrelated. Using equation (18), it is possible to recover vector b as

$$b = \Gamma^{-1}y \tag{21}$$

Using equation (10) and orthonormality property of Γ, it is possible to reconstruct the original block x as

$$x = \Gamma^T y + \mu \tag{22}$$

The above equation leads to exact reconstruction. Suppose that instead of using all the n^2 eigenvectors of R_b, we use only k eigenvectors corresponding to the k largest eigenvalues and form a transformation matrix Γ_k of order $k \times n^2$. The resulting transformed vector $\hat{y}$ therefore becomes k-dimensional and the reconstruction given in equation (23) will not be exact. The reconstructed vector $\hat{x}$ is then given by

$$\hat{x} = \Gamma_k^T \hat{y} + \mu \tag{23}$$

Optimality of K-L Transform

To show that K-L Transform is optimal in the least square error sense, we first establish a relation between the variance of the original data vector x and the eigenvalues.

If we project the mean-removed vector b, defined in equation (24) into any of the eigenvectors e_j (j = 1,2,...., n^2), the projection is defined by the inner product of the vectors b and e_j is given by

$$A = b^T e_j = e_j^T b \tag{24}$$

The variance σ^2 of the projection is therefore given by

$$\begin{aligned}
\sigma^2 &= E\left[A^2\right] \\
&= E\left[e_j^T bb^T e_j\right]. \\
&= e_j^T E\left[bb^T\right] e_j \\
&= e_j^T R_b e_j
\end{aligned} \tag{25}$$

By projecting the vector b into all the n^2 eigenvectors and using equation (26), we obtain the total variance as

$$\sigma_{n^2}^2 = \sum_{j=1}^{n^2} e_j^T R_b e_j = \sum_{j=1}^{n^2} \lambda_j. \tag{26}$$

By considering only the first k eigenvectors out of n^2 , the variance of the approximating signal in the projected space is given by

$$\sigma_k^2 = \sum_{j=1}^{k} \lambda_j. \tag{27}$$

Thus, the mean-square error e_{ms} in the projected space by considering only the first k components can be obtained by subtracting equation (27) from equation (28)

$$\begin{aligned}
e_{ms} &= \sigma_{n^2}^2 - \sigma_k^2 \\
&= \sum_{j=1}^{n^2} \lambda_j - \sum_{j=1}^{k} \lambda_j \\
&= \sum_{j=k+1}^{n^2} \lambda_j
\end{aligned} \tag{28}$$

Since, the transformation is energy-preserving, the same mean-square error exists between the original vector x and its approximation $\hat{x}$. It is evident from the above equation that the mean square error is zero when $k = n^2$, i.e., if all the Eigenvectors are used in the transformation. Since the λ_j's decrease monotonically, the error can be minimized by selecting the first k eigenvectors are associated with the largest eigenvalues. Thus, K-L transform is optimal in the sense that it minimizes the mean-square error between the original input vectors x and their approximations $\hat{x}$.

References

- Jerry D. Gibson; Toby Berger; Tom Lookabaugh (1998). Digital Compression for Multimedia. Morgan Kaufmann. ISBN 978-1-55860-369-1

- Chanda, Elhaik, and Bader (2012). "HapZipper: sharing HapMap populations just got easier". Nucleic Acids Res. 40 (20): 1–7. PMC 3488212. PMID 22844100. doi:10.1093/nar/gks709

- C.E. Shannon, "A Mathematical Theory of Communication", Bell System Technical Journal, vol. 27, pp. 379–423, 623-656, July, October, 1948

- David Salomon, Giovanni Motta, (with contributions by David Bryant), Handbook of Data Compression, 5th edition, Springer, 2009, ISBN 1-84882-902-7, pp. 16–18

- "Milestones:Lempel-Ziv Data Compression Algorithm, 1977". IEEE Global History Network. Institute of Electrical and Electronics Engineers. 2014-07-22. Retrieved 2014-11-09

- Hu, T. C.; Tucker, A. C. (1971). "Optimal Computer Search Trees and Variable-Length Alphabetical Codes". SIAM Journal on Applied Mathematics. 21 (4): 514. JSTOR 2099603. doi:10.1137/0121057

- David J. C. MacKay. Information Theory, Inference, and Learning Algorithms Cambridge: Cambridge University Press, 2003. ISBN 0-521-64298-1

- Feldspar, Antaeus (23 August 1997). "An Explanation of the Deflate Algorithm". comp.compression newsgroup. zlib.net. Retrieved 2014-11-09

- Huffman, D. (1952). "A Method for the Construction of Minimum-Redundancy Codes" (PDF). Proceedings of the IRE. 40 (9): 1098–1101. doi:10.1109/JRPROC.1952.273898

- Rissanen, Jorma (May 1976). "Generalized Kraft Inequality and Arithmetic Coding" (PDF). IBM Journal of Research and Development. 20 (3): 198–203. doi:10.1147/rd.203.0198. Retrieved 2007-09-21

- Cover, Thomas M. (2006). "Chapter 5: Data Compression". Elements of Information Theory. John Wiley & Sons. ISBN 0-471-24195-4

- Alvestrand, Harald Tveit; Salsman, James (May 1999). "RFC 2586 – The Audio/L16 MIME content type". The Internet Society. Retrieved 2010-03-16

- Sears, R. W. (January 1948). "Bell Systems Technical Journal, Vol. 27: Electron Beam Deflection Tube for Pulse Code Modulation". Bell labs. pp. 44–57. Retrieved 14 May 2017

- Press, WH; Teukolsky, SA; Vetterling, WT; Flannery, BP (2007). "Section 22.6. Arithmetic Coding". Numerical Recipes: The Art of Scientific Computing (3rd ed.). New York: Cambridge University Press. ISBN 978-0-521-88068-8

- "RFC 3108 – Conventions for the use of the Session Description Protocol (SDP) for ATM Bearer Connections". May 2001. Retrieved 2010-03-16

- Goodall, W. M. (January 1951). "Bell Systems Technical Journal, Vol. 30: Television by Pulse Code Modulation". Bell labs. pp. 33–49. Retrieved 14 May 2017

- Celebi, M. E. (2011). "Improving the performance of k-means for color quantization". Image and Vision Computing. 29 (4): 260–271. doi:10.1016/j.imavis.2010.10.002

- U.S. patent number 1,608,527; also see p. 8, Data conversion handbook, Walter Allan Kester, ed., Newnes, 2005, ISBN 0-7506-7841-0

- "Differences Between PCM/ADPCM Wave Files Explained". KB 89879 Revision 3.0. Microsoft Knowledge Base. 2011-09-24. Retrieved 2013-12-30

3

JBIG and JPEG: Still Image Compression Standards

There is a need to have uniformity in encoding and decoding so that products are less complex and users need not install separate decoders. This has given birth to coding standards. A few examples of image compression standards are JBIG, JPEG, and JPEG 2000. This chapter has been carefully written to provide an easy understanding of the varied facets of still image compression standards.

JBIG

JBIG is an early lossless image compression standard from the Joint Bi-level Image Experts Group, standardized as ISO/IEC standard 11544 and as ITU-T recommendation T.82 in March 1993. It is widely implemented in fax machines. Now that the newer bi-level image compression standard JBIG2 has been released, JBIG is also known as JBIG1. JBIG was designed for compression of binary images, particularly for faxes, but can also be used on other images. In most situations JBIG offers between a 20% and 50% increase in compression efficiency over the Fax Group 4 standard, and in some situations, it offers a 30-fold improvement.

JBIG is based on a form of arithmetic coding developed by IBM (known as the Q-coder) that also uses a relatively minor refinement developed by Mitsubishi, resulting in what became known as the QM-coder. It bases the probability estimates for each encoded bit on the values of the previous bits and the values in previous lines of the picture. JBIG also supports progressive transmission, which generally incurs a small overhead in bit rate (around 5%).

Patents

Doubts about patent licence requirements for JBIG1 implementations by IBM, Mitsubishi and AT&T prevented the codec from being widely implemented in open-source software. For example, as of 2012, none of the commonly used web browsers supported it. Since 2012, there are now no more JBIG1 patents in force – the last ones to expire were Mitsubishi's patents in Canada and Australia (on 25 February 2011) and in the United States (on 4 April 2012).

JBIG2

JBIG2 is an image compression standard for bi-level images, developed by the Joint Bi-level Image Experts Group. It is suitable for both lossless and lossy compression. According to a press release from the Group, in its lossless mode JBIG2 typically generates files 3–5 times smaller than Fax Group 4 and 2–4 times smaller then JBIG, the previous bi-level compression standard released by the Group. JBIG2 has been published in 2000 as the international standard ITU T.88, and in 2001 as ISO/IEC 14492.

Functionality

Ideally, a JBIG2 encoder will segment the input page into regions of text, regions of halftone images, and regions of other data. Regions that are neither text nor halftones are typically compressed using a context-dependent arithmetic coding algorithm called the MQ coder. Textual regions are compressed as follows: the foreground pixels in the regions are grouped into symbols. A dictionary of symbols is then created and encoded, typically also using context-dependent arithmetic coding, and the regions are encoded by describing which symbols appear where. Typically, a symbol will correspond to a character of text, but this is not required by the compression method. For lossy compression the difference between similar symbols (e.g., slightly different impressions of the same letter) can be neglected; for lossless compression, this difference is taken into account by compressing one similar symbol using another as a template. Halftone images may be compressed by reconstructing the grayscale image used to generate the halftone and then sending this image together with a dictionary of halftone patterns. Overall, the algorithm used by JBIG2 to compress text is very similar to the JB2 compression scheme used in the DjVu file format for coding binary images.

PDF files versions 1.4 and above may contain JBIG2-compressed data. Open-source decoders for JBIG2 are jbig2dec, the java-based jbig2-imageio and the decoder found in versions 2.00 and above of xpdf. An open-source encoder is jbig2enc.

Technical Details

Typically, a bi-level image consists mainly of a large amount of textual and halftone data, in which the same shapes appear repeatedly. The bi-level image is segmented into three regions: text, halftone, and generic regions. Each region is coded differently and the coding methodologies are described in the following passage.

Text Image Data

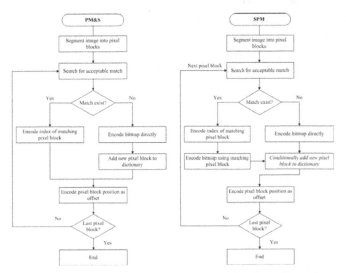

Block diagrams of (left) pattern matching and substitution method and (right) soft pattern matching method

Text coding is based on the nature of human visual interpretation. A human observer cannot tell the difference between two instances of the same characters in a bi-level image even though they may not exactly match pixel by pixel. Therefore, only the bitmap of one representative character instance needs to be coded instead of coding the bitmaps of each occurrence of the same character individually. For each character instance, the coded instance of the character is then stored into a "symbol dictionary". There are two encoding methods for text image data: pattern matching and substitution (PM&S) and soft pattern matching (SPM).

Pattern matching and substitution

> After performing image segmentation and match searching, and if a match exists, we code an index of the corresponding representative bitmap in the dictionary and the position of the character on the page. The position is usually relative to another previously coded character. If a match is not found, the segmented pixel block is coded directly and added into the dictionary. Typical procedures of pattern matching and substitution algorithm are displayed in the left block diagram of the figure above. Although the method of PM&S can achieve outstanding compression, substitution errors could be made during the process if the image resolution is low.

Soft pattern matching

> In addition to a pointer to the dictionary and position information of the character, refinement data is also required because it is a crucial piece of information used to reconstruct the original character in the image. The deployment of refinement data can make the character-substitution error mentioned earlier highly unlikely. The refinement data contains the current desired character instance, which is coded using the pixels of both the current character and the matching character in the dictionary. Since it is known that the current character instance is highly correlated with the matched character, the prediction of the current pixel is more accurate.

Halftones

Halftone images can be compressed using two methods. One of the methods is similar to the context-based arithmetic coding algorithm, which adaptively positions the template pixels in order to obtain correlations between the adjacent pixels. In the second method, descreening is performed on the halftone image so that the image is converted back to grayscale. The converted grayscale values are then used as indexes of fixed-sized tiny bitmap patterns contained in a halftone bitmap dictionary. This allows decoder to successfully render a halftone image by presenting indexed dictionary bitmap patterns neighboring with each other.

Arithmetic Entropy Coding

All three region types including text, halftone, and generic regions may all use arithmetic coding. JBIG2 specifically uses the MQ coder.

Patents

Patents for JBIG2 are owned by IBM and Mitsubishi. Free licenses should be available after a request. JBIG and JBIG2 patents are not the same.

Disadvantages

When used in lossy mode, JBIG2 compression can potentially alter text in a way that's not discernible as corruption. This is in contrast to some other algorithms, which simply degrade into a blur, making the compression artifacts obvious. Since JBIG2 tries to match up similar-looking symbols, the numbers "6" and "8" may get replaced, for example.

In 2013, various substitutions (including replacing "6" with "8") were reported to happen on some Xerox Workcentre photocopier and printer machines, where numbers printed on scanned (but not OCRed) documents could have potentially been altered. This has been demonstrated on construction blueprints and some tables of numbers; the potential impact of such substitution errors in documents such as medical prescriptions was briefly mentioned. David Kriesel and Xerox were investigating this.

Xerox subsequently acknowledged that this was a long-standing software defect, and their initial statements in suggesting that only non-factory settings could introduce the substitution were incorrect. Patches that comprehensively address the problem were published later in August, but no attempt has been made to recall or mandate updates to the affected devices – which was acknowledged to affect more than a dozen product families. Documents previously scanned continue to potentially contain errors making their veracity difficult to substantiate. German and Swiss regulators have subsequently (in 2015) disallowed the JBIG2 encoding in archival documents.

JPEG

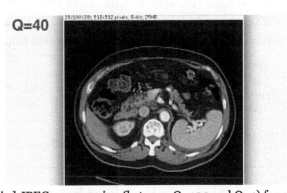

Continuously varied JPEG compression (between Q=100 and Q=1) for an abdominal CT scan

JPEG (*JAY-PEG*) is a commonly used method of lossy compression for digital images, particularly for those images produced by digital photography. The degree of compression can be adjusted, allowing a selectable tradeoff between storage size and image quality. JPEG typically achieves 10:1 compression with little perceptible loss in image quality.

JPEG compression is used in a number of image file formats. JPEG/Exif is the most common image format used by digital cameras and other photographic image capture devices; along with JPEG/JFIF, it is the most common format for storing and transmitting photographic images on the World Wide Web. These format variations are often not distinguished, and are simply called JPEG.

The term "JPEG" is an initialism/acronym for the Joint Photographic Experts Group, which created the standard. The MIME media type for JPEG is *image/jpeg*, except in older Internet Explorer versions, which provides a MIME type of *image/pjpeg* when uploading JPEG images. JPEG files usually have a filename extension of *.jpg* or *.jpeg*.

JPEG/JFIF supports a maximum image size of 65,535×65,535 pixels, hence up to 4 gigapixels for an aspect ratio of 1:1.

The JPEg Standard

"JPEG" stands for Joint Photographic Experts Group, the name of the committee that created the JPEG standard and also other still picture coding standards. The "Joint" stood for ISO TC97 WG8 and CCITT SGVIII. In 1987 ISO TC 97 became ISO/IEC JTC1 and in 1992 CCITT became ITU-T. Currently on the JTC1 side JPEG is one of two sub-groups of ISO/IEC Joint Technical Committee 1, Subcommittee 29, Working Group 1 (ISO/IEC JTC 1/SC 29/WG 1) – titled as *Coding of still pictures*. On the ITU-T side ITU-T SG16 is the respective body. The original JPEG group was organized in 1986, issuing the first JPEG standard in 1992, which was approved in September 1992 as ITU-T Recommendation T.81 and in 1994 as ISO/IEC 10918-1.

The JPEG standard specifies the codec, which defines how an image is compressed into a stream of bytes and decompressed back into an image, but not the file format used to contain that stream. The Exif and JFIF standards define the commonly used file formats for interchange of JPEG-compressed images.

JPEG standards are formally named as *Information technology – Digital compression and coding of continuous-tone still images*. ISO/IEC 10918 consists of the following parts:

Digital compression and coding of continuous-tone still images – Parts						
Part	ISO/IEC standard	ITU-T Rec.	First public release date	Latest amendment	Title	Description
Part 1	ISO/IEC 10918-1:1994	T.81 (09/92)	Sep 18, 1992		Requirements and guidelines	
Part 2	ISO/IEC 10918-2:1995	T.83 (11/94)	Nov 11, 1994		Compliance testing	rules and checks for software conformance (to Part 1)
Part 3	ISO/IEC 10918-3:1997	T.84 (07/96)	Jul 3, 1996	Apr 1, 1999	Extensions	set of extensions to improve the Part 1, including the SPIFF file format
Part 4	ISO/IEC 10918-4:1999	T.86 (06/98)	Jun 18, 1998	Jun 29, 2012	Registration of JPEG profiles, SPIFF profiles, SPIFF tags, SPIFF colour spaces, APPn markers, SPIFF compression types and Registration Authorities (REGAUT)	methods for registering some of the parameters used to extend JPEG

| Part 5 | ISO/IEC 10918-5:2013 | T.871 (05/11) | May 14, 2011 | | JPEG File Interchange Format (JFIF) | A popular format which has been the de facto file format for images encoded by the JPEG standard. In 2009, the JPEG Committee formally established an Ad Hoc Group to standardize JFIF as JPEG Part 5. |
| Part 6 | ISO/IEC 10918-6:2013 | T.872 (06/12) | Jun 2012 | | Application to printing systems | Specifies a subset of features and application tools for the interchange of images encoded according to the ISO/IEC 10918-1 for printing. |

Ecma International TR/98 specifies the JPEG File Interchange Format (JFIF); the first edition was published in June 2009.

Typical Usage

The JPEG compression algorithm is at its best on photographs and paintings of realistic scenes with smooth variations of tone and color. For web usage, where the amount of data used for an image is important, JPEG is very popular. JPEG/Exif is also the most common format saved by digital cameras.

On the other hand, JPEG may not be as well suited for line drawings and other textual or iconic graphics, where the sharp contrasts between adjacent pixels can cause noticeable artifacts. Such images may be better saved in a lossless graphics format such as TIFF, GIF, PNG, or a raw image format. The JPEG standard actually includes a lossless coding mode, but that mode is not supported in most products.

As the typical use of JPEG is a lossy compression method, which somewhat reduces the image fidelity, it should not be used in scenarios where the exact reproduction of the data is required (such as some scientific and medical imaging applications and certain technical image processing work).

JPEG is also not well suited to files that will undergo multiple edits, as some image quality will usually be lost each time the image is decompressed and recompressed, particularly if the image is cropped or shifted, or if encoding parameters are changed. To avoid this, an image that is being modified or may be modified in the future can be saved in a lossless format, with a copy exported as JPEG for distribution.

JPEG Compression

JPEG uses a lossy form of compression based on the discrete cosine transform (DCT). This mathematical operation converts each frame/field of the video source from the spatial (2D) domain into the frequency domain (a.k.a. transform domain). A perceptual model based loosely on the human psychovisual system discards high-frequency information, i.e. sharp transitions in intensity, and color hue. In the transform domain, the process of reducing information is called quantization. In simpler terms, quantization is a method for optimally reducing a large number scale (with different occurrences of each number) into a smaller one, and the transform-domain is a convenient representation of the image because the high-frequency coefficients, which contribute less to the overall picture than other coefficients, are characteristically small-values with high compressibility. The quantized coefficients are then sequenced and losslessly packed into the output bitstream. Nearly all software implementations of JPEG permit user control over the compression-ratio (as well as other optional parameters), allowing the user to trade off picture-quality for smaller file size. In embedded applications (such as miniDV, which uses a similar DCT-compression scheme), the parameters are pre-selected and fixed for the application.

The compression method is usually lossy, meaning that some original image information is lost and cannot be restored, possibly affecting image quality. There is an optional lossless mode defined in the JPEG standard. However, this mode is not widely supported in products.

There is also an interlaced *progressive* JPEG format, in which data is compressed in multiple passes of progressively higher detail. This is ideal for large images that will be displayed while downloading over a slow connection, allowing a reasonable preview after receiving only a portion of the data. However, support for progressive JPEGs is not universal. When progressive JPEGs are received by programs that do not support them (such as versions of Internet Explorer before Windows 7) the software displays the image only after it has been completely downloaded.

There are also many medical imaging and traffic systems that create and process 12-bit JPEG images, normally grayscale images. The 12-bit JPEG format has been part of the JPEG specification for some time, but this format is not as widely supported.

Lossless Editing

A number of alterations to a JPEG image can be performed losslessly (that is, without recompression and the associated quality loss) as long as the image size is a multiple of 1 MCU block (Minimum Coded Unit) (usually 16 pixels in both directions, for 4:2:0 chroma subsampling). Utilities that implement this include jpegtran, with user interface Jpegcrop, and the JPG_TRANSFORM plugin to IrfanView.

Blocks can be rotated in 90-degree increments, flipped in the horizontal, vertical and diagonal axes and moved about in the image. Not all blocks from the original image need to be used in the modified one.

The top and left edge of a JPEG image must lie on an 8 × 8 pixel block boundary, but the bottom and right edge need not do so. This limits the possible lossless crop operations, and also prevents flips and rotations of an image whose bottom or right edge does not lie on a block boundary for all channels (because the edge would end up on top or left, where – as aforementioned – a block boundary is obligatory).

Rotations where the image is not a multiple of 8 or 16, which value depends upon the chroma subsampling, are not lossless. Rotating such an image causes the blocks to be recomputed which results in loss of quality.

When using lossless cropping, if the bottom or right side of the crop region is not on a block boundary then the rest of the data from the partially used blocks will still be present in the cropped file and can be recovered. It is also possible to transform between baseline and progressive formats without any loss of quality, since the only difference is the order in which the coefficients are placed in the file.

Furthermore, several JPEG images can be losslessly joined together, as long as they were saved with the same quality and the edges coincide with block boundaries.

JPEG Files

The file format known as "JPEG Interchange Format" (JIF) is specified in Annex B of the standard. However, this "pure" file format is rarely used, primarily because of the difficulty of programming encoders and decoders that fully implement all aspects of the standard and because of certain shortcomings of the standard:

- Color space definition
- Component sub-sampling registration
- Pixel aspect ratio definition.

Several additional standards have evolved to address these issues. The first of these, released in 1992, was JPEG File Interchange Format (or JFIF), followed in recent years by Exchangeable image file format (Exif) and ICC color profiles. Both of these formats use the actual JIF byte layout, consisting of different *markers*, but in addition employ one of the JIF standard's extension points, namely the *application markers*: JFIF uses APP0, while Exif uses APP1. Within these segments of the file, that were left for future use in the JIF standard and aren't read by it, these standards add specific metadata.

Thus, in some ways JFIF is a cutdown version of the JIF standard in that it specifies certain constraints (such as not allowing all the different encoding modes), while in other ways it is an extension of JIF due to the added metadata. The documentation for the original JFIF standard states:

> JPEG File Interchange Format is a minimal file format which enables JPEG bitstreams to be exchanged between a wide variety of platforms and applications. This minimal format does not include any of the advanced features found in the TIFF JPEG specification or any application specific file format. Nor should it, for the only purpose of this simplified format is to allow the exchange of JPEG compressed images.

Image files that employ JPEG compression are commonly called "JPEG files", and are stored in variants of the JIF image format. Most image capture devices (such as digital cameras) that output JPEG are actually creating files in the Exif format, the format that the camera industry has standardized on for metadata interchange. On the other hand, since the Exif standard does not allow color profiles, most image editing software stores JPEG in JFIF format, and also include the APP1 segment from the Exif file to include the metadata in an almost-compliant way; the JFIF standard is interpreted somewhat flexibly.

Strictly speaking, the JFIF and Exif standards are incompatible because each specifies that its marker segment (APP0 or APP1, respectively) appear first. In practice, most JPEG files contain a JFIF marker segment that precedes the Exif header. This allows older readers to correctly handle the older format JFIF segment, while newer readers also decode the following Exif segment, being less strict about requiring it to appear first.

JPEG Filename Extensions

The most common filename extensions for files employing JPEG compression are .jpg and .jpeg, though .jpe, .jfif and .jif are also used. It is also possible for JPEG data to be embedded in other file types – TIFF encoded files often embed a JPEG image as a thumbnail of the main image; and MP3 files can contain a JPEG of cover art, in the ID3v2 tag.

Color Profile

Many JPEG files embed an ICC color profile (color space). Commonly used color profiles include sRGB and Adobe RGB. Because these color spaces use a non-linear transformation, the dynamic range of an 8-bit JPEG file is about 11 stops.

Syntax and Structure

A JPEG image consists of a sequence of *segments,* each beginning with a *marker,* each of which begins with a 0xFF byte followed by a byte indicating what kind of marker it is. Some markers consist of just those two bytes; others are followed by two bytes (high then low) indicating the length of marker-specific payload data that follows. (The length includes the two bytes for the length, but not the two bytes for the marker.) Some markers are followed by entropy-coded data; the length of such a marker does not include the entropy-coded data. Note that consecutive 0xFF bytes are used as fill bytes for padding purposes, although this fill byte padding should only ever take place for markers immediately following entropy-coded scan data.

Within the entropy-coded data, after any 0xFF byte, a 0x00 byte is inserted by the encoder before the next byte, so that there does not appear to be a marker where none is intended, preventing framing errors. Decoders must skip this 0x00 byte. This technique, called byte stuffing, is only applied to the entropy-coded data, not to marker payload data. Note however that entropy-coded data has a few markers of its own; specifically the Reset markers (0xD0 through 0xD7), which are used to isolate independent chunks of entropy-coded data to allow parallel decoding, and encoders are free to insert these Reset markers at regular intervals (although not all encoders do this).

Common JPEG markers				
Short name	Bytes	Payload	Name	Comments
SOI	0xFF, 0xD8	*none*	Start Of Image	
SOF0	0xFF, 0xC0	*variable size*	Start Of Frame (baseline DCT)	Indicates that this is a baseline DCT-based JPEG, and specifies the width, height, number of components, and component subsampling (e.g., 4:2:0).
SOF2	0xFF, 0xC2	*variable size*	Start Of Frame (progressive DCT)	Indicates that this is a progressive DCT-based JPEG, and specifies the width, height, number of components, and component subsampling (e.g., 4:2:0).
DHT	0xFF, 0xC4	*variable size*	Define Huffman Table(s)	Specifies one or more Huffman tables.
DQT	0xFF, 0xDB	*variable size*	Define Quantization Table(s)	Specifies one or more quantization tables.

DRI	0xFF, 0xDD	4 bytes	Define Restart Interval	Specifies the interval between RST*n* markers, in Minimum Coded Units (MCUs). This marker is followed by two bytes indicating the fixed size so it can be treated like any other variable size segment.
SOS	0xFF, 0xDA	*variable size*	Start Of Scan	Begins a top-to-bottom scan of the image. In baseline DCT JPEG images, there is generally a single scan. Progressive DCT JPEG images usually contain multiple scans. This marker specifies which slice of data it will contain, and is immediately followed by entropy-coded data.
RST*n*	0xFF, 0xD*n* (*n*=0..7)	*none*	Restart	Inserted every *r* macroblocks, where *r* is the restart interval set by a DRI marker. Not used if there was no DRI marker. The low three bits of the marker code cycle in value from 0 to 7.
APP*n*	0xFF, 0xE*n*	*variable size*	Application-specific	For example, an Exif JPEG file uses an APP1 marker to store metadata, laid out in a structure based closely on TIFF.
COM	0xFF, 0xFE	*variable size*	Comment	Contains a text comment.
EOI	0xFF, 0xD9	*none*	End Of Image	

There are other *Start Of Frame* markers that introduce other kinds of JPEG encodings.

Since several vendors might use the same APP*n* marker type, application-specific markers often begin with a standard or vendor name (e.g., "Exif" or "Adobe") or some other identifying string.

At a restart marker, block-to-block predictor variables are reset, and the bitstream is synchronized to a byte boundary. Restart markers provide means for recovery after bitstream error, such as transmission over an unreliable network or file corruption. Since the runs of macroblocks between restart markers may be independently decoded, these runs may be decoded in parallel.

JPEG Codec Example

Although a JPEG file can be encoded in various ways, most commonly it is done with JFIF encoding. The encoding process consists of several steps:

1. The representation of the colors in the image is converted from RGB to $Y'C_BC_R$, consisting of one luma component (Y'), representing brightness, and two chroma components, (C_B and C_R), representing color. This step is sometimes skipped.

2. The resolution of the chroma data is reduced, usually by a factor of 2 or 3. This reflects the fact that the eye is less sensitive to fine color details than to fine brightness details.

3. The image is split into blocks of 8×8 pixels, and for each block, each of the Y, C_B, and C_R data undergoes the discrete cosine transform (DCT), which was developed in 1974 by N. Ahmed, T. Natarajan and K. R. Rao; Citation 1 in discrete cosine transform. A DCT is similar to a Fourier transform in the sense that it produces a kind of spatial frequency spectrum.

4. The amplitudes of the frequency components are quantized. Human vision is much more sensitive to small variations in color or brightness over large areas than to the strength

of high-frequency brightness variations. Therefore, the magnitudes of the high-frequency components are stored with a lower accuracy than the low-frequency components. The quality setting of the encoder (for example 50 or 95 on a scale of 0–100 in the Independent JPEG Group's library) affects to what extent the resolution of each frequency component is reduced. If an excessively low quality setting is used, the high-frequency components are discarded altogether.

5. The resulting data for all 8×8 blocks is further compressed with a lossless algorithm, a variant of Huffman encoding.

The decoding process reverses these steps, except the *quantization* because it is irreversible. In the remainder, the encoding and decoding processes are described in more detail.

Encoding

Many of the options in the JPEG standard are not commonly used, and as mentioned above, most image software uses the simpler JFIF format when creating a JPEG file, which among other things specifies the encoding method. Here is a brief description of one of the more common methods of encoding when applied to an input that has 24 bits per pixel (eight each of red, green, and blue). This particular option is a lossy data compression method.

Color Space Transformation

First, the image should be converted from RGB into a different color space called $Y'C_BC_R$ (or, informally, YCbCr). It has three components Y', C_B and C_R: the Y' component represents the brightness of a pixel, and the C_B and C_R components represent the chrominance (split into blue and red components). This is basically the same color space as used by digital color television as well as digital video including video DVDs, and is similar to the way color is represented in analog PAL video and MAC (but not by analog NTSC, which uses the YIQ color space). The $Y'C_BC_R$ color space conversion allows greater compression without a significant effect on perceptual image quality (or greater perceptual image quality for the same compression). The compression is more efficient because the brightness information, which is more important to the eventual perceptual quality of the image, is confined to a single channel. This more closely corresponds to the perception of color in the human visual system. The color transformation also improves compression by statistical decorrelation.

A particular conversion to $Y'C_BC_R$ is specified in the JFIF standard, and should be performed for the resulting JPEG file to have maximum compatibility. However, some JPEG implementations in "highest quality" mode do not apply this step and instead keep the color information in the RGB color model, where the image is stored in separate channels for red, green and blue brightness components. This results in less efficient compression, and would not likely be used when file size is especially important.

Downsampling

Due to the densities of color- and brightness-sensitive receptors in the human eye, humans can see considerably more fine detail in the brightness of an image (the Y' component) than in the hue and color saturation of an image (the Cb and Cr components). Using this knowledge, encoders can be designed to compress images more efficiently.

The transformation into the $Y'C_BC_R$ color model enables the next usual step, which is to reduce the spatial resolution of the Cb and Cr components (called "downsampling" or "chroma subsampling"). The ratios at which the downsampling is ordinarily done for JPEG images are 4:4:4 (no downsampling), 4:2:2 (reduction by a factor of 2 in the horizontal direction), or (most commonly) 4:2:0 (reduction by a factor of 2 in both the horizontal and vertical directions). For the rest of the compression process, Y', Cb and Cr are processed separately and in a very similar manner.

Block Splitting

After subsampling, each channel must be split into 8×8 blocks. Depending on chroma subsampling, this yields Minimum Coded Unit (MCU) blocks of size 8×8 (4:4:4 – no subsampling), 16×8 (4:2:2), or most commonly 16×16 (4:2:0). In video compression MCUs are called macroblocks.

If the data for a channel does not represent an integer number of blocks then the encoder must fill the remaining area of the incomplete blocks with some form of dummy data. Filling the edges with a fixed color (for example, black) can create ringing artifacts along the visible part of the border; repeating the edge pixels is a common technique that reduces (but does not necessarily completely eliminate) such artifacts, and more sophisticated border filling techniques can also be applied.

Discrete Cosine Transform

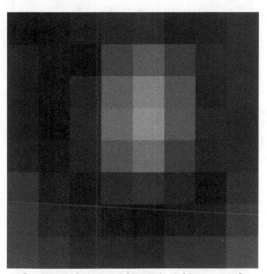

The 8×8 sub-image shown in 8-bit grayscale

Next, each 8×8 block of each component (Y, Cb, Cr) is converted to a frequency-domain representation, using a normalized, two-dimensional type-II discrete cosine transform (DCT), which was introduced by N. Ahmed, T. Natarajan and K. R. Rao in 1974. The DCT is sometimes referred to as "type-II DCT" in the context of a family of transforms as in discrete cosine transform, and the corresponding inverse (IDCT) is denoted as "type-III DCT".

As an example, one such 8×8 8-bit subimage might be:

$$\begin{bmatrix} 52 & 55 & 61 & 66 & 70 & 61 & 64 & 73 \\ 63 & 59 & 55 & 90 & 109 & 85 & 69 & 72 \\ 62 & 59 & 68 & 113 & 144 & 104 & 66 & 73 \\ 63 & 58 & 71 & 122 & 154 & 106 & 70 & 69 \\ 67 & 61 & 68 & 104 & 126 & 88 & 68 & 70 \\ 79 & 65 & 60 & 70 & 77 & 68 & 58 & 75 \\ 85 & 71 & 64 & 59 & 55 & 61 & 65 & 83 \\ 87 & 79 & 69 & 68 & 65 & 76 & 78 & 94 \end{bmatrix}.$$

Before computing the DCT of the 8×8 block, its values are shifted from a positive range to one centered on zero. For an 8-bit image, each entry in the original block falls in the range $[0,255]$. The midpoint of the range (in this case, the value 128) is subtracted from each entry to produce a data range that is centered on zero, so that the modified range is $[-128,127]$. This step reduces the dynamic range requirements in the DCT processing stage that follows. (Aside from the difference in dynamic range within the DCT stage, this step is mathematically equivalent to subtracting 2048 from the DC coefficient after performing the transform – which may be a better way to perform the operation on some architectures since it involves performing only one subtraction rather than 64 of them.)

This step results in the following values:

$$x \\ \rightarrow$$

$$g = \begin{bmatrix} -76 & -73 & -67 & -62 & -58 & -67 & -64 & -55 \\ -65 & -69 & -73 & -38 & -19 & -43 & -59 & -56 \\ -66 & -69 & -60 & -15 & 16 & -24 & -62 & -55 \\ -65 & -70 & -57 & -6 & 26 & -22 & -58 & -59 \\ -61 & -67 & -60 & -24 & -2 & -40 & -60 & -58 \\ -49 & -63 & -68 & -58 & -51 & -60 & -70 & -53 \\ -43 & -57 & -64 & -69 & -73 & -67 & -63 & -45 \\ -41 & -49 & -59 & -60 & -63 & -52 & -50 & -34 \end{bmatrix} \Bigg\downarrow y.$$

The next step is to take the two-dimensional DCT, which is given by:

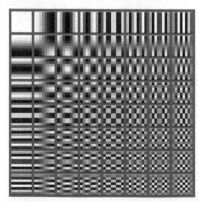

The DCT transforms an 8×8 block of input values to a linear combination of these 64 patterns. The patterns are referred to as the two-dimensional DCT *basis functions*, and the output values are referred to as *transform coefficients*. The horizontal index is u and the vertical index is v.

$$G_{u,v} = \frac{1}{4}\alpha(u)\alpha(v)\sum_{x=0}^{7}\sum_{y=0}^{7}g_{x,y}\cos\left[\frac{(2x+1)u\pi}{16}\right]\cos\left[\frac{(2y+1)v\pi}{16}\right]$$

where

- u i s the horizontal spatial frequency, for the integers $0 \leq u < 8$.

- v is the vertical spatial frequency, for the integers $0 \leq v < 8$.

- $\alpha(u) = \begin{cases} \dfrac{1}{\sqrt{2}}, & \text{if } u = 0 \\ 1, & \text{otherwise} \end{cases}$ is a normalizing scale factor to make the transformation orthonormal

- $g_{x,y}$ is the pixel value at coordinates (x, y)

- $G_{u,v}$ is the DCT coefficient at coordinates (u, v).

If we perform this transformation on our matrix above, we get the following (rounded to the nearest two digits beyond the decimal point):

$$G = \begin{bmatrix} -415.38 & -30.19 & -61.20 & 27.24 & 56.12 & -20.10 & -2.39 & 0.46 \\ 4.47 & -21.86 & -60.76 & 10.25 & 13.15 & -7.09 & -8.54 & 4.88 \\ -46.83 & 7.37 & 77.13 & -24.56 & -28.91 & 9.93 & 5.42 & -5.65 \\ -48.53 & 12.07 & 34.10 & -14.76 & -10.24 & 6.30 & 1.83 & 1.95 \\ 12.12 & -6.55 & -13.20 & -3.95 & -1.87 & 1.75 & -2.79 & 3.14 \\ -7.73 & 2.91 & 2.38 & -5.94 & -2.38 & 0.94 & 4.30 & 1.85 \\ -1.03 & 0.18 & 0.42 & -2.42 & -0.88 & -3.02 & 4.12 & -0.66 \\ -0.17 & 0.14 & -1.07 & -4.19 & -1.17 & -0.10 & 0.50 & 1.68 \end{bmatrix} \downarrow v.$$

Note the top-left corner entry with the rather large magnitude. This is the DC coefficient (also called the constant component), which defines the basic hue for the entire block. The remaining 63 coefficients are the AC coefficients (also called the alternating components). The advantage of the DCT is its tendency to aggregate most of the signal in one corner of the result, as may be seen above. The quantization step to follow accentuates this effect while simultaneously reducing the overall size of the DCT coefficients, resulting in a signal that is easy to compress efficiently in the entropy stage.

The DCT temporarily increases the bit-depth of the data, since the DCT coefficients of an 8-bit/component image take up to 11 or more bits (depending on fidelity of the DCT calculation) to store. This may force the codec to temporarily use 16-bit numbers to hold these coefficients, doubling the size of the image representation at this point; these values are typically reduced back to 8-bit values by the quantization step. The temporary increase in size at this stage is not a performance concern for most JPEG implementations, since typically only a very small part of the image is stored in full DCT form at any given time during the image encoding or decoding process.

Quantization

The human eye is good at seeing small differences in brightness over a relatively large area, but not so good at distinguishing the exact strength of a high frequency brightness variation. This allows one to greatly reduce the amount of information in the high frequency components. This is done by simply dividing each component in the frequency domain by a constant for that component, and then rounding to the nearest integer. This rounding operation is the only lossy operation in the whole process (other than chroma subsampling) if the DCT computation is performed with sufficiently high precision. As a result of this, it is typically the case that many of the higher frequency components are rounded to zero, and many of the rest become small positive or negative numbers, which take many fewer bits to represent.

The elements in the quantization matrix control the compression ratio, with larger values producing greater compression. A typical quantization matrix (for a quality of 50% as specified in the original JPEG Standard), is as follows:

$$Q = \begin{bmatrix} 16 & 11 & 10 & 16 & 24 & 40 & 51 & 61 \\ 12 & 12 & 14 & 19 & 26 & 58 & 60 & 55 \\ 14 & 13 & 16 & 24 & 40 & 57 & 69 & 56 \\ 14 & 17 & 22 & 29 & 51 & 87 & 80 & 62 \\ 18 & 22 & 37 & 56 & 68 & 109 & 103 & 77 \\ 24 & 35 & 55 & 64 & 81 & 104 & 113 & 92 \\ 49 & 64 & 78 & 87 & 103 & 121 & 120 & 101 \\ 72 & 92 & 95 & 98 & 112 & 100 & 103 & 99 \end{bmatrix}.$$

The quantized DCT coefficients are computed with

$$B_{j,k} = \text{round}\left(\frac{G_{j,k}}{Q_{j,k}}\right) \text{ for } j = 0,1,2,\ldots,7; k = 0,1,2,\ldots,7$$

where G is the unquantized DCT coefficients; Q is the quantization matrix above; and B is the quantized DCT coefficients.

Using this quantization matrix with the DCT coefficient matrix from above results in:

$$B = \begin{bmatrix} -26 & -3 & -6 & 2 & 2 & -1 & 0 & 0 \\ 0 & -2 & -4 & 1 & 1 & 0 & 0 & 0 \\ -3 & 1 & 5 & -1 & -1 & 0 & 0 & 0 \\ -3 & 1 & 2 & -1 & 0 & 0 & 0 & 0 \\ 1 & 0 & 0 & 0 & 0 & 0 & 0 & 0 \\ 0 & 0 & 0 & 0 & 0 & 0 & 0 & 0 \\ 0 & 0 & 0 & 0 & 0 & 0 & 0 & 0 \\ 0 & 0 & 0 & 0 & 0 & 0 & 0 & 0 \end{bmatrix}.$$

For example, using −415 (the DC coefficient) and rounding to the nearest integer

$$\text{round}\left(\frac{-415.37}{16}\right) = \text{round}(-25.96) = -26.$$

Notice that most of the higher-frequency elements of the sub-block (i.e., those with an x or y spatial frequency greater than 4) are compressed into zero values.

Entropy Coding

Entropy coding is a special form of lossless data compression. It involves arranging the image components in a "zigzag" order employing run-length encoding (RLE) algorithm that groups similar frequencies together, inserting length coding zeros, and then using Huffman coding on what is left.

The JPEG standard also allows, but does not require, decoders to support the use of arithmetic coding, which is mathematically superior to Huffman coding. However, this feature has rarely been used, as it was historically covered by patents requiring royalty-bearing licenses, and because it is slower to encode and decode compared to Huffman coding. Arithmetic coding typically makes files about 5–7% smaller.

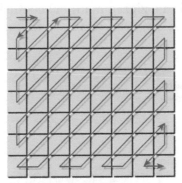

Zigzag ordering of JPEG image components

The previous quantized DC coefficient is used to predict the current quantized DC coefficient. The difference between the two is encoded rather than the actual value. The encoding of the 63 quantized AC coefficients does not use such prediction differencing.

The zigzag sequence for the above quantized coefficients are shown below. (The format shown is just for ease of understanding/viewing.)

```
−26
−3    0
−3   −2   −6
 2   −4    1   −3
 1    1    5    1    2
−1    1   −1    2    0    0
 0    0    0   −1   −1    0    0
 0    0    0    0    0    0    0    0
 0    0    0    0    0    0    0
 0    0    0    0    0    0
 0    0    0    0    0
 0    0    0    0
 0    0    0
 0    0
 0
```

If the i-th block is represented by B_i and positions within each block are represented by (p,q) where $p = 0,1,...,7$ and $q = 0,1,...,7$, then any coefficient in the DCT image can be represented as $B_i(p,q)$. Thus, in the above scheme, the order of encoding pixels (for the i-th block) is $B_i(0,0)$, $B_i(0,1), B_i(1,0), B_i(2,0), B_i(1,1), B_i(0,2), B_i(0,3), B_i(1,2)$ and so on.

This encoding mode is called baseline *sequential* encoding. Baseline JPEG also supports *progressive* encoding. While sequential encoding encodes coefficients of a single block at a time (in a zigzag manner), progressive encoding encodes similar-positioned batch of coefficients of all blocks in one go (called a *scan*), followed by the next batch of coefficients of all blocks, and so on. For example, if the image is divided into N 8×8 blocks $B_0, B_1, B_2, ..., B_{n-1}$, then a 3-scan progressive encoding encodes DC component, $B_i(0,0)$ for all blocks, i.e., for all $i = 0,1,2,...,N-1$, in first scan. This is followed by the second scan which encoding a few more components (assuming four more components, they are $B_i(0,1)$ to $B_i(1,1)$, still in a zigzag manner) coefficients of all blocks (so the sequence is: $B_0(0,1), B_0(1,0), B_0(2,0), B_0(1,1), B_1(0,1), B_1(1,0), ..., B_N(2,0), B_N(1,1)), ...$), followed by all the remained coefficients of all blocks in the last scan.

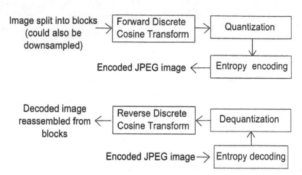

Baseline sequential JPEG encoding and decoding processes

It should be noted here that once all similar-positioned coefficients have been encoded, the next position to be encoded is the one occurring next in the zigzag traversal as indicated in the figure above. It has been found that *baseline progressive* JPEG encoding usually gives better compression as compared to *baseline sequential* JPEG due to the ability to use different Huffman tables tailored for different frequencies on each "scan" or "pass" (which includes similar-positioned coefficients), though the difference is not too large.

In the rest of the lesson, it is assumed that the coefficient pattern generated is due to sequential mode.

In order to encode the above generated coefficient pattern, JPEG uses Huffman encoding. The JPEG standard provides general-purpose Huffman tables; encoders may also choose to generate Huffman tables optimized for the actual frequency distributions in images being encoded.

The process of encoding the zig-zag quantized data begins with a run-length encoding explained below, where:

- x is the non-zero, quantized AC coefficient.

- *RUNLENGTH* is the number of zeroes that came before this non-zero AC coefficient.

- *SIZE* is the number of bits required to represent x.

- *AMPLITUDE* is the bit-representation of x.

The run-length encoding works by examining each non-zero AC coefficient x and determining how many zeroes came before the previous AC coefficient. With this information, two symbols are created:

Symbol 1	Symbol 2
(RUNLENGTH, SIZE)	(AMPLITUDE)

Both *RUNLENGTH* and *SIZE* rest on the same byte, meaning that each only contains four bits of information. The higher bits deal with the number of zeroes, while the lower bits denote the number of bits necessary to encode the value of *x*.

This has the immediate implication of *Symbol 1* being only able store information regarding the first 15 zeroes preceding the non-zero AC coefficient. However, JPEG defines two special Huffman code words. One is for ending the sequence prematurely when the remaining coefficients are zero (called "End-of-Block" or "EOB"), and another when the run of zeroes goes beyond 15 before reaching a non-zero AC coefficient. In such a case where 16 zeroes are encountered before a given non-zero AC coefficient, *Symbol 1* is encoded "specially" as: (15, 0)(0).

The overall process continues until "EOB" – denoted by (0, 0) – is reached.

With this in mind, the sequence from earlier becomes:

(0, 2)(–3); (1, 2)(–3); (0, 2)(–2); (0, 3)(–6); (0, 2)(2); (0, 3)(–4); (0, 1)(1); (0, 2)(–3); (0, 1)(1);

(0, 1)(1); (0, 3)(5); (0, 1)(1); (0, 2)(2); (0, 1)(–1); (0, 1)(1); (0, 1)(–1); (0, 2)(2); (5, 1)(–1);

(0, 1)(–1); (0, 0).

(The first value in the matrix, –26, is the DC coefficient; it is not encoded the same way.)

From here, frequency calculations are made based on occurrences of the coefficients. In our example block, most of the quantized coefficients are small numbers that are not preceded immediately by a zero coefficient. These more-frequent cases will be represented by shorter code words.

Compression Ratio and Artifacts

This image shows the pixels that are different between a non-compressed image and the same image JPEG compressed with a quality setting of 50. Darker means a larger difference. Note especially the changes occurring near sharp edges and having a block-like shape.

The original image

The compressed 8×8 squares are visible in the scaled-up picture,
together with other visual artifacts of the lossy compression

The resulting compression ratio can be varied according to need by being more or less aggressive in the divisors used in the quantization phase. Ten to one compression usually results in an image that cannot be distinguished by eye from the original. A compression ration of 100:1 is usually possible, but will look distinctly artifacted compared to the original. The appropriate level of compression depends on the use to which the image will be put.

Those who use the World Wide Web may be familiar with the irregularities known as compression artifacts that appear in JPEG images, which may take the form of noise around contrasting edges (especially curves and corners), or "blocky" images. These are due to the quantization step of the JPEG algorithm. They are especially noticeable around sharp corners between contrasting colors (text is a good example, as it contains many such corners). The analogous artifacts in MPEG video are referred to as *mosquito noise,* as the resulting "edge busyness" and spurious dots, which change over time, resemble mosquitoes swarming around the object.

These artifacts can be reduced by choosing a lower level of compression; they may be completely avoided by saving an image using a lossless file format, though this will result in a larger file size. The images created with ray-tracing programs have noticeable blocky shapes on the terrain. Certain low-intensity compression artifacts might be acceptable when simply viewing the images, but can be emphasized if the image is subsequently processed, usually resulting in unacceptable quality. Consider the example below, demonstrating the effect of lossy compression on an edge detection processing step.

Image	Lossless compression	Lossy compression
Original	⬤	⬤

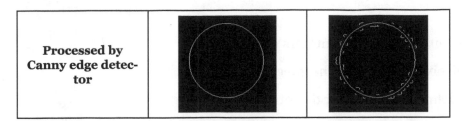

| Processed by Canny edge detector | | |

Some programs allow the user to vary the amount by which individual blocks are compressed. Stronger compression is applied to areas of the image that show fewer artifacts. This way it is possible to manually reduce JPEG file size with less loss of quality.

Since the quantization stage *always* results in a loss of information, JPEG standard is always a lossy compression codec. (Information is lost both in quantizing and rounding of the floating-point numbers.) Even if the quantization matrix is a matrix of ones, information will still be lost in the rounding step.

Decoding

Decoding to display the image consists of doing all the above in reverse.

Taking the DCT coefficient matrix (after adding the difference of the DC coefficient back in)

$$
\begin{bmatrix}
-26 & -3 & -6 & 2 & 2 & -1 & 0 & 0 \\
0 & -2 & -4 & 1 & 1 & 0 & 0 & 0 \\
-3 & 1 & 5 & -1 & -1 & 0 & 0 & 0 \\
-3 & 1 & 2 & -1 & 0 & 0 & 0 & 0 \\
1 & 0 & 0 & 0 & 0 & 0 & 0 & 0 \\
0 & 0 & 0 & 0 & 0 & 0 & 0 & 0 \\
0 & 0 & 0 & 0 & 0 & 0 & 0 & 0 \\
0 & 0 & 0 & 0 & 0 & 0 & 0 & 0
\end{bmatrix}
$$

and taking the entry-for-entry product with the quantization matrix from above results in

$$
\begin{bmatrix}
416 & -33 & -60 & 32 & 48 & -40 & 0 & 0 \\
0 & -24 & -56 & 19 & 26 & 0 & 0 & 0 \\
-42 & 13 & 80 & -24 & -40 & 0 & 0 & 0 \\
-42 & 17 & 44 & -29 & 0 & 0 & 0 & 0 \\
18 & 0 & 0 & 0 & 0 & 0 & 0 & 0 \\
0 & 0 & 0 & 0 & 0 & 0 & 0 & 0 \\
0 & 0 & 0 & 0 & 0 & 0 & 0 & 0 \\
0 & 0 & 0 & 0 & 0 & 0 & 0 & 0
\end{bmatrix}
$$

which closely resembles the original DCT coefficient matrix for the top-left portion.

The next step is to take the two-dimensional inverse DCT (a 2D type-III DCT), which is given by:

$$
f_{x,y} = \frac{1}{4} \sum_{u=0}^{7} \sum_{v=0}^{7} \alpha(u)\alpha(v)F_{u,v} \cos\left[\frac{(2x+1)u\pi}{16}\right]\cos\left[\frac{(2y+1)v\pi}{16}\right]
$$

where

- x is the pixel row, for the integers $0 \leq x < 8$.

- y is the pixel column, for the integers $0 \leq < 8$.

- $\alpha(u)$ is defined as above, for the integers $0 \leq u < 8$.

- $F_{u,v}$ is the reconstructed approximate coefficient at coordinates (u,v).

- $f_{x,y}$ is the reconstructed pixel value at coordinates (x,y)

Rounding the output to integer values (since the original had integer values) results in an image with values (still shifted down by 128)

Notice the slight differences between the original (top) and decompressed image (bottom), which is most readily seen in the bottom-left corner.

$$\begin{bmatrix} -66 & -63 & -71 & -68 & -56 & -65 & -68 & -46 \\ -71 & -73 & -72 & -46 & -20 & -41 & -66 & -57 \\ -70 & -78 & -68 & -17 & 20 & -14 & -61 & -63 \\ -63 & -73 & -62 & -8 & 27 & -14 & -60 & -58 \\ -58 & -65 & -61 & -27 & -6 & -40 & -68 & -50 \\ -57 & -57 & -64 & -58 & -48 & -66 & -72 & -47 \\ -53 & -46 & -61 & -74 & -65 & -63 & -62 & -45 \\ -47 & -34 & -53 & -74 & -60 & -47 & -47 & -41 \end{bmatrix}$$

and adding 128 to each entry

$$\begin{bmatrix} 62 & 65 & 57 & 60 & 72 & 63 & 60 & 82 \\ 57 & 55 & 56 & 82 & 108 & 87 & 62 & 71 \\ 58 & 50 & 60 & 111 & 148 & 114 & 67 & 65 \\ 65 & 55 & 66 & 120 & 155 & 114 & 68 & 70 \\ 70 & 63 & 67 & 101 & 122 & 88 & 60 & 78 \\ 71 & 71 & 64 & 70 & 80 & 62 & 56 & 81 \\ 75 & 82 & 67 & 54 & 63 & 65 & 66 & 83 \\ 81 & 94 & 75 & 54 & 68 & 81 & 81 & 87 \end{bmatrix}.$$

This is the decompressed subimage. In general, the decompression process may produce values outside the original input range of $[0, 255]$. If this occurs, the decoder needs to clip the output values keep them within that range to prevent overflow when storing the decompressed image with the original bit depth.

The decompressed subimage can be compared to the original subimage by taking the difference (original – uncompressed) results in the following error values:

$$\begin{bmatrix} -10 & -10 & 4 & 6 & -2 & -2 & 4 & -9 \\ 6 & 4 & -1 & 8 & 1 & -2 & 7 & 1 \\ 4 & 9 & 8 & 2 & -4 & -10 & -1 & 8 \\ -2 & 3 & 5 & 2 & -1 & -8 & 2 & -1 \\ -3 & -2 & 1 & 3 & 4 & 0 & 8 & -8 \\ 8 & -6 & -4 & -0 & -3 & 6 & 2 & -6 \\ 10 & -11 & -3 & 5 & -8 & -4 & -1 & -0 \\ 6 & -15 & -6 & 14 & -3 & -5 & -3 & 7 \end{bmatrix}$$

with an average absolute error of about 5 values per pixels (i.e., $\frac{1}{64} \sum\limits_{x=0}^{7} \sum\limits_{y=0}^{7} |e(x,y)| = 4.8750$).

The error is most noticeable in the bottom-left corner where the bottom-left pixel becomes darker than the pixel to its immediate right.

Required Precision

The encoding description in the JPEG standard does not fix the precision needed for the output compressed image. However, the JPEG standard (and the similar MPEG standards) includes some precision requirements for the *de*coding, including all parts of the decoding process (variable length decoding, inverse DCT, dequantization, renormalization of outputs); the output from the reference algorithm must not exceed:

- a maximum of one bit of difference for each pixel component

- low mean square error over each 8×8-pixel block

- very low mean error over each 8×8-pixel block

- very low mean square error over the whole image

- extremely low mean error over the whole image

These assertions are tested on a large set of randomized input images, to handle the worst cases. The former IEEE 1180–1990 standard contained some similar precision requirements. The precision has a consequence on the implementation of decoders, and it is critical because some encoding processes (notably used for encoding sequences of images like MPEG) need to be able to construct, on the encoder side, a reference decoded image. In order to support 8-bit precision per pixel component output, dequantization and inverse DCT transforms are typically implemented with at least 14-bit precision in optimized decoders.

Effects of JPEG Compression

JPEG compression artifacts blend well into photographs with detailed non-uniform textures, allowing higher compression ratios. Notice how a higher compression ratio first affects the high-frequency textures in the upper-left corner of the image, and how the contrasting lines become more fuzzy. The very high compression ratio severely affects the quality of the image, although the overall colors and image form are still recognizable. However, the precision of colors suffer less (for a human eye) than the precision of contours (based on luminance). This justifies the fact that images should be first transformed in a color model separating the luminance from the chromatic information, before subsampling the chromatic planes (which may also use lower quality quantization) in order to preserve the precision of the luminance plane with more information bits.

Sample Photographs

For information, the uncompressed 24-bit RGB bitmap image below (73,242 pixels) would require 219,726 bytes (excluding all other information headers). The filesizes indicated below include the internal JPEG information headers and some meta-data. For highest quality images (Q=100), about 8.25 bits per color pixel is required. On grayscale images, a minimum of 6.5 bits per pixel is enough (a comparable Q=100 quality color information requires about 25% more encoded bits). The highest quality image below (Q=100) is encoded at nine bits per color pixel, the medium quality image (Q=25) uses one bit per color pixel. For most applications, the quality factor should not go below 0.75 bit per pixel (Q=12.5), as demonstrated by the low quality image. The image at lowest quality uses only 0.13 bit per pixel, and displays very poor color. This is useful when the image will be displayed in a significantly scaled-down size. A method for creating better quantization matrices for a given image quality using PSNR instead of the Q factor is described in Minguillón & Pujol (2001).

Image	Quality	Size (bytes)	Compression ratio	Comment
	Highest quality (Q = 100)	83,261	2.6:1	Extremely minor artifacts
	High quality (Q = 50)	15,138	15:1	Initial signs of subimage artifacts

	Medium quality (Q = 25)	9,553	23:1	Stronger artifacts; loss of high frequency information
	Low quality (Q = 10)	4,787	46:1	Severe high frequency loss; artifacts on subimage boundaries ("macroblocking") are obvious
	Lowest quality (Q = 1)	1,523	144:1	Extreme loss of color and detail; the leaves are nearly unrecognizable
Note: The above images are not IEEE / CCIR / EBU test images, and the encoder settings are not specified or available.				

The medium quality photo uses only 4.3% of the storage space required for the uncompressed image, but has little noticeable loss of detail or visible artifacts. However, once a certain threshold of compression is passed, compressed images show increasingly visible defects. A particular limitation of JPEG in this regard is its non-overlapped 8×8 block transform structure. More modern designs such as JPEG 2000 and JPEG XR exhibit a more graceful degradation of quality as the bit usage decreases – by using transforms with a larger spatial extent for the lower frequency coefficients and by using overlapping transform basis functions.

Lossless Further Compression

From 2004 to 2008 new research emerged on ways to further compress the data contained in JPEG images without modifying the represented image. This has applications in scenarios where the original image is only available in JPEG format, and its size needs to be reduced for archiving or transmission. Standard general-purpose compression tools cannot significantly compress JPEG files.

Typically, such schemes take advantage of improvements to the naive scheme for coding DCT coefficients, which fails to take into account:

- Correlations between magnitudes of adjacent coefficients in the same block;

- Correlations between magnitudes of the same coefficient in adjacent blocks;

- Correlations between magnitudes of the same coefficient/block in different channels;

- The DC coefficients when taken together resemble a downscale version of the original image multiplied by a scaling factor. Well-known schemes for lossless coding of continuous-tone images can be applied, achieving somewhat better compression than the Huffman coded DPCM used in JPEG.

Some standard but rarely used options already exist in JPEG to improve the efficiency of coding DCT coefficients: the arithmetic coding option, and the progressive coding option (which produces lower bitrates because values for each coefficient are coded independently, and each coefficient has a significantly different distribution). Modern methods have improved on these techniques by reordering coefficients to group coefficients of larger magnitude together; using adjacent coefficients and blocks to predict new coefficient values; dividing blocks or coefficients up among a small number of independently coded models based on their statistics and adjacent values; and most recently, by decoding blocks, predicting subsequent blocks in the spatial domain, and then encoding these to generate predictions for DCT coefficients.

Typically, such methods can compress existing JPEG files between 15 and 25 percent, and for JPEGs compressed at low-quality settings, can produce improvements of up to 65%.

A freely available tool called packJPG is based on the 2007 paper "Improved Redundancy Reduction for JPEG Files."

Derived Formats for Stereoscopic 3D

JPEG Stereoscopic

An example of a stereoscopic .JPS file

JPS is a stereoscopic JPEG image used for creating 3D effects from 2D images. It contains two static images, one for the left eye and one for the right eye; encoded as two side-by-side images in a single JPG file. JPEG Stereoscopic (JPS, extension .jps) is a JPEG-based format for stereoscopic images. It has a range of configurations stored in the JPEG APP3 marker field, but usually contains one image of double width, representing two images of identical size in cross-eyed (i.e. left frame on the right half of the image and vice versa) side-by-side arrangement. This file format can be viewed as a JPEG without any special software, or can be processed for rendering in other modes.

JPEG Multi-picture Format

JPEG Multi-Picture Format (MPO, extension .mpo) is a JPEG-based format for multi-view images. It contains two or more JPEG files concatenated together. There are also special EXIF fields describing its purpose. This is used by the Fujifilm FinePix Real 3D W1 camera, Panasonic Lumix DMC-TZ20, DMC-TZ30, DMC-TZ60& DMC-TS4 (FT4), Sony DSC-HX7V, HTC Evo 3D, the JVC GY-HMZ1U AVCHD/MVC extension camcorder and by the Nintendo 3DS for its 3D Camera. In the last few years, due to the growing use of stereoscopic images, much effort has been spent by the scientific community to develop algorithms for stereoscopic image compression.

Patent Issues

In 2002, Forgent Networks asserted that it owned and would enforce patent rights on the JPEG technology, arising from a patent that had been filed on October 27, 1986, and granted on October 6, 1987 (U.S. Patent 4,698,672). The announcement created a furor reminiscent of Unisys' attempts to assert its rights over the GIF image compression standard.

The JPEG committee investigated the patent claims in 2002 and were of the opinion that they were invalidated by prior art. Others also concluded that Forgent did not have a patent that covered JPEG. Nevertheless, between 2002 and 2004 Forgent was able to obtain about US$105 million by licensing their patent to some 30 companies. In April 2004, Forgent sued 31 other companies to enforce further license payments. In July of the same year, a consortium of 21 large computer companies filed a countersuit, with the goal of invalidating the patent. In addition, Microsoft launched a separate lawsuit against Forgent in April 2005. In February 2006, the United States Patent and Trademark Office agreed to re-examine Forgent's JPEG patent at the request of the Public Patent Foundation. On May 26, 2006 the USPTO found the patent invalid based on prior art. The USPTO also found that Forgent knew about the prior art, and did not tell the Patent Office, making any appeal to reinstate the patent highly unlikely to succeed.

Forgent also possesses a similar patent granted by the European Patent Office in 1994, though it is unclear how enforceable it is.

As of October 27, 2006, the U.S. patent's 20-year term appears to have expired, and in November 2006, Forgent agreed to abandon enforcement of patent claims against use of the JPEG standard.

The JPEG committee has as one of its explicit goals that their standards (in particular their baseline methods) be implementable without payment of license fees, and they have secured appropriate license rights for their JPEG 2000 standard from over 20 large organizations.

Beginning in August 2007, another company, Global Patent Holdings, LLC claimed that its patent (U.S. Patent 5,253,341) issued in 1993, is infringed by the downloading of JPEG images on either a website or through e-mail. If not invalidated, this patent could apply to any website that displays JPEG images. The patent emerged in July 2007 following a seven-year reexamination by the U.S. Patent and Trademark Office in which all of the original claims of the patent were revoked, but an additional claim (claim 17) was confirmed.

In its first two lawsuits following the reexamination, both filed in Chicago, Illinois, Global Patent Holdings sued the Green Bay Packers, CDW, Motorola, Apple, Orbitz, Officemax, Caterpillar, Kraft and Peapod as defendants. A third lawsuit was filed on December 5, 2007 in South Florida against ADT Security Services, AutoNation, Florida Crystals Corp., HearUSA, MovieTickets.com, Ocwen Financial Corp. and Tire Kingdom, and a fourth lawsuit on January 8, 2008 in South Florida against the Boca Raton Resort & Club. A fifth lawsuit was filed against Global Patent Holdings in Nevada. That lawsuit was filed by Zappos.com, Inc., which was allegedly threatened by Global Patent Holdings, and seeks a judicial declaration that the '341 patent is invalid and not infringed.

Global Patent Holdings had also used the '341 patent to sue or threaten outspoken critics of broad software patents, including Gregory Aharonian and the anonymous operator of a website blog known as the "Patent Troll Tracker." On December 21, 2007, patent lawyer Vernon Francissen of Chicago asked the U.S. Patent and Trademark Office to reexamine the sole remaining claim of the '341 patent on the basis of new prior art.

On March 5, 2008, the U.S. Patent and Trademark Office agreed to reexamine the '341 patent, finding that the new prior art raised substantial new questions regarding the patent's validity. In light of the reexamination, the accused infringers in four of the five pending lawsuits have filed motions to suspend (stay) their cases until completion of the U.S. Patent and Trademark Office's review of the '341 patent. On April 23, 2008, a judge presiding over the two lawsuits in Chicago, Illinois granted the motions in those cases. On July 22, 2008, the Patent Office issued the first "Office Action" of the second reexamination, finding the claim invalid based on nineteen separate grounds. On Nov. 24, 2009, a Reexamination Certificate was issued cancelling all claims.

Beginning in 2011 and continuing as of early 2013, an entity known as Princeton Digital Image Corporation, based in Eastern Texas, began suing large numbers of companies for alleged infringement of U.S. Patent 4,813,056. Princeton claims that the JPEG image compression standard infringes the '056 patent and has sued large numbers of websites, retailers, camera and device manufacturers and resellers. The patent was originally owned and assigned to General Electric. The patent expired in December 2007, but Princeton has sued large numbers of companies for "past infringement" of this patent. (Under U.S. patent laws, a patent owner can sue for "past infringement" up to six years before the filing of a lawsuit, so Princeton could theoretically have continued suing companies until December 2013.) As of March 2013, Princeton had suits pending in New York and Delaware against more than 55 companies. General Electric's involvement in the suit is unknown, although court records indicate that it assigned the patent to Princeton in 2009 and retains certain rights in the patent.

Implementations

A very important implementation of a JPEG codec is the free programming library *libjpeg* of the Independent JPEG Group. It was first published in 1991 and was key for the success of the standard. This library or a direct derivative of it is used in countless applications.

In March 2017, Google released the open source project Guetzli, which trades off a much longer encoding time for better appearance and smaller file size (similar to what Zopfli does for PNG and other lossless data formats).

Continuous Tone Still Image Coding Standards

A different set of standards had to be created for compressing and coding continuous tone mono-chrome and color images of any size and sampling rate. Of these, the Joint Photographic Expert Group (JPEG)'s first standard, known as JPEG is the most widely used one. Only in recent times, the new standard JPEG-2000 has its implementations in still image coding systems. JPEG is a very simple and easy to use standard that is based on the Discrete Cosine Transform (DCT).

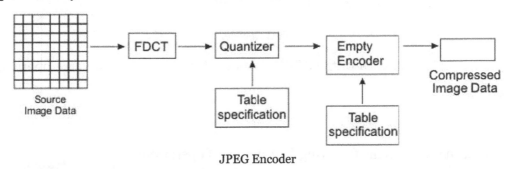

JPEG Encoder

Figure shows the block diagram of a JPEG encoder, which has the following components:

(a) Forward Discrete Cosine Transform (FDCT): The still images are first partitioned into non-overlapping blocks of size 8x8 and the image samples are shifted from unsigned integers with range $[0, 2^p -1]$ to signed integers with range $[-2^{p-1}, 2^{p-1}]$, where p is the number of bits (here, $p = 8$). The theory of the DCT has been already discussed and will not be repeated here. It should however be mentioned that to preserve freedom for innovation and customization within implementations, JPEG neither specifies any unique FDCT algorithm, nor any unique IDCT algorithms.

The implementations may therefore differ in precision and JPEG has specified an accuracy test as a part of the compliance test.

(b) Quantization: Each of the 64 coefficients from the FDCT outputs of a block is uniformly quantized according to a quantization table. Since the aim is to compress the images without visible artifacts, each step-size should be chosen as the perceptual threshold or for "just noticeable distortion". Psycho-visual experiments have led to a set of quantization tables and these appear in ISO-JPEG standard as a matter of information, but not a requirement.

The quantized coefficients are zig-zag scanned, as described in lesson-8. The DC coefficient is encoded as a difference from the DC coefficient of the previous block and the 63 AC coefficients are encoded into (run, level) pair.

(c) Entropy Coder: This is the final processing step of the JPEG encoder. The JPEG standard specifies two entropy coding methods – Huffman and arithmetic coding. The baseline sequential JPEG uses Huffman only, but codecs with both methods are specified for the other modes of operation. Huffman coding requires that one or more sets of coding tables are specified by the application. The same table used for compression is used needed to decompress it. The baseline JPEG uses only two sets of Huffman tables – one for DC and the other for AC.

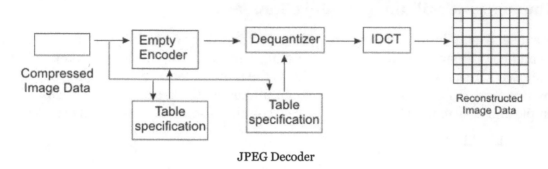

JPEG Decoder

Figure shows the block diagram of the JPEG decoder. It performs the inverse operation of the JPEG encoder.

Modes of Operation in JPEG

The JPEG standard supports the following four modes of operation:

- Baseline or sequential encoding

- Progressive encoding (includes spectral selection and successive approximation approaches).

- Hierarchical encoding

- Lossless encoding

Baseline Encoding: Baseline sequential coding is for images with 8-bit samples and uses Huffman coding only. In baseline encoding, each block is encoded in a single left-to-right and top-to-bottom scan. It encodes and decodes complete 8x8 blocks with full precision one at a time and supports interleaving of color components. The FDCT, quantization, DC difference and zig-zag ordering proceeds in exactly the manner described . In order to claim JPEG compatibility of a product it must include the support for at least the baseline encoding system.

Progressive Encoding: Unlike baseline encoding, each block in progressive encoding is encoded in multiple scans, rather than a single one. Each scan follows the zig zag ordering, quantization and entropy coding, as done in baseline encoding, but takes much less time to encode and decode, as compared to the single scan of baseline encoding, since each scan contains only a part of the complete information. With the first scan, a crude form of image can be reconstructed at the decoder and with successive scans, the quality of the image is refined. You must have experienced this while downloading web pages containing images. It is very convenient for browsing applications, where crude reconstruction quality at the early scans may be sufficient for quick browsing of a page.

There are two forms of progressive encoding: (a) spectral selection approach and (b) successive approximation approach. Each of these approaches is described below.

Progressive scanning through spectral selection: In this approach, the first scan sends some specified low frequency DCT coefficients within each block. The corresponding reconstructed image obtained at the decoder from the first scan therefore appears blurred as the details in the forms of high frequency components are missing. In subsequent scans, bands of coefficients, which are higher in frequency than the previous scan, are encoded and therefore the reconstructed image gets richer with details. This procedure is called spectral selection, because each band typically contains coefficients which occupy a lower or higher part of the frequency spectrum for that 8x8 block.

Progressive scanning through successive approximation: This is also a multiple scan approach. Here, each scan encodes all the coefficients within a block, but not to their full quantized accuracy. In the first scan, only the N most significant bits of each coefficient are encoded (N is specifiable) and in successive scans, the next lower significant bits of the coefficients are added and so on until all the bits are sent. The resulting reconstruction quality is good even from the early scans, as the high frequency coefficients are present from the initial scans.

Hierarchical encoding: The hierarchical encoding is also known as the pyramidal encoding in which the image to be encoded is organized in a pyramidal structure of multiple resolutions, with the original, that is, the finest resolution image on the lowermost layer and reduced resolution images on the successive upper layers. Each layer decreases its resolution with respect to its adjacent lower layer by a factor of two in either the horizontal or the vertical direction or both. Hierarchical encoding may be regarded as a special case of progressive encoding with increasing spatial resolution between the progressive stages.

The steps involved in hierarchical encoding may be summarized below:

- Obtain the reduced resolution images starting with the original and for each, reduce the resolution by a factor of two, as described above.

- Encode the reduced resolution image from the topmost layer of the pyramid (that is, the coarsest form of the image) using baseline (sequential) encoding, progressive encoding or lossless encoding.

- Decode the above reduced resolution image. Interpolate and up-sample it by a factor of two horizontally and/or vertically, using the identical interpolation filter which the decoder must use. Use this interpolated and up-sampled image as a predicted image for encoding the next lower layer (finer resolution) of the pyramid.

- Encode the difference between the image in the next lower layer and the predicted image using baseline, progressive or lossless encoding.

- Repeat the steps of encoding and decoding until the lowermost layer (finest resolution) of the pyramid is encoded.

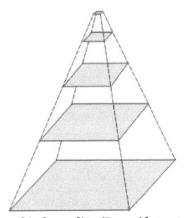

Hierarchical encoding (Pyramid structure)

Figure above illustrates the hierarchical encoding process. In hierarchical encoding, the image quality at low bit rates surpass the other JPEG encoding methods, but at the cost of increased number of bits at the full resolution. Hierarchical encoding is used for applications in which a high-resolution image should be accessed by a low resolution display device. For example, the image may be printed by a high-resolution printer, while it is being displayed on a low resolution monitor.

Lossless encoding: The lossless mode of encoding in JPEG follows a simple predictive coding mechanism, rather than having FDCT + Entropy coder for encoding and Entropy decoder + IDCT for decoding. Theoretically, it should have been possible to achieve lossless encoding by eliminating the quantization block, but because of finite precision representation of the cosine kernels, IDCT can not exactly recover what the image was before IDCT. This led to a modified and simpler mechanism of predictive coding.

In lossless encoding, the 8x8 block structure is not used and each pixel is predicted based on three adjacent pixels, as illustrated in the figure below using one of the eight possible predictor modes, listed in table.

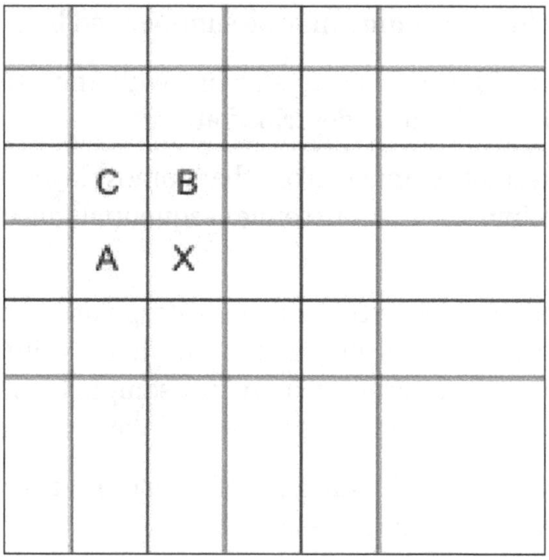

Predictive coding for lossless JPEG

An entropy encoder is then used to encode the predicted pixel obtained from the lossless encoder. Lossless codecs typically produce around 2:1 compression for color images with moderately complex scenes. Lossless JPEG encoding finds applications in transmission and storage of medical images.

Selection Value	Prediction
0	None
1	A
2	B
3	C

4	A+B-C
5	A+(B-C)/2
6	B+(A-C)/2
7	(A+B)/2

Predictors in lossless JPEG mode

Color Image Formats and Interleaving

The most commonly used color image representation format is RGB, the encoding of which may be regarded as three independent gray scale image encoding. However, from efficient encoding considerations, RGB is not the best format. Color spaces such as YUV, CIELUV, CIELAB and others represent the chromatic (color) information in two components and the luminance (intensity) information in one component. These formats are more efficient from image compression considerations, since our eyes are relatively insensitive to the high frequency information from the chrominance channels and thus the chrominance components can be represented at a reduced resolution as compared to the luminance components for which full resolution representation is necessary.

It is possible to convert an RGB image into YUV, using the following relations:

$$Y = 0.3R + 0.6G + 0.1B$$

$$U = \frac{B-Y}{2} + 0.5$$

$$V = \frac{R-Y}{1.6} + 0.5$$

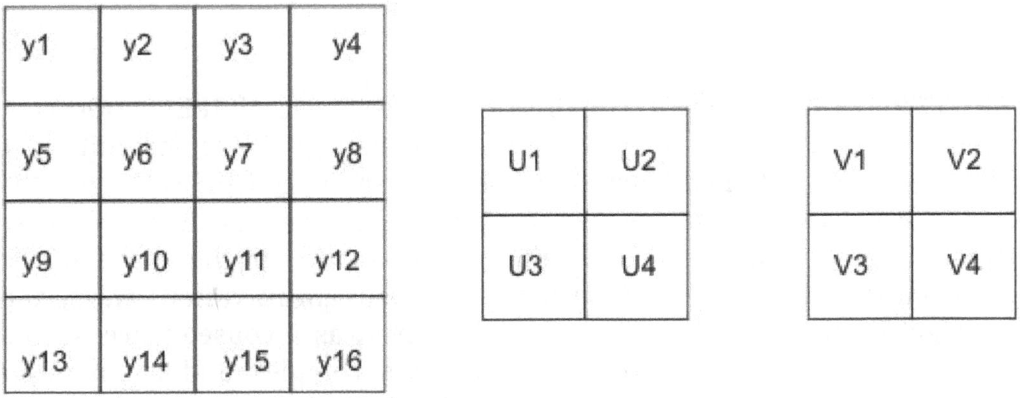

y1	y2	y3	y4
y5	y6	y7	y8
y9	y10	y11	y12
y13	y14	y15	y16

U1	U2
U3	U4

V1	V2
V3	V4

YUV representation of an example 4x4 image

Figure above illustrates the YUV representation by considering an example of a 4x4 image. The Y components are shown as Y1, Y2, ..., Y16. The U and the V components are sub-sampled by a factor of two in both horizontal and vertical directions and are therefore of 2x2 size. The three components may be transmitted in either a non-interleaved manner or an interleaved manner.

The non-interleaved ordering can be shown as

Scan-1: Y1,Y2,Y3,.......,Y15,Y16.

Scan-2: U1,U2,U3,U4.

Scan-3: V1,V2,V3,V4.

The interleaved ordering encodes in a single scan and proceeds like

Y1, Y2, Y3, Y4, U1, V1, Y5, Y6, Y7, Y8, U2, V2, ...

Interleaving requires minimum of buffering to decode the image at the decoder.

JPEG 2000

JPEG 2000 (JP2) is an image compression standard and coding system. It was created by the Joint Photographic Experts Group committee in 2000 with the intention of superseding their original discrete cosine transform-based JPEG standard (created in 1992) with a newly designed, wavelet-based method. The standardized filename extension is .jp2 for ISO/IEC 15444-1 conforming files and .jpx for the extended part-2 specifications, published as ISO/IEC 15444-2. The registered MIME types are defined in RFC 3745. For ISO/IEC 15444-1 it is image/jp2.

JPEG 2000 code streams are regions of interest that offer several mechanisms to support spatial random access or region of interest access at varying degrees of granularity. It is possible to store different parts of the same picture using different quality.

As of 2017, there are very few digital cameras that shoot photos in the JPEG 2000 format, and support for viewing and editing photos in this format remains limited.

Aims of the Standard

While there is a modest increase in compression performance of JPEG 2000 compared to JPEG, the main advantage offered by JPEG 2000 is the significant flexibility of the codestream. The codestream obtained after compression of an image with JPEG 2000 is scalable in nature, meaning that it can be decoded in a number of ways; for instance, by truncating the codestream at any point, one may obtain a representation of the image at a lower resolution, or signal-to-noise ratio. By ordering the codestream in various ways, applications can achieve significant performance increases. However, as a consequence of this flexibility, JPEG 2000 requires encoders/decoders that are complex and computationally demanding. Another difference, in comparison with JPEG, is in terms of visual artifacts: JPEG 2000 only produces ringing artifacts, manifested as blur and rings near edges in the image, while JPEG produces both ringing artifacts and 'blocking' artifacts, due to its 8×8 blocks.

JPEG 2000 has been published as an ISO standard, ISO/IEC 15444. As of 2013, JPEG 2000 is not widely supported in web browsers, and hence is not generally used on the Internet.

Improvements Over the 1992 JPEG Standard

Top-to-bottom demonstration of the artifacts of JPEG 2000 compression.
The numbers indicate the compression ratio used.

Superior Compression Ratio

At high bit rates, artifacts become nearly imperceptible, JPEG 2000 has a small machine-measured fidelity advantage over JPEG. At lower bit rates (e.g., less than 0.25 bits/pixel for grayscale images), JPEG 2000 has a significant advantage over certain modes of JPEG: artifacts are less visible and there is almost no blocking. The compression gains over JPEG are attributed to the use of DWT and a more sophisticated entropy encoding scheme.

Multiple Resolution Representation

JPEG 2000 decomposes the image into a multiple resolution representation in the course of its compression process. This pyramid representation can be put to use for other image presentation purposes beyond compression.

Progressive Transmission by Pixel and Resolution Accuracy

These features are more commonly known as *progressive decoding* and *signal-to-noise ratio (SNR) scalability*. JPEG 2000 provides efficient code-stream organizations which are progressive by pixel accuracy and by image resolution (or by image size). This way, after a smaller part of the whole file has been received, the viewer can see a lower quality version of the final picture. The quality then improves progressively through downloading more data bits from the source.

Choice of Lossless or Lossy Compression

Like the Lossless JPEG standard, the JPEG 2000 standard provides both lossless and lossy compression in a single compression architecture. Lossless compression is provided by the use of a reversible integer wavelet transform in JPEG 2000.

Error Resilience

Like JPEG 1992, JPEG 2000 is robust to bit errors introduced by noisy communication channels, due to the coding of data in relatively small independent blocks.

Flexible File Format

The JP2 and JPX file formats allow for handling of color-space information, metadata, and for interactivity in networked applications as developed in the JPEG Part 9 JPIP protocol.

High Dynamic Range Support

JPEG 2000 supports any bit depth, such as 16- and 32-bit floating point pixel images, and any color space.

Side Channel Spatial Information

Full support for transparency and alpha planes.

JPEG 2000 Image Coding System - Parts

The JPEG 2000 image coding system (ISO/IEC 15444) consists of following parts:

JPEG 2000 image coding system - Parts							
Part	Number	First public release date (First edition)	Latest public release date (edition)	Latest amendment	Identical ITU-T standard	Title	Description
Part 1	ISO/IEC 15444-1	2000	2004	2006	T.800	Core coding system	the basic characteristics of JPEG 2000 compression (.jp2)
Part 2	ISO/IEC 15444-2	2004	2004	2006	T.801	Extensions	(.jpx, .jpf, floating points)
Part 3	ISO/IEC 15444-3	2002	2007		T.802	Motion JPEG 2000	(.mj2)

JPEG 2000 image coding system - Parts							
Part	Number	First public release date (First edition)	Latest public release date (edition)	Latest amendment	Identical ITU-T standard	Title	Description
Part 4	ISO/IEC 15444-4	2002	2004		T.803	Conformance testing	
Part 5	ISO/IEC 15444-5	2003	2003	2003	T.804	Reference software	Java and C implementations
Part 6	ISO/IEC 15444-6	2003	2003	2007	T.805	Compound image file format	(.jpm) e.g. document imaging, for prepress and fax-like applications
Part 7	abandoned					Guideline of minimum support function of ISO/IEC 15444-1	(Technical Report on Minimum Support Functions)
Part 8	ISO/IEC 15444-8	2007	2007	2008	T.807	Secure JPEG 2000	JPSEC (security aspects)
Part 9	ISO/IEC 15444-9	2005	2005	2008	T.808	Interactivity tools, APIs and protocols	JPIP (interactive protocols and API)
Part 10	ISO/IEC 15444-10	2008	2008	2008	T.809	Extensions for three-dimensional data	JP3D (volumetric imaging)
Part 11	ISO/IEC 15444-11	2007	2007		T.810	Wireless	JPWL (wireless applications)
Part 12	ISO/IEC 15444-12	2004	2008			ISO base media file format	
Part 13	ISO/IEC 15444-13	2008	2008		T.812	An entry level JPEG 2000 encoder	
Part 14	ISO/IEC 15444-14	2013			T.813	XML structural representation and reference	JPXML

Technical Discussion

The aim of JPEG 2000 is not only improving compression performance over JPEG but also adding (or improving) features such as scalability and editability. JPEG 2000's improvement in compression performance relative to the original JPEG standard is actually rather modest and should not ordinarily be the primary consideration for evaluating the design. Very low and very high compression rates are supported in JPEG 2000. The ability of the design to handle a very large range of effective bit rates is one of the strengths of JPEG 2000. For example, to reduce the number of bits for a picture below a certain amount, the advisable thing to do with the first JPEG standard is to reduce the resolution of the input image before encoding it. That is unnecessary when using JPEG 2000, because JPEG 2000 already does this automatically through its multiresolution decomposition structure.

According to KB, "the current JP2 format specification leaves room for multiple interpretations when it comes to the support of ICC profiles, and the handling of grid resolution information".

Color Components Transformation

Initially images have to be transformed from the RGB color space to another color space, leading to three *components* that are handled separately. There are two possible choices:

1. Irreversible Color Transform (ICT) uses the well known YC_BC_R color space. It is called "irreversible" because it has to be implemented in floating or fix-point and causes round-off errors.

2. Reversible Color Transform (RCT) uses a modified YUV color space that does not introduce quantization errors, so it is fully reversible. Proper implementation of the RCT requires that numbers are rounded as specified that cannot be expressed exactly in matrix form. The transformation is:

$$Y = \left\lfloor \frac{R + 2G + B}{4} \right\rfloor; C_B = B - G; C_R = R - G;$$

and

$$G = Y - \left\lfloor \frac{C_B + C_R}{4} \right\rfloor; R = C_R + G; B = C_B + G.$$

The chrominance components can be, but do not necessarily have to be, down-scaled in resolution; in fact, since the wavelet transformation already separates images into scales, downsampling is more effectively handled by dropping the finest wavelet scale. This step is called *multiple component transformation* in the JPEG 2000 language since its usage is not restricted to the RGB color model.

Tiling

After color transformation, the image is split into so-called *tiles*, rectangular regions of the image that are transformed and encoded separately. Tiles can be any size, and it is also possible to consider the whole image as one single tile. Once the size is chosen, all the tiles will have the same size (except optionally those on the right and bottom borders). Dividing the image into tiles is advantageous in that the decoder will need less memory to decode the image and it can opt to decode only selected tiles to achieve a partial decoding of the image. The disadvantage of this approach is that the quality of the picture decreases due to a lower peak signal-to-noise ratio. Using many tiles can create a blocking effect similar to the older JPEG 1992 standard.

Wavelet Transform

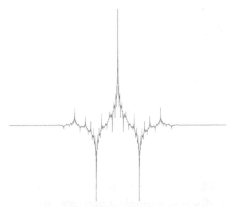

CDF 5/3 wavelet used for lossless compression.

An example of the wavelet transform that is used in JPEG 2000.
This is a 2nd-level CDF 9/7 wavelet transform.

These tiles are then wavelet transformed to an arbitrary depth, in contrast to JPEG 1992 which uses an 8×8 block-size discrete cosine transform. JPEG 2000 uses two different wavelet transforms:

1. *irreversible*: the CDF 9/7 wavelet transform. It is said to be "irreversible" because it introduces quantization noise that depends on the precision of the decoder.

2. *reversible*: a rounded version of the biorthogonal CDF 5/3 wavelet transform. It uses only integer coefficients, so the output does not require rounding (quantization) and so it does not introduce any quantization noise. It is used in lossless coding.

The wavelet transforms are implemented by the lifting scheme or by convolution.

Quantization

After the wavelet transform, the coefficients are scalar-quantized to reduce the number of bits to represent them, at the expense of quality. The output is a set of integer numbers which have to be encoded bit-by-bit. The parameter that can be changed to set the final quality is the quantization step: the greater the step, the greater is the compression and the loss of quality. With a quantization step that equals 1, no quantization is performed (it is used in lossless compression).

Coding

The result of the previous process is a collection of *sub-bands* which represent several approximation scales. A sub-band is a set of *coefficients*—real numbers which represent aspects of the image associated with a certain frequency range as well as a spatial area of the image.

The quantized sub-bands are split further into *precincts*, rectangular regions in the wavelet domain. They are typically selected in a way that the coefficients within them across the sub-bands form approximately spatial blocks in the (reconstructed) image domain, though this is not a requirement.

Precincts are split further into *code blocks*. Code blocks are located in a single sub-band and have equal sizes—except those located at the edges of the image. The encoder has to encode the bits of all quantized coefficients of a code block, starting with the most significant bits and progressing to less significant bits by a process called the *EBCOT* scheme. *EBCOT* here stands for *Embedded Block Coding with Optimal Truncation*. In this encoding process, each bit plane of the code block gets encoded in three so-called *coding passes*, first encoding bits (and signs) of insignificant coefficients with significant neighbors (i.e., with 1-bits in higher bit planes), then refinement bits of significant coefficients and finally coefficients without significant neighbors. The three passes are called *Significance Propagation*, *Magnitude Refinement* and *Cleanup* pass, respectively.

Clearly, in lossless mode all bit planes have to be encoded by the EBCOT, and no bit planes can be dropped.

The bits selected by these coding passes then get encoded by a context-driven binary arithmetic coder, namely the binary MQ-coder. The context of a coefficient is formed by the state of its nine neighbors in the code block.

The result is a bit-stream that is split into *packets* where a *packet* groups selected passes of all code blocks from a precinct into one indivisible unit. Packets are the key to quality scalability (i.e., packets containing less significant bits can be discarded to achieve lower bit rates and higher distortion).

Packets from all sub-bands are then collected in so-called *layers*. The way the packets are built up from the code-block coding passes, and thus which packets a layer will contain, is not defined by the JPEG 2000 standard, but in general a codec will try to build layers in such a way that the image quality will increase monotonically with each layer, and the image distortion will shrink from layer to layer. Thus, layers define the progression by image quality within the code stream.

The problem is now to find the optimal packet length for all code blocks which minimizes the overall distortion in a way that the generated target bitrate equals the demanded bit rate.

While the standard does not define a procedure as to how to perform this form of rate–distortion optimization, the general outline is given in one of its many appendices: For each bit encoded by the EBCOT coder, the improvement in image quality, defined as mean square error, gets measured; this can be implemented by an easy table-lookup algorithm. Furthermore, the length of the resulting code stream gets measured. This forms for each code block a graph in the rate–distortion plane, giving image quality over bitstream length. The optimal selection for the truncation points, thus for the packet-build-up points is then given by defining critical *slopes* of these curves, and picking all those coding passes whose curve in the rate–distortion graph is steeper than the given critical slope. This method can be seen as a special application of the method of *Lagrange multiplier* which is used for optimization problems under constraints. The Lagrange multiplier, typically denoted by λ, turns out to be the critical slope, the constraint is the demanded target bitrate, and the value to optimize is the overall distortion.

Packets can be reordered almost arbitrarily in the JPEG 2000 bit-stream; this gives the encoder as well as image servers a high degree of freedom.

Already encoded images can be sent over networks with arbitrary bit rates by using a layer-progressive encoding order. On the other hand, color components can be moved back in the bit-stream; lower resolutions (corresponding to low-frequency sub-bands) could be sent first for image previewing. Finally, spatial browsing of large images is possible through appropriate tile and/or partition selection. All these operations do not require any re-encoding but only byte-wise copy operations.

Compression Ratio

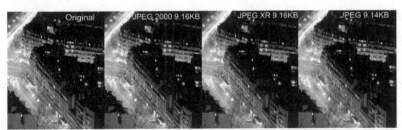

Comparison between JPEG 2000, JPEG XR, and JPEG.

Compared to the previous JPEG standard, JPEG 2000 delivers a typical compression gain in the range of 20%, depending on the image characteristics. Higher-resolution images tend to benefit more, where JPEG-2000's spatial-redundancy prediction can contribute more to the compression process. In very low-bitrate applications, studies have shown JPEG 2000 to be outperformed by the intra-frame coding mode of H.264. Good applications for JPEG 2000 are large images, images with low-contrast edges — e.g., medical images.

Computational Complexity and Performance

JPEG2000 is much more complicated in terms of computational complexity in comparison with JPEG standard. Tiling, color component transform, discrete wavelet transform, and quantization could be done pretty fast, though entropy codec is time consuming and quite complicated. EBCOT context modelling and arithmetic MQ-coder take most of the time of JPEG2000 codec.

On CPU the main idea of getting fast JPEG2000 encoding and decoding is closely connected with AVX/SSE and multithreading to process each tile in separate thread. The fastest JPEG2000 solutions utilize both CPU and GPU power to get high performance benchmarks.

File Format and Code Stream

Similar to JPEG-1, JPEG 2000 defines both a file format and a code stream. Whereas JPEG 2000 entirely describes the image samples, JPEG-1 includes additional meta-information such as the resolution of the image or the color space that has been used to encode the image. JPEG 2000 images should — if stored as files — be boxed in the JPEG 2000 file format, where they get the .jp2 extension. The part-2 extension to JPEG 2000, i.e., ISO/IEC 15444-2, also enriches this file format by including mechanisms for animation or composition of several code streams into one single image. Images in this extended file-format use the .jpx extension.

There is no standardized extension for code-stream data because code-stream data is not to be considered to be stored in files in the first place, though when done for testing purposes, the extension .jpc or .j2k appear frequently.

Metadata

For traditional JPEG, additional metadata, e.g. lighting and exposure conditions, is kept in an application marker in the Exif format specified by the JEITA. JPEG 2000 chooses a different route, encoding the same metadata in XML form. The reference between the Exif tags and the XML elements is standardized by the ISO TC42 committee in the standard 12234-1.4.

Extensible Metadata Platform can also be embedded in JPEG 2000.

Applications

Some markets and applications intended to be served by this standard are listed below:

- Consumer applications such as multimedia devices (e.g., digital cameras, personal digital assistants, 3G mobile phones, color facsimile, printers, scanners, etc.)

- Client/server communication (e.g., the Internet, Image database, Video streaming, video server, etc.)

- Military/surveillance (e.g., HD satellite images, Motion detection, network distribution and storage, etc.)

- Medical imagery, esp. the DICOM specifications for medical data interchange.

- Biometrics.

- Remote sensing

- High-quality frame-based video recording, editing and storage.

- Live HDTV feed contribution (I-frame only video compression with low transmission latency), such as live HDTV feed of a sport event linked to the TV station studio

- Digital cinema

- JPEG 2000 has many design commonalities with the ICER image compression format that is used to send images back from the Mars rovers.

- Digitized Audio-visual contents and Images for Long term digital preservation
- World Meteorological Organization has built JPEG 2000 Compression into the new GRIB2 file format. The GRIB file structure is designed for global distribution of meteorological data. The implementation of JPEG 2000 compression in GRIB2 has reduced file sizes up to 80%.

Comparison with PNG Format

Although JPEG 2000 format supports lossless encoding, it is not intended to completely supersede today's dominant lossless image file formats.

The PNG (Portable Network Graphics) format is still more space-efficient in the case of images with many pixels of the same color, such as diagrams, and supports special compression features that JPEG 2000 does not.

Legal Status

JPEG 2000 is covered by patents, but the contributing companies and organizations agreed that licenses for its first part—the core coding system—can be obtained free of charge from all contributors.

The JPEG committee has stated:

It has always been a strong goal of the JPEG committee that its standards should be implementable in their baseline form without payment of royalty and license fees... The up and coming JPEG 2000 standard has been prepared along these lines, and agreement reached with over 20 large organizations holding many patents in this area to allow use of their intellectual property in connection with the standard without payment of license fees or royalties.

However, the JPEG committee has acknowledged that undeclared submarine patents may still present a hazard:

It is of course still possible that other organizations or individuals may claim intellectual property rights that affect implementation of the standard, and any implementers are urged to carry out their own searches and investigations in this area.

Related Standards

Several additional parts of the JPEG 2000 standard exist; Amongst them are ISO/IEC 15444-2:2000, JPEG 2000 extensions defining the .jpx file format, featuring for example Trellis quantization, an extended file format and additional color spaces, ISO/IEC 15444-4:2000, the reference testing and ISO/IEC 15444-6:2000, the compound image file format (.jpm), allowing compression of compound text/image graphics.

Extensions for secure image transfer, *JPSEC* (ISO/IEC 15444-8), enhanced error-correction schemes for wireless applications, *JPWL* (ISO/IEC 15444-11) and extensions for encoding of volumetric images, *JP3D* (ISO/IEC 15444-10) are also already available from the ISO.

JPIP Protocol for Streaming JPEG 2000 Images

In 2005, a JPEG 2000 based image browsing protocol, called JPIP has been published as ISO/IEC 15444-9. Within this framework, only selected regions of potentially huge images have to be transmitted from an image server on the request of a client, thus reducing the required bandwidth.

JPEG 2000 data may also be streamed using the ECWP and ECWPS protocols found within the ERDAS ECW/JP2 SDK.

Motion JPEG 2000

Motion JPEG 2000, (MJ2), originally defined in Part 3 of the ISO Standard for JPEG2000 (ISO/IEC 15444-3:2002,) as a standalone document, has now been expressed by ISO/IEC 15444-3:2002/Amd 2:2003 in terms of the ISO Base format, ISO/IEC 15444-12 and in ITU-T Recommendation T.802. It specifies the use of the JPEG 2000 format for timed sequences of images (motion sequences), possibly combined with audio, and composed into an overall presentation. It also defines a file format, based on ISO base media file format (ISO 15444-12). Filename extensions for Motion JPEG 2000 video files are .mj2 and .mjp2 according to RFC 3745.

It is an open ISO standard and an advanced update to MJPEG (or MJ), which was based on the legacy JPEG format. Unlike common video formats, such as MPEG-4 Part 2, WMV, and H.264, MJ2 does not employ temporal or inter-frame compression. Instead, each frame is an independent entity encoded by either a lossy or lossless variant of JPEG 2000. Its physical structure does not depend on time ordering, but it does employ a separate profile to complement the data. For audio, it supports LPCM encoding, as well as various MPEG-4 variants, as "raw" or complement data.

Motion JPEG 2000 (often referenced as MJ2 or MJP2) was considered as a digital archival format by the Library of Congress. In June 2013, in an interview with Bertram Lyons from the Library of Congress for *The New York Times Magazine*, about "Tips on Archiving Family History", codecs like FFV1, H264 or Apple ProRes are mentioned, but JPEG 2000 is not.

ISO Base Media File Format

ISO/IEC 15444-12 is identical with ISO/IEC 14496-12 (MPEG-4 Part 12) and it defines ISO base media file format. For example, Motion JPEG 2000 file format, MP4 file format or 3GP file format are also based on this ISO base media file format.

GML JP2 Georeferencing

The Open Geospatial Consortium (OGC) has defined a metadata standard for georeferencing JPEG 2000 images with embedded XML using the Geography Markup Language (GML) format: *GML in JPEG 2000 for Geographic Imagery Encoding (GMLJP2)*, version 1.0.0, dated 2006-01-18. Version 2.0, entitled *GML in JPEG 2000 (GMLJP2) Encoding Standard Part 1: Core* was approved 2014-06-30.

JP2 and JPX files containing GMLJP2 markup can be located and displayed in the correct position on the Earth's surface by a suitable Geographic Information System (GIS), in a similar way to GeoTIFF images.

Application Support

Applications

	Application support for JPEG 2000				
Program	**Basic**		**Advanced**		**License**
	Read	**Write**	**Read**	**Write**	
ACDSee	Yes	Yes	?	?	Proprietary
Adobe Photoshop	Yes	Yes	Yes	Yes	Proprietary
Adobe Lightroom	No	No	No	No	Proprietary
Apple iPhoto	Yes	No	Yes	No	Proprietary
Apple Preview	Yes	Yes	Yes	Yes	Proprietary
Autodesk AutoCAD	Yes	Yes	Yes	?	Proprietary
BAE Systems CoMPASS	Yes	No	Yes	No	Proprietary
Blender	Yes	Yes	?	?	GPL
Phase One Capture One	Yes	Yes	Yes	Yes	Proprietary
Chasys Draw IES	Yes	Yes	Yes	Yes	Freeware
CineAsset	Yes	Yes	Yes	Yes	Proprietary
CompuPic Pro	Yes	Yes	?	?	Proprietary
Corel Photo-Paint	Yes	Yes	Yes	Yes	Proprietary
Daminion	Yes	No	Yes	No	Proprietary
darktable	?	Yes	?	?	GPL
DBGallery	Yes	No	Yes	No	Proprietary
digiKam (KDE)	Yes	Yes	?	?	GPL
ECognition	Yes	Yes	?	?	Proprietary
ENVI	Yes	Yes	?	?	Proprietary
ERDAS IMAGINE	Yes	Yes	?	?	Proprietary
evince (PDF 1.5 embedding)	Yes	No	No	No	GPL v2
FastStone Image Viewer	Yes	Yes	Yes	Yes	Freeware
FastStone MaxView	Yes	No	Yes	No	Proprietary
FotoGrafix 2.0	No	No	No	No	Proprietary
FotoSketcher 2.70	No	No	No	No	Proprietary
GIMP 2.8	Yes	No	?	No	GPL
Google Chrome	No	No	No	No	Proprietary
GraphicConverter	Yes	Yes	Yes	?	Shareware
Gwenview (KDE)	Yes	Yes	?	?	GPL
IDL	Yes	Yes	?	?	Proprietary
ImageMagick	Yes	Yes	No	No	ImageMagick License
IrfanView	Yes	Partial	No	No	Proprietary
KolourPaint (KDE)	Yes	Yes	?	?	2-clause BSD
Mathematica	Yes	Yes	?	?	Proprietary
Matlab	via toolbox	via toolbox	via toolbox	via toolbox	Proprietary

Application support for JPEG 2000					
Program	**Basic**		**Advanced**		**License**
	Read	**Write**	**Read**	**Write**	
Mozilla Firefox	No	No	No	No	MPL
Opera	via Quick-Time	-	?	-	Proprietary
Paint Shop Pro	Yes	Yes	Yes	Yes	Proprietary
PhotoFiltre 7.1	No	No	No	No	Proprietary
PhotoLine	Yes	Yes	?	?	Proprietary
Pixel image editor	Yes	Yes	?	?	Proprietary
QGIS (with a plugin)	Yes	Yes	?	?	GPL
Safari	Yes	-	?	-	Proprietary
SilverFast	Yes	Yes	Yes	Yes	Proprietary
XnView	Yes	Yes	Yes	Yes	Proprietary
Ziproxy	Yes	Yes	No	No	GPL

Libraries

Library support for JPEG 2000						
Program	**Basic**		**Advanced**		**Language**	**License**
	Read	**Write**	**Read**	**Write**		
Comprimato	Yes	Yes	Yes	Yes	C, C++	Proprietary
ERDAS ECW JPEG2000 SDK	Yes	Yes	?	?	C, C++	Proprietary
Fastvideo SDK	No	Yes	No	No	C, C++	Proprietary
FFmpeg	Yes	Yes	?	?	C	LGPL
Grok	Yes	Yes	Yes	Yes	C, C++	AGPL
GTK+ (from 2.14)	Yes	No	?	No	C/GTK	LGPL
J2K-Codec	Yes	No	Yes	No	C++	Proprietary
JasPer	Yes	Yes	No	No	C	MIT License-style
Kakadu	Yes	Yes	Yes	Yes	C++	Proprietary
LEADTOOLS	Yes	Yes	Yes	Yes	C++, .NET	Proprietary
OpenJPEG	Yes	Yes	Yes	Yes	C	BSD
BOI codec	Yes	Yes	No	No	Java	BOI License

References

- "ITU-T Recommendation T.88 – T.88 : Information technology - Coded representation of picture and audio information - Lossy/lossless coding of bi-level images". Retrieved 2011-02-19

- Akramullah, Shahriar (2014). "Video Coding Standards". Digital Video Concepts, Methods, and Metrics. Apress. pp. 55–100. ISBN 978-1-4302-6712-6. doi:10.1007/978-1-4302-6713-3_3

- Kriesel, David. "Video and Slides of my Xerox Talk at 31C3". D. Kriesel Data Science, Machine Learning, BBQ, Photos, and Ants in a Terrarium. Retrieved 31 July 2016

- "T.81 : Information technology – Digital compression and coding of continuous-tone still images – Requirements and guidelines". Retrieved 2009-11-07

- William B. Pennebaker; Joan L. Mitchell (1993). JPEG still image data compression standard (3rd ed.). Springer. p. 291. ISBN 978-0-442-01272-4

- Workgroup. "Article on Princeton Court Ruling Regarding GE License Agreement". Archived from the original on 2016-03-09. Retrieved 2013-05-01

4

An Overview of Audio and Video Coding Standards

A video codec is a form of encoder that compresses or decompresses a digital video. A few examples of video codecs are MPEG-1, MPEG-2, and MPEG-4. An audio codec is an encoder that compresses and decompresses digital audio data as per an audio coding format. A content representation format for transmitting and storing audio is known as audio coding format. MP3 is its most popular form. Audio and video coding is best understood in confluence with the major topics listed in the following section.

Audio Codec

An audio codec is a device or computer program capable of coding or decoding a digital data stream of audio.

In software, an audio codec is a computer program implementing an algorithm that compresses and decompresses digital audio data according to a given audio file or streaming media audio coding format. The objective of the algorithm is to represent the high-fidelity audio signal with minimum number of bits while retaining the quality. This can effectively reduce the storage space and the bandwidth required for transmission of the stored audio file. Most codecs are implemented as libraries which interface to one or more multimedia players.

In hardware, audio codec refers to a single device that encodes analog audio as digital signals and decodes digital back into analog. In other words, it contains both an analog-to-digital converter (ADC) and digital-to-analog converter (DAC) running off the same clock. This is used in sound cards that support both audio in and out, for instance.

Audio Coding Format

An audio coding format (or sometimes audio compression format) is a content representation format for storage or transmission of digital audio (such as in digital television, digital radio and in audio and video files). Examples of audio coding formats include MP3, AAC, Vorbis, FLAC, and Opus. A specific software or hardware implementation capable of audio compression and decompression to/from a specific audio coding format is called an audio codec; an example of an audio codec is LAME, which is one of several different codecs which implements encoding and decoding audio in the MP3 audio coding format in software.

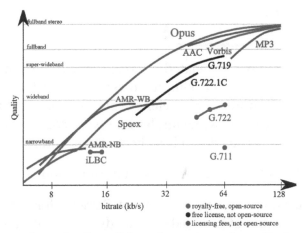

Comparison of coding efficiency between popular audio formats

Some audio coding formats are documented by a detailed technical specification document known as an audio coding specification. Some such specifications are written and approved by standardization organizations as technical standards, and are thus known as an audio coding standard. The term 'standard' is also sometimes used for *de facto* standards as well as formal standards.

Audio content encoded in a particular audio coding format is normally encapsulated within a container format. As such, the user normally doesn't have a raw AAC file, but instead has a .m4a audio file, which is a MPEG-4 Part 14 container containing AAC-encoded audio. The container also contains metadata such as title and other tags, and perhaps an index for fast seeking. A notable exception is MP3 files, which are raw audio coding without a container format. De facto standards for adding metadata tags such as title and artist to MP3s, such as ID3, are hacks which work by appending the tags to the MP3, and then relying on the MP3 player to recognize the chunk as malformed audio coding and therefore skip it. In video files with audio, the encoded audio content is bundled with video (in a video coding format) inside a multimedia container format.

An audio coding format does not dictate all algorithms used by a codec implementing the format. An important part of how lossy audio compression works is by removing data in ways humans can't hear, according to a psychoacoustic model; the implementer of an encoder has some freedom of choice in which data to remove (according to their psychoacoustic model).

Lossless, Lossy, and Uncompressed Audio Coding Formats

A lossless audio coding format reduces the total data needed to represent a sound but can be de-coded to its original, uncompressed form. A lossy audio coding format additionally reduces the bit resolution of the sound on top of compression, which results in far less data at the cost of irretrievably lost information.

Consumer audio is most often compressed using lossy audio codecs as the smaller size is far more convenient for distribution. Lossless audio coding formats such as FLAC and Apple Lossless are sometimes available, though at the cost of larger files.

Uncompressed audio formats, such as pulse-code modulation (.wav), are also sometimes used.

MPEG-1 Audio Layer I

MPEG-1 Audio Layer I, commonly abbreviated to MP1, is one of three audio formats included in the MPEG-1 standard. It is a deliberately simplified version of MPEG-1 Audio Layer II, created for applications where lower compression efficiency could be tolerated in return for a less complex algorithm that could be executed with simpler hardware requirements. While supported by most media players, the codec is considered largely obsolete, and replaced by MP2 or MP3.

For files only containing MP1 audio, the file extension .mp1 is used.

MPEG-1 layer I was also used by the Digital Compact Cassette format, in the form of the PASC audio compression codec. Because of the need of a steady stream of frames per second on a tape-based medium, PASC uses the rarely used (and under-documented) padding bit in the MPEG header to indicate that a frame was padded with 32 extra 0-bits (four 0-bytes) to change a short 416-byte frame into 420 bytes. The varying frame size only occurs when a 44.1 kHz 16-bit stereo audio signal is encoded at 384 kilobits per second, because the bitrate of the uncompressed signal is not an exact multiple of the bitrate of the compressed bit stream.

Specification

MPEG-1 Layer I is defined in ISO/IEC 11172-3, which first version was published in 1993.

- Sampling rates: 32, 44.1 and 48 kHz

- Bitrates: 32, 64, 96, 128, 160, 192, 224, 256, 288, 320, 352, 384, 416 and 448 kbit/s

An extension has been provided in MPEG-2 Layer I and is defined in ISO/IEC 13818-3, which first version was published in 1995.

- Additional sampling rates: 16, 22.05 and 24 kHz

- Additional bitrates: 48, 56, 80, 112, 144 and 176 kbit/s

MP1 uses a comparatively simple sub-band coding, using 32 sub-bands.

Layers of Audio Compression

The MPEG-1 audio coding standard supports the following three coding layers with increasing complexity, delay and subjective performance –

(a) Layer –I: This is the simplest layer and best suits bit rates above 128 Kbps per channel. Relatively lower compression ratio as compared to the higher layers makes this layer simple. Layer-1 encoding is used in digital audiocassettes that use compressed bit rates of 192 Kbps per channel.

(b) Layer – II: This layer is of intermediate complexity and supports compressed bit stream up to 128 Kbps per channel. Applications of this layer include digital audio in CDs, VCDs.

(c) Layer – III: This is the most complicated of the three layers. The target bit rate is around 64 Kbps per channel. This layer is suitable for ISDN.

Modes of MPEG-1 Audio

MPEG-1 supports upto two channels of audio with four modes as follows.

    (a) Monophonic mode for single channels audio

    (b) Dual monophonic mode for two independent channels of audio. This is useful for bilingual presentations

    (c) Stereo mode for stereo channels that share bits but do not exploit correlations between the stereo channels.

    (d) Joint stereo mode which exploits correlations between the stereo channels and uses an irrevancy reduction technique called *intensity stereo.*

Structure of MPEG-1 Audio Codec

Figure shows the structure of MPEG-1 audio codec for layer-I and II. To allocate bits to the audio samples, the samples are passed through an analysis filter bank, which filters the signal into 32 subbands. To derive the audio spectrum, performing FFT on the samples carries out a time to frequency conversion. The psychoacoustic models identify the tonal and the non-tonal components to derive the masking thresholds and hence the Signal to Mask Ratio (SMR). Bits are allocated on a block by block basis for each subband. Each block has 12 samples per subband for Layer-I of audio i.e., total 384 samples considering 32 sub bands and 36 subband samples (total of 1152 samples) for Layer-II and III. MPEG-1 audio codec supports two psychoacoustics' models. The psychoacoustics model I is used in Layer I. and II. and the model-II is used for Layer-III. The subband codewords, the scale factor and the bit allocation information are multiplexed into one bitstream, together with a header and optional ancillary data. At the decoder, the synthesis filter bank reconstructs the audio output from the demultiplexed bitstream.

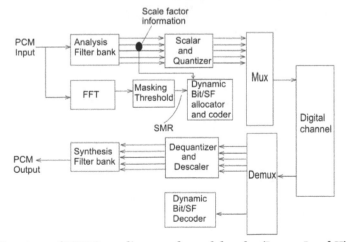

Structure of MPEG.1 audio enconder and decoder (Layers I and II)

Psychoacoustics Models

As already mentioned, MPEG-1 audio codec design is based on two psychoacoustic models. This model computes the *SMR* s, considering the short term spectrum of the audio block to be coded. Only the encoder requires this model. Both model-I and II determine the masking characteristics for either "tone masks noise" or "noise masks tone" types and calculate the global masking thresholds. In both the models, the audio samples are Hann weighted.

The Psychoacoustics model II is more complex than the model- I. It takes into consideration the properties of the inner ear and the effects of pre-echoes.

Design Issues of Analysis and Synthesis Filters

The basic framework for an analysis / synthesis system is shown in figure. The analysis filer bank segments the input samples $x(n)$ into a number of contiguous filter banks, whose outputs are shown as $X_k(m)$, where k=0,1,...,K-1 are the subband numbers and m=0,1... are the sample indices. The synthesis filterbanks receive the subband samples $\hat{X}_k(m)$ from the digital channel. For a lossless channel, $\hat{X}_k(m) = X_k(m)$, but this is not true for a noisy channel. The synthesis filter bank reconstructs the signal as $\hat{x}(n)$ which should be ideally an exact replica of the input signal.

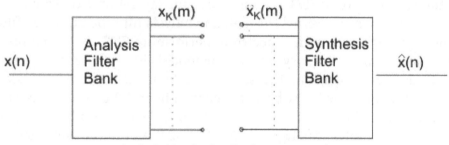

Analysis/Synthesis Filtering Framework

There are two different approaches to the design of such analysis and synthesis filters. The first is based on a bank of lowpass and bandpass filters. We conveniently express these filters in frequency domain. Exact reconstruction can be achieved only if the composite analysis-synthesis filter channel responses overlap and add, such that their sum indicates a flat response in the figure below indicates this concept. All the filters are non-ideal and have definite roll-offs, which must match.

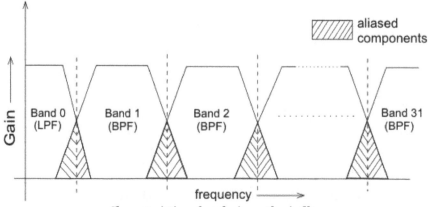

Characteristics of analysis synthesis filter

In this scheme, it is necessary that any frequency domain aliasing introduced by representing the narrow band analysis signals at a reduced sampling rate must be removed at the synthesis filter.

A second approach towards the realization of analysis / synthesis system is to use frequency domain transform. The analysis filter first windows the samples before applying transforms like DFT, DCT etc. The transform domain samples form the channel signals. To synthesize, the channel signals are inverse transformed and the resulting time sequence is multiplied by a synthesis window, overlapped and added to generate the reconstructed signal. By a similar argument we followed for a first approach, we can say that reconstruction of $x(n)$ will be perfect if the composite analysis-synthesis window responses overlap and add in the time domain is flat and any time domain aliasing introduced by the frequency domain representation is removed in the synthesis process.

Such Time Domain Alias Cancellation (TDAC) may be seen as the dual of Frequency Domain Alias Cancellation (FDAC). The analysis-synthesis systems for coding applications are so designed that the overall sampling rate at the output is same as that of the input systems satisfying such conditions are referred to as *critically sampled system*. In a K-band filtering approach, this can be achieved by decimating each channel signal by a factor of K. For the frequency domain, i.,e subband filtering approach critical sampling introduces frequency domain aliasing except in the case where the analysis and synthesis filters have rectangular response equal to the channel width. In time domain approach, the dual of subband filtering is time domain windowing and there, critical sampling introduces time domain aliasing, except if the analysis and synthesis windows are rectangular and equal to the decimation factor.

One popular techniques of critically sampled analysis-synthesis system having overlapped channel frequency responses and reconstruction is the Quandrature mirror filtering (QMF). Overlap exists only between adjacent channel filters. For these systems, frequency domain aliasing is introduced by the analysis filters, but these are corrected by the synthesis filters. The techniques can be best described by single sideband modulation (SSB), since the channel signals are real.

A corresponding time domain description of SSB results in a block transform implementation of filter banks, using DCT and Discrete Sine Transforms (DST). An efficient weighted overlap-add (OLA) analysis and synthesis can be used to reconstruct the samples through time-domain alias cancellation. A detailed mathematical analysis of such system, along with the necessary conditions for perfect reconstruction are described by Princen et al and is not repeated here.

Mechanism of Time-domain Aliasing Cancellation

Figure above illustrates the mechanism for time-domain alias cancellation. The input signal is first windowed with overlap between the adjacent windows. Let us first consider that the block time m is even. The recovered sequence after the forward and the inverse transform (in this case, the DCT) contains time reversed aliasing distortion, shown by the dashed curve. Although, for illustration purposes we have shown the original signal and the aliased signal separate, in practice the sum of these two would be observed. The sequence can be interpreted as periodic with period K. The synthesis window extracts a portion of the sequence of length K. In the next block time that is with m odd, the window is shifted by K/2 and a forward and an inverse DST are performed on the windowed sequence. The output contains time-reversed aliasing distortion, as shown by the dashed curve. It may be noted that the aliased samples in odd block time is opposite in sign as compared to those in even block time. The aliasing terms from the upper edge of segment from block time m, and from the lower edge of segment from block time m+1 are equal and opposite and hence cancelled when these are overlapped and added.

Implementation and Window Design for TDAC

Implementation of the TDAC approach follows the block diagram shown in the first figure. The input signal is multiplied by an analysis window and then a transform (DCT/DST) is applied. The syntheses involve a corresponding inverse transform (IDCT/IDST), multiplication by a synthesis window, followed by overlap and add to obtain alias-free time samples. Time domain designs are more efficient for a given number of bands as compared to the frequency-based designs. For example, a critically sampled design for a 32-band system using frequency domain techniques, having stop-band attenuation greater than 40 dB and passband ripple less than 0.2 dB would require an 80-sample window. A critically sampled time domain design, in contrast requires just a window of 32 samples to implement filters with the same characteristics.

Two possible window design using TDAD are shown in the second figure and the corresponding coefficient values are shown in table. The Modified Discrete Cosine Transform (MDCT) approach, adopted in MPEG-1 audio coding standard is a variant of the TDAC approach developed by Princen and Bradley.

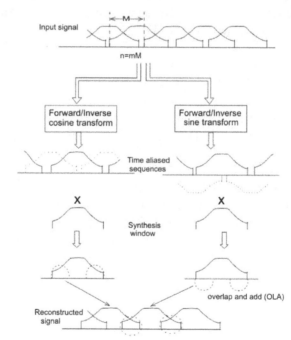

The mechanism of aliasing cancellation through DCT/DST and OLA

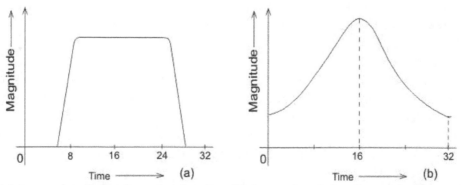

(a) A 20- point window for 32-band system; (b) A 32-point window for a 32-band system

Table: Window coefficient for two possible design in a 32 band system. Note that the windows are symmetric, i.,e h(31-r)=h(r))

Coefficient no (r)	Design −1 (20 point window)	Design −2 (32-point windows)
0	0	0.18332
1	0	0.26722
2	0	0.36390
3	0	0.47162
4	0	0.58798
5	0	0.70847
6	0.5000	0.82932
7	0.86603	0.94553
8	1.11803	1.05202
9	1.32287	1.14558
10	1.41421	1.22396
11	1.41421	1.28610
12	1.41421	1.33307
13	1.41421	1.36655
14	1.41421	1.38866
15	1.41421	1.40212

Theory of Polyphase Filters

We have discussed that the design of a multiband filter requires alias cancellation between adjacent bands and that the filter shapes be controlled such that the transition bands of adjacent filters add to produce a flat response.

Following Rothwieter's approach, a filter bank fulfilling these requirements can be formed by first designing a low pass prototype filter with a controlled transition band frequency response. The filter bank can then be composed by multiplying the impulse response of the prototype low pass filter with a sinusoid having frequencies equal to the centre frequencies of the desired filters.

We assume the sampling frequency to be unity, so that the frequency range to be covered is 0 to π radians/sec. A bank of M filters to be synthesized as shown in the figure. The nominal bandwidth of each filter is π/M and the filter centre frequencies are at add multiples of $\pi/2M$.

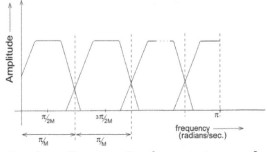

A bank of bandpass filter. Sampling frequency is assuned to be 1 Hz

Real bandpass filters are composed of two complex filters $F_i(z)$ and $G_i(z)$ located respectively at the positive and negative centre frequencies. If the prototype lowpass filter is a FIR filter with impulse response $h(n)$ and z- transform $H(z)$ we can express $F_i(Z)$ and $G_i(Z)$ as

$$F_i(z) = H\left(e^{-\frac{j\pi(2i+1)}{2M}} z\right)$$

$$G_i(z) = H\left(e^{\frac{j\pi(2i+1)}{2M}} z\right). \quad (1)$$

In equations (1), the complex filters in z-domain are derived by multiplying the Z with complex exponentials located of odd multiples of $\pi/2M$. We therefore obtain a band of filers with $i=0,1,...,M-1$ and the corresponding composite filters may be expressed as

$$H_i(z) = a_i F_i(z) + b_i G_i(z)$$

$$K_i(z) = c_i F_i(z) + d_i G_i(z) \quad (2)$$

where a_i, b_i, c_i and d_i are complex constants. $H_i(Z)$ and $K_i(z)$ form the analysis and the synthesis filter banks respectively, as shown in the figure.

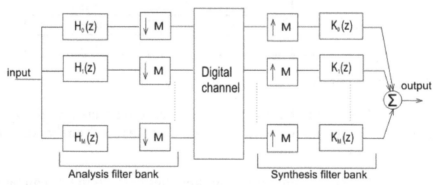

Analysis and Synthesis filter banks

If $a_i = b_i^*$ the impulse response of H_i is real and is given by

$$h_i(n) = \left\{ \begin{array}{l} \mathrm{Re}(a_i)\cos\left[\pi(2i+1)(2n+1)/4M\right] \\ -\mathrm{Im}(a_i)\sin\left[\pi(2i+1)(2n+1)/4M\right] \end{array} \right\} h(n). \quad (3)$$

Replacing a_i and b_i with c_i and d_i, a corresponding equation results for $k_i(n)$.

From equation (3), it is evident that the $h_i(n)$ contains odd number of half cycles of sinusoids in 2M points ($n=0,1....., 2M-1$)

If the input samples are given by $x(n)$, $n=0,1,.......$, then the filtered output of bank-i is given by the famous convolution equation

$$s_i(i) = \sum_{n=0}^{L-1} x(l-n)h_i(n) \quad (4)$$

where L is the length of the filter's tap.

Substituting equation (3) in (4) we obtain DCT/DST of the input samples, multiplied by the prototype low pass filter's impulse. The latter serves as the windowing of the time domain samples.

The equation (3) involving $h_i(n)$ clearly shows that the response of each band i is a modulation of the prototype response with a cosine term to shift the low pass response to the appropriate band. Hence, these are called polyphase filters.

One efficient implementation of a polyphase filter bank is shown in the first figure. The input samples are first multiplied by lowpass prototype filter h(n). Blocks of 2M products of the multiplications are accumulated with the sign of alternate blocks negated. These 2M values are then multiplied by M sinusoids to generate the M output values. A typical response of low-pass prototype analysis filter h(n) is sketched in the second figure. Negating the signs of alternate blocks result in a net windowing function c(n) as sketched in the last figure.

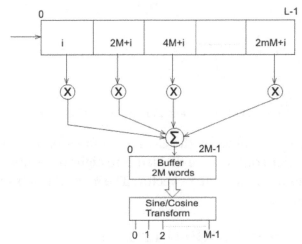

Implementation of polyphase filter

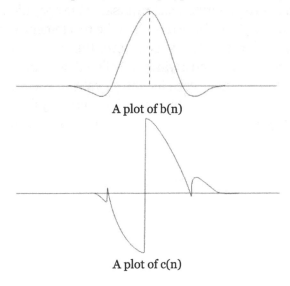

A plot of b(n)

A plot of c(n)

For audio signals, since the flat response to DC is not required, the coefficient a_i in equation (3) can be either pure real or pure imaginary. Hence, equation (3) contains either the sine terms or the cosine terms, but not both. In MPEG-1, a modified discrete cosine transforms (MDCT) is applied to obtain M subband samples out of 2M words

Polyphase Analysis Filter for MPEG-1 Audio

Figure below shows the polyphase implementation of MPEG-1 analysis filter bank which is a variant of Rothweller's implementation described above. During the analysis, the audio signal is shifted into a 512 samples X buffer, 32 samples at a time.

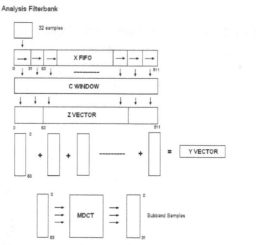

Polyphase implementation of analysis filterbank.

The content of X buffer are multiplied by the C-window function c(n) and the results are stored into the Z-buffer. The Z-buffer contents are divided into eight 64-element vectors (taking M=32), which are summed to form a 64-element Y- vector. The Y-vector is transformed using MDCT to yield the 32-subband samples.

Polyphase Synthesis Filter for MPEG-1 Audio

The synthesis filter shown in figure performs exact reversal of the operations performed by the analysis filter. The 32 subband samples are transformed back to the 64 element V vector, using inverse MDCT (IMDCT). The V-vector is pushed into a FIFO which stores the last 16 V vectors. A U-vector is created from the alternate 32 component blocks and a window (called D-window) is applied to U to produce the W-vector, which is divided into 16 vectors, each having 32 values. These 16 vectors are added together to obtain 32 sample output. It may therefore be noted that the analysis synthesis filtering operation is critically sampled, since exactly 32-sampled output is obtained for 32-sampled input.

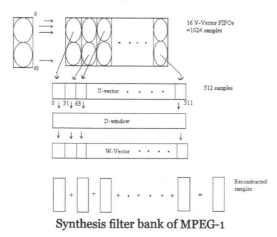

Synthesis filter bank of MPEG-1

Video Codec

A video codec is an electronic circuit or software that compresses or decompresses digital video. It converts raw (uncompressed) digital video to a compressed format or vice versa. In the context of video compression, "codec" is a concatenation of "encoder" and "decoder"—a device that only compresses is typically called an *encoder*, and one that only decompresses is a *decoder*.

The compressed data format usually conforms to a standard video compression specification. The compression is typically lossy, meaning that the compressed video lacks some information present in the original video. A consequence of this is that decompressed video has lower quality than the original, uncompressed video because there is insufficient information to accurately reconstruct the original video.

There are complex relationships between the video quality, the amount of data used to represent the video (determined by the bit rate), the complexity of the encoding and decoding algorithms, sensitivity to data losses and errors, ease of editing, random access, and end-to-end delay (latency).

History

Historically, video was stored as an analog signal on magnetic tape. Around the time when the compact disc entered the market as a digital-format replacement for analog audio, it became feasible to also store and convey video in digital form. Because of the large amount of storage and bandwidth needed to record and convey raw video, a method was needed to reduce the amount of data used to represent the raw video. Since then, engineers and mathematicians have developed a number of solutions for achieving this goal that involve compressing the digital video data.

Applications

Video codecs are used in DVD and video CD players and recorders, video broadcast systems, personal computers, and a variety of other applications. In particular, they are widely used in applications that record or transmit video, which may not be feasible with the high data volumes and bandwidths of uncompressed video. For example, they are used in operating theaters to record surgical operations, in IP-based security systems, and in remotely operated vehicles such as ROVs and UAVs.

Video Codec Design

Video codecs seek to represent a fundamentally analog data set in a digital format. Because of the design of analog video signals, which represent luminance ("luma") and color information (chrominance, "chroma") separately, a common first step in image compression in codec design is to represent and store the image in a YCbCr color space. The conversion to YCbCr provides two benefits: first, it improves compressibility by providing decorrelation of the color signals; and second, it separates the luma signal, which is perceptually much more important, from the chroma signal, which is less perceptually important and which can be represented at lower resolution to achieve more efficient data compression. It is common to represent the ratios of information stored in these different channels in the following way Y:Cb:Cr.

Different codecs use different chroma subsampling ratios as appropriate to their compression needs. Video compression schemes for Web and DVD make use of a 4:2:1 color sampling pattern, and the DV standard uses 4:1:1 sampling ratios. Professional video codecs designed to function at much higher bitrates and to record a greater amount of color information for post-production manipulation sample in 3:1:1 (uncommon), 4:2:2 and 4:4:4 ratios. Examples of these codecs include Panasonic's DVCPRO50 and DVCPROHD codecs (4:2:2), and then Sony's HDCAM-SR (4:4:4) or Panasonic's HDD5 (4:2:2). Apple's Prores HQ 422 codec also samples in 4:2:2 color space. More codecs that sample in 4:4:4 patterns exist as well, but are less common, and tend to be used internally in post-production houses. It is also worth noting that video codecs can operate in RGB space as well. These codecs tend not to sample the red, green, and blue channels in different ratios, since there is less perceptual motivation for doing so—just the blue channel could be undersampled.

Some amount of spatial and temporal downsampling may also be used to reduce the raw data rate before the basic encoding process. The most popular such transform is the 8x8 discrete cosine transform (DCT). Codecs which make use of a wavelet transform are also entering the market, especially in camera workflows which involve dealing with RAW image formatting in motion sequences. The output of the transform is first quantized, then entropy encoding is applied to the quantized values. When a DCT has been used, the coefficients are typically scanned using a zig-zag scan order, and the entropy coding typically combines a number of consecutive zero-valued quantized coefficients with the value of the next non-zero quantized coefficient into a single symbol, and also has special ways of indicating when all of the remaining quantized coefficient values are equal to zero. The entropy coding method typically uses variable-length coding tables. Some encoders can compress the video in a multiple step process called *n-pass* encoding (e.g. 2-pass), which performs a slower but potentially better quality compression.

The decoding process consists of performing, to the extent possible, an inversion of each stage of the encoding process. The one stage that cannot be exactly inverted is the quantization stage. There, a best-effort approximation of inversion is performed. This part of the process is often called "inverse quantization" or "dequantization", although quantization is an inherently non-invertible process.

This process involves representing the video image as a set of macroblocks. For more information about this critical facet of video codec design.

Video codec designs are usually standardized or eventually become standardized—i.e., specified precisely in a published document. However, only the decoding process need be standardized to enable interoperability. The encoding process is typically not specified at all in a standard, and implementers are free to design their encoder however they want, as long as the video can be decoded in the specified manner. For this reason, the quality of the video produced by decoding the results of different encoders that use the same video codec standard can vary dramatically from one encoder implementation to another.

Commonly used Video Codecs

A variety of video compression formats can be implemented on PCs and in consumer electronics equipment. It is therefore possible for multiple codecs to be available in the same product, avoiding the need to choose a single dominant video compression format for compatibility reasons.

Video in most of the publicly documented or standardized video compression formats can be created with multiple encoders made by different people. Many video codecs use common, standard video compression formats, which makes them compatible. For example, video created with a standard MPEG-4 Part 2 codec such as Xvid can be decoded (played back) using any other standard MPEG-4 Part 2 codec such as FFmpeg MPEG-4 or DivX Pro Codec, because they all use the same video format.

Some widely used software codecs are listed below, grouped by which video compression format they implement.

H.265/MPEG-H HEVC Codecs

- x265: A GPL-licensed implementation of the H.265 video standard. x265 is only an encoder.

H.264/MPEG-4 AVC Codecs

- x264: A GPL-licensed implementation of the H.264 video standard. x264 is only an encoder.

- Nero Digital: Commercial MPEG-4 ASP and AVC codecs developed by Nero AG.

- QuickTime H.264: H.264 implementation released by Apple.

- DivX Pro Codec: An H.264 decoder and encoder was added in version 7.

H.263/MPEG-4 Part 2 Codecs

- DivX Pro Codec: A proprietary MPEG-4 ASP codec made by DivX, Inc.

- Xvid: Free/open-source implementation of MPEG-4 ASP, originally based on the OpenDivX project.

- FFmpeg MPEG-4: Included in the open-source libavcodec codec library, which is used by default for decoding or encoding in many open-source video players, frameworks, editors and encoding tools such as MPlayer, VLC, ffdshow or GStreamer. Compatible with other standard MPEG-4 codecs like Xvid or DivX Pro Codec.

- 3ivx: A commercial MPEG-4 codec created by 3ivx Technologies.

H.262/MPEG-2 Codecs

- x262: A GPL-licensed implementation of the H.262 video standard. x262 is only an encoder.

Microsoft Codecs

- WMV (Windows Media Video): Microsoft's family of proprietary video codec designs including WMV 7, WMV 8, and WMV 9. The latest generation of WMV is standardized by SMPTE as the VC-1 standard.

- MS MPEG-4v3: A proprietary and not MPEG-4 compliant video codec created by Microsoft. Released as a part of Windows Media Tools 4. A hacked version of Microsoft's MPEG-4v3 codec became known as DivX.

Google (On2) Codecs

- VP6, VP6-E, VP6-S, VP7, VP8, VP9: Proprietary high definition video compression formats and codecs developed by On2 Technologies used in platforms such as Adobe Flash Player 8 and above, Adobe Flash Lite, Java FX and other mobile and desktop video platforms. Supports resolution up to 720p and 1080p. VP9 supports resolutions up to 2160p. VP8 and VP9 have been available under the New BSD License by Google with source code available as the libvpx VP8/VP9 codec SDK.

- libtheora: A reference implementation of the Theora video compression format developed by the Xiph.org Foundation, based upon On2 Technologies' VP3 codec, and christened by On2 as the successor in VP3's lineage. Theora is targeted at competing with MPEG-4 video and similar lower-bitrate video compression schemes.

Other Codecs

- Apple ProRes: Is a lossy video compression format developed by Apple Inc.

- Schrödinger and dirac-research: implementations of the Dirac compression format developed by BBC Research at the BBC. Dirac provides video compression from web video up to ultra HD and beyond.

- DNxHD codec: a lossy high-definition video production codec developed by Avid Technology. It is an implementation of VC-3.

- Sorenson 3: A video compression format and codec that is popularly used by Apple's Quick-Time, sharing many features with H.264. Many movie trailers found on the web use this compression format.

- Sorenson Spark: A codec and compression format that was licensed to Macromedia for use in its Flash Video starting with Flash Player 6. It is considered as an incomplete implementation of the H.263 standard.

- RealVideo: Developed by RealNetworks. A popular compression format and codec technology a few years ago, now fading in importance for a variety of reasons.

- Cinepak: A very early codec used by Apple's QuickTime.

- Indeo, an older video compression format and codec initially developed by Intel.

All of the codecs above have their qualities and drawbacks. Comparisons are frequently published. The trade-off between compression power, speed, and fidelity (including artifacts) is usually considered the most important figure of technical merit.

Codec Packs

Online video material is encoded by a variety of codecs, and this has led to the availability of codec packs — a pre-assembled set of commonly used codecs combined with an installer available as a software package for PCs, such as K-Lite Codec Pack.

MPEG-1

MPEG-1 is a standard for lossy compression of video and audio. It is designed to compress VHS-quality raw digital video and CD audio down to 1.5 Mbit/s (26:1 and 6:1 compression ratios respectively) without excessive quality loss, making video CDs, digital cable/satellite TV and digital audio broadcasting (DAB) possible.

Today, MPEG-1 has become the most widely compatible lossy audio/video format in the world, and is used in a large number of products and technologies. Perhaps the best-known part of the MPEG-1 standard is the MP3 audio format it introduced.

The MPEG-1 standard is published as ISO/IEC 11172 – Information technology—Coding of moving pictures and associated audio for digital storage media at up to about 1.5 Mbit/s. The standard consists of the following five *Parts*:

1. Systems (storage and synchronization of video, audio, and other data together)

2. Video (compressed video content)

3. Audio (compressed audio content)

4. Conformance testing (testing the correctness of implementations of the standard)

5. Reference software (example software showing how to encode and decode according to the standard)

History

Modeled on the successful collaborative approach and the compression technologies developed by the Joint Photographic Experts Group and CCITT's Experts Group on Telephony (creators of the JPEG image compression standard and the H.261 standard for video conferencing respectively), the Moving Picture Experts Group (MPEG) working group was established in January 1988. MPEG was formed to address the need for standard video and audio formats, and to build on H.261 to get better quality through the use of more complex encoding methods.

Development of the MPEG-1 standard began in May 1988. Fourteen video and fourteen audio codec proposals were submitted by individual companies and institutions for evaluation. The codecs were extensively tested for computational complexity and subjective (human perceived) quality, at data rates of 1.5 Mbit/s. This specific bitrate was chosen for transmission over T-1/E-1 lines and as the approximate data rate of audio CDs. The codecs that excelled in this testing were utilized as the basis for the standard and refined further, with additional features and other improvements being incorporated in the process.

After 20 meetings of the full group in various cities around the world, and 4½ years of development and testing, the final standard (for parts 1–3) was approved in early November 1992 and published a few months later. The reported completion date of the MPEG-1 standard varies greatly: a largely complete draft standard was produced in September 1990, and from that point on, only minor changes were introduced. The draft standard was publicly available for purchase. The standard was finished with the 6 November 1992 meeting. The Berkeley Plateau Multimedia Research Group developed an MPEG-1 decoder in November 1992. In July 1990, before the first draft of the MPEG-1 standard had even been written, work began on a second standard, MPEG-2, intended to extend MPEG-1 technology to provide full broadcast-quality video (as per CCIR 601) at high bitrates (3–15 Mbit/s) and support for interlaced video. Due in part to the similarity between the two codecs, the MPEG-2 standard includes full backwards compatibility with MPEG-1 video, so any MPEG-2 decoder can play MPEG-1 videos.

Notably, the MPEG-1 standard very strictly defines the bitstream, and decoder function, but does not define how MPEG-1 encoding is to be performed, although a reference implementation is provided in ISO/IEC-11172-5. This means that MPEG-1 coding efficiency can drastically vary depending on the encoder used, and generally means that newer encoders perform significantly better than their predecessors. The first three parts (Systems, Video and Audio) of ISO/IEC 11172 were published in August 1993.

MPEG-1 Parts				
Part	Number	First public release date (First edition)	Latest correction	Title
Part 1	ISO/IEC 11172-1	1993	1999	Systems
Part 2	ISO/IEC 11172-2	1993	2006	Video
Part 3	ISO/IEC 11172-3	1993	1996	Audio
Part 4	ISO/IEC 11172-4	1995	2007	Compliance testing
Part 5	ISO/IEC TR 11172-5	1998	2007	Software simulation

Patents

All widely known patent searches suggest that, due to its age, MPEG-1 video and Layer I/II audio is no longer covered by any patents and can thus be used without obtaining a licence or paying any fees. The ISO patent database lists one patent for ISO 11172, US 4,472,747, which expired in 2003. The near-complete draft of the MPEG-1 standard was publicly available as ISO CD 11172 by December 6, 1991. Neither the July 2008 Kuro5hin article "Patent Status of MPEG-1, H.261 and MPEG-2", nor an August 2008 thread on the gstreamer-devel mailing list were able to list a single unexpired MPEG-1 video and Layer I/II audio patent. A May 2009 discussion on the whatwg mailing list mentioned US 5,214,678 patent as possibly covering MPEG audio layer II. Filed in 1990 and published in 1993, this patent is now expired.

A full MPEG-1 decoder and encoder, with "Layer 3 audio", cannot be implemented royalty free since there are companies that require patent fees for implementations of MPEG-1.

Applications

- Most popular software for video playback includes MPEG-1 decoding, in addition to any other supported formats.

- The popularity of MP3 audio has established a massive installed base of hardware that can play back MPEG-1 Audio (all three layers).

- "Virtually all digital audio devices" can play back MPEG-1 Audio. Many millions have been sold to-date.

- Before MPEG-2 became widespread, many digital satellite/cable TV services used MPEG-1 exclusively.

- The widespread popularity of MPEG-2 with broadcasters means MPEG-1 is playable by most digital cable and satellite set-top boxes, and digital disc and tape players, due to backwards compatibility.

- MPEG-1 was used for full-screen video on Green Book CD-i, and on Video CD (VCD).

- The Super Video CD standard, based on VCD, uses MPEG-1 audio exclusively, as well as MPEG-2 video.

- The DVD-Video format uses MPEG-2 video primarily, but MPEG-1 support is explicitly defined in the standard.

- The DVD-Video standard originally required MPEG-1 Layer II audio for PAL countries, but was changed to allow AC-3/Dolby Digital-only discs. MPEG-1 Layer II audio is still allowed on DVDs, although newer extensions to the format, like MPEG Multichannel, are rarely supported.

- Most DVD players also support Video CD and MP3 CD playback, which use MPEG-1.

- The international Digital Video Broadcasting (DVB) standard primarily uses MPEG-1 Layer II audio, and MPEG-2 video.

- The international Digital Audio Broadcasting (DAB) standard uses MPEG-1 Layer II audio exclusively, due to MP2's especially high quality, modest decoder performance requirements, and tolerance of errors.

Part 1: Systems

Part 1 of the MPEG-1 standard covers *systems*, and is defined in ISO/IEC-11172-1.

MPEG-1 Systems specifies the logical layout and methods used to store the encoded audio, video, and other data into a standard bitstream, and to maintain synchronization between the different contents. This file format is specifically designed for storage on media, and transmission over data channels, that are considered relatively reliable. Only limited error protection is defined by the standard, and small errors in the bitstream may cause noticeable defects.

This structure was later named an MPEG program stream: "The MPEG-1 Systems design is essentially identical to the MPEG-2 Program Stream structure." This terminology is more popular, precise (differentiates it from an MPEG transport stream) and will be used here.

Elementary Streams

Elementary Streams (ES) are the raw bitstreams of MPEG-1 audio and video encoded data (output from an encoder). These files can be distributed on their own, such as is the case with MP3 files.

Packetized Elementary Streams (*PES*) are elementary streams packetized into packets of variable lengths, i.e., divided ES into independent chunks where cyclic redundancy check (CRC) checksum was added to each packet for error detection.

System Clock Reference (SCR) is a timing value stored in a 33-bit header of each PES, at a frequency/precision of 90 kHz, with an extra 9-bit extension that stores additional timing data with a precision of 27 MHz. These are inserted by the encoder, derived from the system time clock (STC). Simultaneously encoded audio and video streams will not have identical SCR values, however, due to buffering, encoding, jitter, and other delay.

Program Streams

Program Streams (PS) are concerned with combining multiple packetized elementary streams (usually just one audio and video PES) into a single stream, ensuring simultaneous delivery, and maintaining synchronization. The PS structure is known as a multiplex, or a container format.

Presentation time stamps (PTS) exist in PS to correct the inevitable disparity between audio and video SCR values (time-base correction). 90 kHz PTS values in the PS header tell the decoder which video SCR values match which audio SCR values. PTS determines when to display a portion of an MPEG program, and is also used by the decoder to determine when data can be discarded from the buffer. Either video or audio will be delayed by the decoder until the corresponding segment of the other arrives and can be decoded.

PTS handling can be problematic. Decoders must accept multiple *program streams* that have been concatenated (joined sequentially). This causes PTS values in the middle of the video to reset to zero, which then begin incrementing again. Such PTS wraparound disparities can cause timing issues that must be specially handled by the decoder.

Decoding Time Stamps (DTS), additionally, are required because of B-frames. With B-frames in the video stream, adjacent frames have to be encoded and decoded out-of-order (re-ordered frames). DTS is quite similar to PTS, but instead of just handling sequential frames, it contains the proper time-stamps to tell the decoder when to decode and display the next B-frame (types of frames explained below), ahead of its anchor (P- or I-) frame. Without B-frames in the video, PTS and DTS values are identical.

Multiplexing

To generate the PS, the multiplexer will interleave the (two or more) packetized elementary streams. This is done so the packets of the simultaneous streams can be transferred over the same channel and are guaranteed to both arrive at the decoder at precisely the same time. This is a case of time-division multiplexing.

Determining how much data from each stream should be in each interleaved segment (the size of the interleave) is complicated, yet an important requirement. Improper interleaving will result in buffer underflows or overflows, as the receiver gets more of one stream than it can store (e.g. audio), before it gets enough data to decode the other simultaneous stream (e.g. video). The MPEG Video Buffering Verifier (VBV) assists in determining if a multiplexed PS can be decoded by a device with a specified data throughput rate and buffer size. This offers feedback to the muxer and the encoder, so that they can change the mux size or adjust bitrates as needed for compliance.

Part 2: Video

Part 2 of the MPEG-1 standard covers video and is defined in ISO/IEC-11172-2. The design was heavily influenced by H.261.

MPEG-1 Video exploits perceptual compression methods to significantly reduce the data rate required by a video stream. It reduces or completely discards information in certain frequencies and areas of the picture that the human eye has limited ability to fully perceive. It also exploits temporal (over time) and spatial (across a picture) redundancy common in video to achieve better data compression than would be possible otherwise.

Color Space

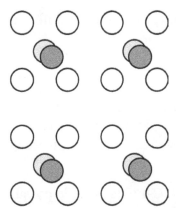

Example of 4:2:0 subsampling. The two overlapping center circles represent chroma blue and chroma red (color) pixels, while the 4 outside circles represent the luma (brightness).

Before encoding video to MPEG-1, the color-space is transformed to Y'CbCr (Y'=Luma, Cb=Chroma Blue, Cr=Chroma Red). Luma (brightness, resolution) is stored separately from chroma (color, hue, phase) and even further separated into red and blue components. The chroma is also subsampled to 4:2:0, meaning it is reduced by one half vertically and one half horizontally, to just one quarter the resolution of the video. This software algorithm also has analogies in hardware, such as the output from a Bayer pattern filter, common in digital colour cameras.

Because the human eye is much more sensitive to small changes in brightness (the Y component) than in color (the Cr and Cb components), chroma subsampling is a very effective way to reduce the amount of video data that needs to be compressed. On videos with fine detail (high spatial complexity) this can manifest as chroma aliasing artifacts. Compared to other digital compression artifacts, this issue seems to be very rarely a source of annoyance.

Because of subsampling, Y'CbCr video must always be stored using even dimensions (divisible by 2), otherwise chroma mismatch ("ghosts") will occur, and it will appear as if the color is ahead of, or behind the rest of the video, much like a shadow.

Y'CbCr is often inaccurately called YUV which is only used in the domain of analog video signals. Similarly, the terms luminance and chrominance are often used instead of the (more accurate) terms luma and chroma.

Resolution/Bitrate

MPEG-1 supports resolutions up to 4095×4095 (12-bits), and bitrates up to 100 Mbit/s.

MPEG-1 videos are most commonly seen using Source Input Format (SIF) resolution: 352x240, 352x288, or 320x240. These low resolutions, combined with a bitrate less than 1.5 Mbit/s, make up what is known as a constrained parameters bitstream (CPB), later renamed the "Low Level" (LL) profile in MPEG-2. This is the minimum video specifications any decoder should be able to handle, to be considered MPEG-1 compliant. This was selected to provide a good balance between quality and performance, allowing the use of reasonably inexpensive hardware of the time.

Frame/Picture/Block Types

MPEG-1 has several frame/picture types that serve different purposes. The most important, yet simplest, is I-frame.

I-frames

I-frame is an abbreviation for Intra-frame, so-called because they can be decoded independently of any other frames. They may also be known as I-pictures, or keyframes due to their somewhat similar function to the key frames used in animation. I-frames can be considered effectively identical to baseline JPEG images.

High-speed seeking through an MPEG-1 video is only possible to the nearest I-frame. When cutting a video it is not possible to start playback of a segment of video before the first I-frame in the segment (at least not without computationally intensive re-encoding). For this reason, I-frame-only MPEG videos are used in editing applications.

I-frame only compression is very fast, but produces very large file sizes: a factor of 3× (or more) larger than normally encoded MPEG-1 video, depending on how temporally complex a specific video is. I-frame only MPEG-1 video is very similar to MJPEG video. So much so that very high-speed and theoretically lossless (in reality, there are rounding errors) conversion can be made from one format to the other, provided a couple of restrictions (color space and quantization matrix) are followed in the creation of the bitstream.

The length between I-frames is known as the group of pictures (GOP) size. MPEG-1 most commonly uses a GOP size of 15-18. i.e. 1 I-frame for every 14-17 non-I-frames (some combination of P- and B- frames). With more intelligent encoders, GOP size is dynamically chosen, up to some pre-selected maximum limit.

Limits are placed on the maximum number of frames between I-frames due to decoding complexing, decoder buffer size, recovery time after data errors, seeking ability, and accumulation of IDCT errors in low-precision implementations most common in hardware decoders.

P-frames

P-frame is an abbreviation for Predicted-frame. They may also be called forward-predicted frames, or inter-frames (B-frames are also inter-frames).

P-frames exist to improve compression by exploiting the temporal (over time) redundancy in a video. P-frames store only the *difference* in image from the frame (either an I-frame or P-frame) immediately preceding it (this reference frame is also called the *anchor frame*).

The difference between a P-frame and its anchor frame is calculated using *motion vectors* on each *macroblock* of the frame. Such motion vector data will be embedded in the P-frame for use by the decoder.

A P-frame can contain any number of intra-coded blocks, in addition to any forward-predicted blocks.

If a video drastically changes from one frame to the next (such as a cut), it is more efficient to encode it as an I-frame.

B-frames

B-frame stands for bidirectional-frame. They may also be known as backwards-predicted frames or B-pictures. B-frames are quite similar to P-frames, except they can make predictions using both the previous and future frames (i.e. two anchor frames).

It is therefore necessary for the player to first decode the next I- or P- anchor frame sequentially after the B-frame, before the B-frame can be decoded and displayed. This means decoding B-frames requires larger data buffers and causes an increased delay on both decoding and during encoding. This also necessitates the decoding time stamps (DTS) feature in the container/system stream. As such, B-frames have long been subject of much controversy, they are often avoided in videos, and are sometimes not fully supported by hardware decoders.

No other frames are predicted from a B-frame. Because of this, a very low bitrate B-frame can be inserted, where needed, to help control the bitrate. If this was done with a P-frame, future P-frames would be predicted from it and would lower the quality of the entire sequence. However, similarly, the future P-frame must still encode all the changes between it and the previous I- or P- anchor frame. B-frames can also be beneficial in videos where the background behind an object is being revealed over several frames, or in fading transitions, such as scene changes.

A B-frame can contain any number of intra-coded blocks and forward-predicted blocks, in addition to backwards-predicted, or bidirectionally predicted blocks.

D-frames

MPEG-1 has a unique frame type not found in later video standards. D-frames or DC-pictures are independent images (intra-frames) that have been encoded using DC transform coefficients only (AC coefficients are removed when encoding D-frames) and hence are very low quality. D-frames are never referenced by I-, P- or B- frames. D-frames are only used for fast previews of video, for instance when seeking through a video at high speed.

Given moderately higher-performance decoding equipment, fast preview can be accomplished by decoding I-frames instead of D-frames. This provides higher quality previews, since I-frames contain AC coefficients as well as DC coefficients. If the encoder can assume that rapid I-frame decoding capability is available in decoders, it can save bits by not sending D-frames (thus improving compression of the video content). For this reason, D-frames are seldom actually used in MPEG-1 video encoding, and the D-frame feature has not been included in any later video coding standards.

Macroblocks

MPEG-1 operates on video in a series of 8x8 blocks for quantization. However, because chroma (color) is subsampled by a factor of 4, each pair of (red and blue) chroma blocks corresponds to 4 different luma blocks. This set of 6 blocks, with a resolution of 16x16, is called a macroblock.

A macroblock is the smallest independent unit of (color) video. Motion vectors operate solely at the macroblock level.

If the height or width of the video are not exact multiples of 16, full rows and full columns of macroblocks must still be encoded and decoded to fill out the picture (though the extra decoded pixels are not displayed).

Motion Vectors

To decrease the amount of temporal redundancy in a video, only blocks that change are updated, (up to the maximum GOP size). This is known as conditional replenishment. However, this is not very effective by itself. Movement of the objects, and/or the camera may result in large portions of the frame needing to be updated, even though only the position of the previously encoded objects has changed. Through motion estimation the encoder can compensate for this movement and remove a large amount of redundant information.

The encoder compares the current frame with adjacent parts of the video from the anchor frame (previous I- or P- frame) in a diamond pattern, up to a (encoder-specific) predefined radius limit from the area of the current macroblock. If a match is found, only the direction and distance (i.e. the *vector* of the *motion*) from the previous video area to the current macroblock need to be encoded into the inter-frame (P- or B- frame). The reverse of this process, performed by the decoder to reconstruct the picture, is called motion compensation.

A predicted macroblock rarely matches the current picture perfectly, however. The differences between the estimated matching area, and the real frame/macroblock is called the prediction error. The larger the error, the more data must be additionally encoded in the frame. For efficient video compression, it is very important that the encoder is capable of effectively and precisely performing motion estimation.

Motion vectors record the *distance* between two areas on screen based on the number of pixels (called pels). MPEG-1 video uses a motion vector (MV) precision of one half of one pixel, or half-pel. The finer the precision of the MVs, the more accurate the match is likely to be, and the more efficient the compression. There are trade-offs to higher precision, however. Finer MVs result in larger data size, as larger numbers must be stored in the frame for every single MV, increased coding complexity as increasing levels of interpolation on the macroblock are required for both the encoder and decoder, and diminishing returns (minimal gains) with higher precision MVs. Half-pel was chosen as the ideal trade-off.

Because neighboring macroblocks are likely to have very similar motion vectors, this redundant information can be compressed quite effectively by being stored DPCM-encoded. Only the (smaller) amount of difference between the MVs for each macroblock needs to be stored in the final bitstream.

P-frames have one motion vector per macroblock, relative to the previous anchor frame. B-frames, however, can use two motion vectors; one from the previous anchor frame, and one from the future anchor frame.

Partial macroblocks, and black borders/bars encoded into the video that do not fall exactly on a macroblock boundary, cause havoc with motion prediction. The block padding/border information prevents the macroblock from closely matching with any other area of the video, and so, significantly larger prediction error information must be encoded for every one of the several dozen partial macroblocks along the screen border. DCT encoding and quantization also isn't nearly as effective when there is large/sharp picture contrast in a block.

An even more serious problem exists with macroblocks that contain significant, random, *edge noise*, where the picture transitions to (typically) black. All the above problems also apply to edge noise. In addition, the added randomness is simply impossible to compress significantly. All of these effects will lower the quality (or increase the bitrate) of the video substantially.

DCT

Each 8x8 block is encoded by first applying a *forward* discrete cosine transform (FDCT) and then a quantization process. The FDCT process (by itself) is theoretically lossless, and can be reversed by applying an *Inverse* DCT (IDCT) to reproduce the original values (in the absence of any quantization and rounding errors). In reality, there are some (sometimes large) rounding errors introduced both by quantization in the encoder and by IDCT approximation error in the decoder. The minimum allowed accuracy of a decoder IDCT approximation is defined by ISO/IEC 23002-1. (Prior to 2006, it was specified by IEEE 1180-1990.)

The FDCT process converts the 8x8 block of uncompressed pixel values (brightness or color difference values) into an 8x8 indexed array of *frequency coefficient* values. One of these is the (statistically high in variance) DC coefficient, which represents the average value of the entire 8x8 block. The other 63 coefficients are the statistically smaller AC coefficients, which are positive or negative values each representing sinusoidal deviations from the flat block value represented by the *DC coefficient*.

An example of an encoded 8x8 FDCT block:

$$
\begin{bmatrix}
-415 & -30 & -61 & 27 & 56 & -20 & -2 & 0 \\
4 & -22 & -61 & 10 & 13 & -7 & -9 & 5 \\
-47 & 7 & 77 & -25 & -29 & 10 & 5 & -6 \\
-49 & 12 & 34 & -15 & -10 & 6 & 2 & 2 \\
12 & -7 & -13 & -4 & -2 & 2 & -3 & 3 \\
-8 & 3 & 2 & -6 & -2 & 1 & 4 & 2 \\
-1 & 0 & 0 & -2 & -1 & -3 & 4 & -1 \\
0 & 0 & -1 & -4 & -1 & 0 & 1 & 2
\end{bmatrix}
$$

Since the DC coefficient value is statistically correlated from one block to the next, it is compressed using DPCM encoding. Only the (smaller) amount of difference between each DC value and the value of the DC coefficient in the block to its left needs to be represented in the final bitstream.

Additionally, the frequency conversion performed by applying the DCT provides a statistical decorrelation function to efficiently concentrate the signal into fewer high-amplitude values prior to applying quantization.

Quantization

Quantization (of digital data) is, essentially, the process of reducing the accuracy of a signal, by dividing it into some larger step size (i.e. finding the nearest multiple, and discarding the remainder/modulus).

The frame-level quantizer is a number from 0 to 31 (although encoders will usually omit/disable some of the extreme values) which determines how much information will be removed from a given frame. The frame-level quantizer is either dynamically selected by the encoder to maintain a certain user-specified bitrate, or (much less commonly) directly specified by the user.

Contrary to popular belief, a fixed frame-level quantizer (set by the user) does not deliver a constant level of quality. Instead, it is an arbitrary metric that will provide a somewhat varying level of quality, depending on the contents of each frame. Given two files of identical sizes, the one encoded at an average bitrate should look better than the one encoded with a fixed quantizer (variable bitrate). Constant quantizer encoding can be used, however, to accurately determine the minimum and maximum bitrates possible for encoding a given video.

A quantization matrix is a string of 64-numbers (0-255) which tells the encoder how relatively important or unimportant each piece of visual information is. Each number in the matrix corresponds to a certain frequency component of the video image.

An example quantization matrix:

$$
\begin{bmatrix}
16 & 11 & 10 & 16 & 24 & 40 & 51 & 61 \\
12 & 12 & 14 & 19 & 26 & 58 & 60 & 55 \\
14 & 13 & 16 & 24 & 40 & 57 & 69 & 56 \\
14 & 17 & 22 & 29 & 51 & 87 & 80 & 62 \\
18 & 22 & 37 & 56 & 68 & 109 & 103 & 77 \\
24 & 35 & 55 & 64 & 81 & 104 & 113 & 92 \\
49 & 64 & 78 & 87 & 103 & 121 & 120 & 101 \\
72 & 92 & 95 & 98 & 112 & 100 & 103 & 99
\end{bmatrix}
$$

Quantization is performed by taking each of the 64 *frequency* values of the DCT block, dividing them by the frame-level quantizer, then dividing them by their corresponding values in the quantization matrix. Finally, the result is rounded down. This significantly reduces, or completely eliminates, the information in some frequency components of the picture. Typically, high frequency information is less visually important, and so high frequencies are much more *strongly quantized* (drastically reduced). MPEG-1 actually uses two separate quantization matrices, one for intra-blocks (I-blocks) and one for inter-block (P- and B- blocks) so quantization of different block types can be done independently, and so, more effectively.

This quantization process usually reduces a significant number of the *AC coefficients* to zero, (known as sparse data) which can then be more efficiently compressed by entropy coding (lossless compression) in the next step.

An example quantized DCT block:

$$\begin{bmatrix} -26 & -3 & -6 & 2 & 2 & -1 & 0 & 0 \\ 0 & -2 & -4 & 1 & 1 & 0 & 0 & 0 \\ -3 & 1 & 5 & -1 & -1 & 0 & 0 & 0 \\ -4 & 1 & 2 & -1 & 0 & 0 & 0 & 0 \\ 1 & 0 & 0 & 0 & 0 & 0 & 0 & 0 \\ 0 & 0 & 0 & 0 & 0 & 0 & 0 & 0 \\ 0 & 0 & 0 & 0 & 0 & 0 & 0 & 0 \\ 0 & 0 & 0 & 0 & 0 & 0 & 0 & 0 \end{bmatrix}$$

Quantization eliminates a large amount of data, and is the main lossy processing step in MPEG-1 video encoding. This is also the primary source of most MPEG-1 video compression artifacts, like blockiness, color banding, noise, ringing, discoloration, et al. This happens when video is encoded with an insufficient bitrate, and the encoder is therefore forced to use high frame-level quantizers (*strong quantization*) through much of the video.

Entropy Coding

Several steps in the encoding of MPEG-1 video are lossless, meaning they will be reversed upon decoding, to produce exactly the same (original) values. Since these lossless data compression steps don't add noise into, or otherwise change the contents (unlike quantization), it is sometimes referred to as noiseless coding. Since lossless compression aims to remove as much redundancy as possible, it is known as entropy coding in the field of information theory.

The coefficients of quantized DCT blocks tend to zero towards the bottom-right. Maximum compression can be achieved by a zig-zag scanning of the DCT block starting from the top left and using Run-length encoding techniques.

The DC coefficients and motion vectors are DPCM-encoded.

Run-length encoding (RLE) is a very simple method of compressing repetition. A sequential string of characters, no matter how long, can be replaced with a few bytes, noting the value that repeats, and how many times. For example, if someone were to say "five nines", you would know they mean the number: 99999.

RLE is particularly effective after quantization, as a significant number of the AC coefficients are now zero (called sparse data), and can be represented with just a couple of bytes. This is stored in a special 2-dimensional Huffman table that codes the run-length and the run-ending character.

Huffman Coding is a very popular method of entropy coding, and used in MPEG-1 video to reduce the data size. The data is analyzed to find strings that repeat often. Those strings are then put into a special table, with the most frequently repeating data assigned the shortest code. This keeps the data as small as possible with this form of compression. Once the table is constructed, those strings in the data are replaced with their (much smaller) codes, which reference the appropriate entry in the table. The decoder simply reverses this process to produce the original data.

This is the final step in the video encoding process, so the result of Huffman coding is known as the MPEG-1 video "bitstream."

GOP Configurations for Specific Applications

I-frames store complete frame info within the frame and are therefore suited for random access. P-frames provide compression using motion vectors relative to the previous frame (I or P). B-frames provide maximum compression but require the previous as well as next frame for computation. Therefore, processing of B-frames requires more buffer on the decoded side. A configuration of the Group of Pictures (GOP) should be selected based on these factors. I-frame only sequences give least compression, but are useful for random access, FF/FR and editability. I- and P-frame sequences give moderate compression but add a certain degree of random access, FF/FR functionality. I-, P- and B-frame sequences give very high compression but also increase the coding/decoding delay significantly. Such configurations are therefore not suited for video-telephony or video-conferencing applications.

The typical data rate of an I-frame is 1 bit per pixel while that of a P-frame is 0.1 bit per pixel and for a B-frame, 0.015 bit per pixel.

Part 3: Audio

Part 3 of the MPEG-1 standard covers audio and is defined in ISO/IEC-11172-3.

MPEG-1 Audio utilizes psychoacoustics to significantly reduce the data rate required by an audio stream. It reduces or completely discards certain parts of the audio that it deduces that the human ear can't *hear*, either because they are in frequencies where the ear has limited sensitivity, or are *masked* by other (typically louder) sounds.

Channel Encoding:

- Mono

- Joint Stereo – intensity encoded

- Joint Stereo – M/S encoded for Layer 3 only

- Stereo

- Dual (two uncorrelated mono channels)

- Sampling rates: 32000, 44100, and 48000 Hz

- Bitrates for Layer I: 32, 64, 96, 128, 160, 192, 224, 256, 288, 320, 352, 384, 416 and 448 kbit/s

- Bitrates for Layer II: 32, 48, 56, 64, 80, 96, 112, 128, 160, 192, 224, 256, 320 and 384 kbit/s

- Bitrates for Layer III: 32, 40, 48, 56, 64, 80, 96, 112, 128, 160, 192, 224, 256 and 320 kbit/s

MPEG-1 Audio is divided into 3 layers. Each higher layer is more computationally complex, and generally more efficient at lower bitrates than the previous. The layers are semi backwards compatible as higher layers reuse technologies implemented by the lower layers. A "Full" Layer II decoder can also play Layer I audio, but not Layer III audio, although not all higher level players are "full".

Layer I

MPEG-1 Layer I is nothing more than a simplified version of Layer II. Layer I uses a smaller 384-sample frame size for very low delay, and finer resolution. This is advantageous for applications like teleconferencing, studio editing, etc. It has lower complexity than Layer II to facilitate real-time encoding on the hardware available circa 1990.

Layer I saw limited adoption in its time, and most notably was used on Philips' defunct Digital Compact Cassette at a bitrate of 384 kbit/s. With the substantial performance improvements in digital processing since its introduction, Layer I quickly became unnecessary and obsolete.

Layer I audio files typically use the extension .mp1 or sometimes .m1a

Layer II

MPEG-1 Layer II (MP2—often incorrectly called MUSICAM) is a lossy audio format designed to provide high quality at about 192 kbit/s for stereo sound. Decoding MP2 audio is computationally simple, relative to MP3, AAC, etc.

History/MUSICAM

MPEG-1 Layer II was derived from the MUSICAM (*Masking pattern adapted Universal Subband Integrated Coding And Multiplexing*) audio codec, developed by Centre commun d'études de télévision et télécommunications (CCETT), Philips, and Institut für Rundfunktechnik (IRT/CNET) as part of the EUREKA 147 pan-European inter-governmental research and development initiative for the development of digital audio broadcasting.

Most key features of MPEG-1 Audio were directly inherited from MUSICAM, including the filter bank, time-domain processing, audio frame sizes, etc. However, improvements were made, and the actual MUSICAM algorithm was not used in the final MPEG-1 Layer II audio standard. The widespread usage of the term MUSICAM to refer to Layer II is entirely incorrect and discouraged for both technical and legal reasons.

Technical Details

Layer II/MP2 is a time-domain encoder. It uses a low-delay 32 sub-band polyphased filter bank for time-frequency mapping; having overlapping ranges (i.e. polyphased) to prevent aliasing. The psychoacoustic model is based on the principles of auditory masking, simultaneous masking effects, and the absolute threshold of hearing (ATH). The size of a Layer II frame is fixed at 1152-samples (coefficients).

Time domain refers to how analysis and quantization is performed on short, discrete samples/

chunks of the audio waveform. This offers low delay as only a small number of samples are analyzed before encoding, as opposed to frequency domain encoding (like MP3) which must analyze many times more samples before it can decide how to transform and output encoded audio. This also offers higher performance on complex, random and transient impulses (such as percussive instruments, and applause), offering avoidance of artifacts like pre-echo.

The 32 sub-band filter bank returns 32 amplitude coefficients, one for each equal-sized frequency band/segment of the audio, which is about 700 Hz wide (depending on the audio's sampling frequency). The encoder then utilizes the psychoacoustic model to determine which sub-bands contain audio information that is less important, and so, where quantization will be inaudible, or at least much less noticeable.

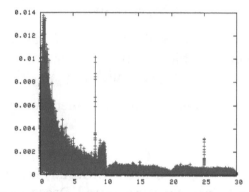

Example FFT analysis on an audio wave sample.

The psychoacoustic model is applied using a 1024-point Fast Fourier Transform (FFT). Of the 1152 samples per frame, 64 samples at the top and bottom of the frequency range are ignored for this analysis. They are presumably not significant enough to change the result. The psychoacoustic model uses an empirically determined masking model to determine which sub-bands contribute more to the masking threshold, and how much quantization noise each can contain without being perceived. Any sounds below the absolute threshold of hearing (ATH) are completely discarded. The available bits are then assigned to each sub-band accordingly.

Typically, sub-bands are less important if they contain quieter sounds (smaller coefficient) than a neighboring (i.e. similar frequency) sub-band with louder sounds (larger coefficient). Also, "noise" components typically have a more significant masking effect than "tonal" components.

Less significant sub-bands are reduced in accuracy by quantization. This basically involves compressing the frequency range (amplitude of the coefficient), i.e. raising the noise floor. Then computing an amplification factor, for the decoder to use to re-expand each sub-band to the proper frequency range.

Layer II can also optionally use intensity stereo coding, a form of joint stereo. This means that the frequencies above 6 kHz of both channels are combined/down-mixed into one single (mono) channel, but the "side channel" information on the relative intensity (volume, amplitude) of each channel is preserved and encoded into the bitstream separately. On playback, the single channel is played through left and right speakers, with the intensity information applied to each channel to give the illusion of stereo sound. This perceptual trick is known as stereo irrelevancy. This can allow further reduction of the audio bitrate without much perceivable loss of fidelity, but is generally not used with higher bitrates as it does not provide very high quality (transparent) audio.

Quality

Subjective audio testing by experts, in the most critical conditions ever implemented, has shown MP2 to offer transparent audio compression at 256 kbit/s for 16-bit 44.1 kHz CD audio using the earliest reference implementation (more recent encoders should presumably perform even better). That (approximately) 1:6 compression ratio for CD audio is particularly impressive because it is quite close to the estimated upper limit of perceptual entropy, at just over 1:8. Achieving much higher compression is simply not possible without discarding some perceptible information.

MP2 remains a favoured lossy audio coding standard due to its particularly high audio coding performances on important audio material such as castanet, symphonic orchestra, male and female voices and particularly complex and high energy transients (impulses) like percussive sounds: triangle, glockenspiel and audience applause. More recent testing has shown that MPEG Multichannel (based on MP2), despite being compromised by an inferior matrixed mode (for the sake of backwards compatibility) rates just slightly lower than much more recent audio codecs, such as Dolby Digital (AC-3) and Advanced Audio Coding (AAC) (mostly within the margin of error—and substantially superior in some cases, such as audience applause). This is one reason that MP2 audio continues to be used extensively. The MPEG-2 AAC Stereo verification tests reached a vastly different conclusion, however, showing AAC to provide superior performance to MP2 at half the bitrate. The reason for this disparity with both earlier and later tests is not clear, but strangely, a sample of applause is notably absent from the latter test.

Layer II audio files typically use the extension .mp2 or sometimes .m2a

Layer III/MP3

MPEG-1 Layer III (MP3) is a lossy audio format designed to provide acceptable quality at about 64 kbit/s for monaural audio over single-channel (BRI) ISDN links, and 128 kbit/s for stereo sound.

History/ASPEC

ASPEC 91 in the Deutsches Museum Bonn, with encoder (below) and decoder

Layer III/MP3 was derived from the *Adaptive Spectral Perceptual Entropy Coding* (ASPEC) codec developed by Fraunhofer as part of the EUREKA 147 pan-European inter-governmental research and development initiative for the development of digital audio broadcasting. ASPEC was adapted to fit in with the Layer II/MUSICAM model (frame size, filter bank, FFT, etc.), to become Layer III.

ASPEC was itself based on *Multiple adaptive Spectral audio Coding* (MSC) by E. F. Schroeder, *Optimum Coding in the Frequency domain* (OCF) the doctoral thesis by Karlheinz Brandenburg at the University of Erlangen-Nuremberg, *Perceptual Transform Coding* (PXFM) by J. D. Johnston at AT&T Bell Labs, and *Transform coding of audio signals* by Y. Mahieux and J. Petit at Institut für Rundfunktechnik (IRT/CNET).

Technical Details

MP3 is a frequency-domain audio transform encoder. Even though it utilizes some of the lower layer functions, MP3 is quite different from Layer II/MP2.

MP3 works on 1152 samples like Layer II, but needs to take multiple frames for analysis before frequency-domain (MDCT) processing and quantization can be effective. It outputs a variable number of samples, using a bit buffer to enable this variable bitrate (VBR) encoding while maintaining 1152 sample size output frames. This causes a significantly longer delay before output, which has caused MP3 to be considered unsuitable for studio applications where editing or other processing needs to take place.

MP3 does not benefit from the 32 sub-band polyphased filter bank, instead just using an 18-point MDCT transformation on each output to split the data into 576 frequency components, and processing it in the frequency domain. This extra granularity allows MP3 to have a much finer psycho-acoustic model, and more carefully apply appropriate quantization to each band, providing much better low-bitrate performance.

Frequency-domain processing imposes some limitations as well, causing a factor of 12 or 36 × worse temporal resolution than Layer II. This causes quantization artifacts, due to transient sounds like percussive events and other high-frequency events that spread over a larger window. This results in audible smearing and pre-echo. MP3 uses pre-echo detection routines, and VBR encoding, which allows it to temporarily increase the bitrate during difficult passages, in an attempt to reduce this effect. It is also able to switch between the normal 36 sample quantization window, and instead using 3× short 12 sample windows instead, to reduce the temporal (time) length of quantization artifacts. And yet in choosing a fairly small window size to make MP3's temporal response adequate enough to avoid the most serious artifacts, MP3 becomes much less efficient in frequency domain compression of stationary, tonal components.

Being forced to use a *hybrid* time domain (filter bank) /frequency domain (MDCT) model to fit in with Layer II simply wastes processing time and compromises quality by introducing aliasing artifacts. MP3 has an aliasing cancellation stage specifically to mask this problem, but which instead produces frequency domain energy which must be encoded in the audio. This is pushed to the top of the frequency range, where most people have limited hearing, in hopes the distortion it causes will be less audible.

Layer II's 1024 point FFT doesn't entirely cover all samples, and would omit several entire MP3 sub-bands, where quantization factors must be determined. MP3 instead uses two passes of FFT analysis for spectral estimation, to calculate the global and individual masking thresholds. This allows it to cover all 1152 samples. Of the two, it utilizes the global masking threshold level from the more critical pass, with the most difficult audio.

In addition to Layer II's intensity encoded joint stereo, MP3 can use middle/side (mid/side, m/s, MS, matrixed) joint stereo. With mid/side stereo, certain frequency ranges of both channels are merged into a single (middle, mid, L+R) mono channel, while the sound difference between the left and right channels is stored as a separate (side, L-R) channel. Unlike intensity stereo, this process does not discard any audio information. When combined with quantization, however, it can exaggerate artifacts.

If the difference between the left and right channels is small, the side channel will be small, which will offer as much as a 50% bitrate savings, and associated quality improvement. If the difference between left and right is large, standard (discrete, left/right) stereo encoding may be preferred, as mid/side joint stereo will not provide any benefits. An MP3 encoder can switch between m/s stereo and full stereo on a frame-by-frame basis.

Unlike Layers I/II, MP3 uses variable-length Huffman coding (after perceptual) to further reduce the bitrate, without any further quality loss.

Quality

These technical limitations inherently prevent MP3 from providing critically transparent quality at any bitrate. This makes Layer II sound quality actually superior to MP3 audio, when it is used at a high enough bitrate to avoid noticeable artifacts. The term "transparent" often gets misused, however. The quality of MP3 (and other codecs) is sometimes called "transparent," even at impossibly low bitrates, when what is really meant is "good quality on average/non-critical material," or perhaps "exhibiting only non-annoying artifacts."

MP3's more fine-grained and selective quantization does prove notably superior to Layer II/MP2 at lower-bitrates, however. It is able to provide nearly equivalent audio quality to Layer II, at a 15% lower bitrate (approximately). 128 kbit/s is considered the "sweet spot" for MP3; meaning it provides generally acceptable quality stereo sound on most music, and there are diminishing quality improvements from increasing the bitrate further. MP3 is also regarded as exhibiting artifacts that are less annoying than Layer II, when both are used at bitrates that are too low to possibly provide faithful reproduction.

Layer III audio files use the extension .mp3.

MPEG-2 Audio Extensions

The MPEG-2 standard includes several extensions to MPEG-1 Audio. These are known as MPEG-2 BC – backwards compatible with MPEG-1 Audio. MPEG-2 Audio is defined in ISO/IEC 13818-3

- MPEG Multichannel – Backward compatible 5.1-channel surround sound.

- Sampling rates: 16000, 22050, and 24000 Hz

- Bitrates: 8, 16, 24, 32, 40, 48, 56, 64, 80, 96, 112, 128, 144 and 160 kbit/s

These sampling rates are exactly half that of those originally defined for MPEG-1 Audio. They were introduced to maintain higher quality sound when encoding audio at lower-bitrates. The even-lower bitrates were introduced because tests showed that MPEG-1 Audio could provide higher quality than any existing (circa 1994) very low bitrate (i.e. speech) audio codecs.

Part 4: Conformance Testing

Part 4 of the MPEG-1 standard covers conformance testing, and is defined in ISO/IEC-11172-4.

Conformance: Procedures for testing conformance.

Provides two sets of guidelines and reference bitstreams for testing the conformance of MPEG-1 audio and video decoders, as well as the bitstreams produced by an encoder.

Part 5: Reference Software

Part 5 of the MPEG-1 standard includes reference software, and is defined in ISO/IEC TR 11172-5.

Simulation: Reference software.

C reference code for encoding and decoding of audio and video, as well as multiplexing and de-multiplexing.

This includes the *ISO Dist10* audio encoder code, which LAME and TooLAME were originally based upon.

File Extension

.mpg is one of a number of file extensions for MPEG-1 or MPEG-2 audio and video compression. MPEG-1 Part 2 video is rare nowadays, and this extension typically refers to an MPEG program stream (defined in MPEG-1 and MPEG-2) or MPEG transport stream (defined in MPEG-2). Other suffixes such as .m2ts also exists specifying the precise container, in this case MPEG-2 TS, but this has little relevance to MPEG-1 media.

.mp3 is the most common extension for files containing MPEG-1 Layer 3 audio. An MP3 file is typically an uncontained stream of raw audio; the conventional way to tag MP3 files is by writing data to "garbage" segments of each frame, which preserve the media information but are discarded by the player. This is similar in many respects to how raw .AAC files are tagged (but this is less supported nowadays, e.g. iTunes).

Note that although it would apply, .mpg does not normally append raw AAC or AAC in MPEG-2 Part 7 Containers. The .aac extension normally denotes these audio files.

Basic Objectives of MPEG-1 Standard

The MPEG-1 standard was primarily targeted for multimedia CD-ROM applications at a bit rate of 1.5 Mbits/sec.

The standard is generic in the sense that it specifics a syntax for the representation of the encoded bitstream and a method of decoding. Unlike JPEG, MPEG-1 does not stipulate use of specific algorithms for bitstream generation and allows substantial flexibility. The syntax supports operations such as motion estimation; motion compensated prediction; Discrete Cosine transforms (DCT); quantization and variable length coding. The standard supports a number of parameters that can be specified in the bit-stream itself and a variety of picture sizes, aspect ratios etc. are permissible.

In addition, MPEG-1 standard supports the following application specified features:

- *Frame–based random access of video*: This is achieved by allowing independent access-points (I-frames) to the bit-stream.

- *Fast-forward and fast reverse (FF/FR) searches*: This refers to the scanning of the compressed bitstream to search for the desired portions of the video stream.

- *Reverse playback of video*

- *Edit ability of the compressed bit stream*

- *Reasonable coding / decoding delay* of about 1 sec. To give the impression of interactivity.

MPEG-2

MPEG-2 (a.k.a. H.222/H.262 as defined by the ITU) is a standard for "the generic coding of moving pictures and associated audio information". It describes a combination of lossy video compression and lossy audio data compression methods, which permit storage and transmission of movies using currently available storage media and transmission bandwidth. While MPEG-2 is not as efficient as newer standards such as H.264/AVC and H.265/HEVC, backwards compatibility with existing hardware and software means it is still widely used, for example in over-the-air digital television broadcasting and in the DVD-Video standard.

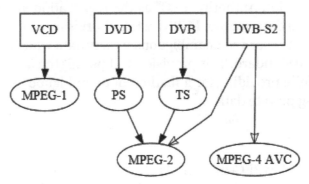

MPEG-2 is used in Digital Video Broadcast and DVDs. The MPEG transport stream, TS, and MPEG program stream, PS, are container formats.

Main Characteristics

MPEG-2 is widely used as the format of digital television signals that are broadcast by terrestrial (over-the-air), cable, and direct broadcast satellite TV systems. It also specifies the format of movies and other programs that are distributed on DVD and similar discs. TV stations, TV receivers, DVD players, and other equipment are often designed to this standard. MPEG-2 was the second of several standards developed by the Moving Pictures Expert Group (MPEG) and is an international standard (ISO/IEC 13818). Parts 1 and 2 of MPEG-2 were developed in a collaboration with ITU-T, and they have a respective catalog number in the ITU-T Recommendation Series.

While MPEG-2 is the core of most digital television and DVD formats, it does not completely specify them. Regional institutions can adapt it to their needs by restricting and augmenting aspects of the standard.

Systems

MPEG-2 includes a Systems section, part 1, that defines two distinct, but related, container formats. One is the *transport stream*, a data packet format designed to transmit one data packet in four ATM data packets for streaming digital video and audio over fixed or mobile transmission mediums, where the beginning and the end of the stream may not be identified, such as radio frequency, cable and linear recording mediums, examples of which include ATSC/DVB/ISDB/SBTVD broadcasting, and HDV recording on tape. The other is the *program stream*, an extended version of the MPEG-1 container format without the extra overhead of previously mentioned *transport stream* designed for random access storage mediums such as hard disk drives, optical discs and flash memory.

Program stream exceptions are M2TS, which is used on Blu-ray discs, AVCHD on re-writable DVDs and HDV on compact flash cards all use the unnecessary overhead of a *transport stream*. While VOB on DVDs and Enhanced VOB on the short lived HD DVD do not waste storage space and just use the *program stream*. M2TS also adds an incompatible private extension of four network ordered bytes to the end of every transport stream packet, which is used as a random access timing reference for faster read times over using the *Program Clock Reference* contained in the adaption section of the primary stream.

MPEG-2 Systems is formally known as ISO/IEC 13818-1 and as ITU-T Rec. H.222.0. ISO authorized the "SMPTE Registration Authority, LLC" as the registration authority for MPEG-2 format identifiers. The registration descriptor of MPEG-2 transport is provided by ISO/IEC 13818-1 in order to enable users of the standard to unambiguously carry data when its format is not necessarily a recognized international standard. This provision will permit the MPEG-2 transport standard to carry all types of data while providing for a method of unambiguous identification of the characteristics of the underlying private data.

Video

The Video section, part 2 of MPEG-2, is similar to the previous MPEG-1 standard, but also provides support for interlaced video, the format used by analog broadcast TV systems. MPEG-2 video is not optimized for low bit-rates, especially less than 1 Mbit/s at standard definition resolutions. All standards-compliant MPEG-2 Video decoders are fully capable of playing back MPEG-1 Video streams conforming to the Constrained Parameters Bitstream syntax. MPEG-2/Video is formally known as ISO/IEC 13818-2 and as ITU-T Rec. H.262.

With some enhancements, MPEG-2 Video and Systems are also used in some HDTV transmission systems, and is the standard format for over-the-air ATSC digital television.

Audio

MPEG-2 introduces new audio encoding methods compared to MPEG-1:

MPEG-2 Part 3

The MPEG-2 Audio section, defined in Part 3 (ISO/IEC 13818-3) of the standard, enhances MPEG-1's audio by allowing the coding of audio programs with more than two channels, up to 5.1 multichannel. This method is backwards-compatible (also known as MPEG-2 BC), allowing MPEG-1 audio decoders to decode the two main stereo components of the presentation. MPEG-2 part 3 also defined additional bit rates and sample rates for MPEG-1 Audio Layer I, II and III.

MPEG-2 BC (backward compatible with MPEG-1 audio formats)

- low bitrate encoding with halved sampling rate (MPEG-1 Layer 1/2/3 LSF - a.k.a. MPEG-2 LSF - "Low Sampling Frequencies")

- multichannel encoding with up to 5.1 channels, a.k.a. MPEG Multichannel

MPEG-2 Part 7

Part 7 (ISO/IEC 13818-7) of the MPEG-2 standard specifies a rather different, non-backwards-compatible audio format (also known as MPEG-2 NBC). Part 7 is referred to as MPEG-2 AAC. AAC is more efficient than the previous MPEG audio standards, and is in some ways less complicated than its predecessor, MPEG-1 Audio, Layer 3, in that it does not have the hybrid filter bank. It supports from 1 to 48 channels at sampling rates of 8 to 96 kHz, with multichannel, multilingual, and multiprogram capabilities. Advanced Audio is also defined in Part 3 of the MPEG-4 standard.

MPEG-2 NBC (Non-Backward Compatible)

- MPEG-2 AAC

- multichannel encoding with up to 48 channels

ISO/IEC 13818

MPEG-2 standards are published as parts of ISO/IEC 13818. Each part covers a certain aspect of the whole specification.

Part 1

> Systems – describes synchronization and multiplexing of video and audio. (It is also known as ITU-T Rec. H.222.0.) MPEG transport stream and MPEG program stream.

Part 2

> Video – video coding format for interlaced and non-interlaced video signals (Also known as ITU-T Rec. H.262).

Part 3

> Audio – audio coding format for perceptual coding of audio signals. A multichannel-enabled extension and extension of bit rates and sample rates for MPEG-1 Audio Layer I, II and III of MPEG-1 audio.

Part 4

Describes procedures for testing compliance.

Part 5

Describes systems for Software simulation.

Part 6

Describes extensions for DSM-CC (Digital Storage Media Command and Control).

Part 7

Advanced Audio Coding (AAC).

Part 8

10-bit video extension. Primary application was studio video, allowing artifact-free processing without giving up compression. Part 8 has been withdrawn due to lack of interest by industry.

Part 9

Extension for real time interfaces.

Part 10

Conformance extensions for DSM-CC.

Part 11

Intellectual property management (IPMP)

MPEG-2 Parts							
Part	Number	First public release date (First edition)	Latest public release date (edition)	Latest amendment	Identical ITU-T Rec.	Title	Description
Part 1	ISO/IEC 13818-1	1996	2013	2014	H.222.0	Systems	
Part 2	ISO/IEC 13818-2	1996	2013		H.262	Video	
Part 3	ISO/IEC 13818-3	1995	1998			Audio	MPEG-2 BC - backwards compatible with MPEG-1 Audio
Part 4	ISO/IEC 13818-4	1998	2004	2009		Conformance testing	
Part 5	ISO/IEC TR 13818-5	1997	2005			Software simulation	

MPEG-2 Parts							
Part	Number	First public release date (First edition)	Latest public release date (edition)	Latest amendment	Identical ITU-T Rec.	Title	Description
Part 6	ISO/IEC 13818-6	1998	1998	2001		Extensions for DSM-CC	extensions for Digital Storage Media Command and Control
Part 7	ISO/IEC 13818-7	1997	2006	2007		Advanced Audio Coding (AAC)	MPEG-2 NBC Audio - Non-Backwards Compatible with MPEG-1 Audio
Part 8	dropped					10-Bit Video	The work began in 1995, but was terminated in 2007 because of low industry interest.
Part 9	ISO/IEC 13818-9	1996	1996			Extension for real time interface for systems decoders	
Part 10	ISO/IEC 13818-10	1999	1999			Conformance extensions for Digital Storage Media Command and Control (DSM-CC)	
Part 11	ISO/IEC 13818-11	2004	2004			IPMP on MPEG-2 systems	Intellectual Property Management and Protection on the MPEG-2 system (XML IPMP messages are also defined in ISO/IEC 23001-3)

History

MPEG-2 evolved out of the shortcomings of MPEG-1.

MPEG-1's known weaknesses:

- An audio compression system limited to two channels (stereo).

- No standardized support for interlaced video with poor compression when used for interlaced video

- Only one standardized "profile" (Constrained Parameters Bitstream), which was unsuited for higher resolution video. MPEG-1 could support 4k video but there was no easy way to encode video for higher resolutions, and identify hardware capable of supporting it, as the limitations of such hardware were not defined.

- Support for only one chroma subsampling, 4:2:0.

Filename Extensions

.mpg, .mpeg, .m2v, .mp2, mp3 are some of a number of filename extensions used for MPEG-1 or MPEG-2 audio and video file formats.

Applications

DVD-video

The DVD-Video standard uses MPEG-2 video, but imposes some restrictions:

- Allowed Dimensions

  o 720 × 480, 704 × 480, 352 × 480, 352 × 240 pixel (NTSC)

  o 720 × 576, 704 × 576, 352 × 576, 352 × 288 pixel (PAL)

- Allowed Aspect ratios (Display AR)

  o 4:3 (for letterboxed widescreen and non-widescreen frames)

  o 16:9 (for anamorphic widescreen)

- Allowed frame rates

  o 29.97 interlaced frame/s (NTSC)

  o 23.978 progressive frame/s (for NTSC 2:3 pull-down to 29.97)

  o 25 interlaced frame/s (PAL)

- Audio + video bitrate

  o Video peak 9.8 Mbit/s

  o Total peak 10.08 Mbit/s

  o Minimum 300 kbit/s

- YUV 4:2:0

- Additional subtitles possible

- Closed captioning (NTSC only)

- Audio

  o Linear Pulse Code Modulation (LPCM): 48 kHz or 96 kHz; 16- or 24-bit; up to six channels (not all combinations possible due to bitrate constraints)

  o MPEG Layer 2 (MP2): 48 kHz, up to 5.1 channels (required in PAL players only)

  o Dolby Digital (DD, also known as AC-3): 48 kHz, 32–448 kbit/s, up to 5.1 channels

- o Digital Theater Systems (DTS): 754 kbit/s or 1510 kbit/s (not required for DVD player compliance)

- o NTSC DVDs must contain at least one LPCM or Dolby Digital audio track.

- o PAL DVDs must contain at least one MPEG Layer 2, LPCM, or Dolby Digital audio track.

- o Players are not required to play back audio with more than two channels, but must be able to downmix multichannel audio to two channels.

- GOP structure (Group Of Pictures)

- o Sequence header must be present at the beginning of every GOP

- o Maximum frames per GOP: 18 (NTSC) / 15 (PAL), i.e. 0.6 seconds both

- o Closed GOP required for multi-angle DVDs

HDV

HDV is a format for recording and playback of high-definition MPEG-2 video on a DV cassette tape.

MOD and TOD

MOD and TOD are recording formats for use in consumer digital file-based camcorders.

XDCAM

XDCAM is a professional file-based video recording format.

DVB

Application-specific restrictions on MPEG-2 video in the DVB standard:

Allowed resolutions for SDTV:

- 720, 640, 544, 528, 480 or 352 × 480 pixel, 24/1.001, 24, 30/1.001 or 30 frame/s

- 352 × 240 pixel, 24/1.001, 24, 30/1.001 or 30 frame/s

- 720, 704, 544, 528, 480 or 352 × 576 pixel, 25 frame/s

- 352 × 288 pixel, 25 frame/s

For HDTV:

- 720 x 576 x 50 frame/s progressive (576p50)

- 1280 x 720 x 25 or 50 frame/s progressive (720p50)

- 1440 or 1920 x 1080 x 25 frame/s progressive (1080p25 = film mode)

- 1440 or 1920 x 1080 x 25 frame/s interlace (1080i50)

ATSC

The ATSC A/53 standard used in the United States, uses MPEG-2 video at the Main Profile @ High Level (MP@HL), with additional restrictions such as the maximum bitrate of 19.4 Mbit/s for broadcast television and 38.8 Mbit/s for cable television, 4:2:0 chroma subsampling format, and mandatory colorimetry information.

ATSC allows the following video resolutions, aspect ratios, and frame/field rates:

- 1920 × 1080 pixel (16:9, square pixels), at 30p, 29.97p, 24p, 23.976p, 60i, 59.94i.

- 1280 × 720 pixel (16:9, square pixels), at 60p, 59.94p, 30p, 29.97p, 24p, or 23.976p

- 704 × 480 pixel (4:3 or 16:9, non-square pixels), at 60p, 59.94p, 30p, 29.97p, 24p, 23.976p, 60i, or 59.94i

- 640 × 480 pixel (4:3, square pixels), at 60p, 59.94p, 30p, 29.97p, 24p, 23.976p, 60i, or 59.94i

ATSC standard A/63 defines additional resolutions and aspect rates for 50 Hz (PAL) signal.

The ATSC specification and MPEG-2 allow the use of progressive frames, even within an interlaced video sequence. For example, a station that transmits 1080i60 video sequence can use a coding method where those 60 fields are coded with 24 progressive frames and metadata instructs the decoder to interlace them and perform 3:2 pulldown before display. This allows broadcasters to switch between 60 Hz interlaced (news, soap operas) and 24 Hz progressive (prime-time) content without ending the MPEG-2 sequence and introducing a several seconds of delay as the TV switches formats. This is the reason why 1080p30 and 1080p24 sequences allowed by the ATSC specification are not used in practice.

The 1080-line formats are encoded with 1920 × 1088 pixel luma matrices and 960 × 540 chroma matrices, but the last 8 lines are discarded by the MPEG-2 decoding and display process.

ATSC A/72 is the newest revision of ATSC standards for digital television, which allows the use of H.264/AVC video coding format and 1080p60 signal.

MPEG-2 audio was a contender for the ATSC standard during the DTV "Grand Alliance" shootout, but lost out to Dolby AC-3.

ISDB-T

Technical features of MPEG-2 in ATSC are also valid for ISDB-T, except that in the main TS has aggregated a second program for mobile devices compressed in MPEG-4 H.264 AVC for video and AAC-LC for audio, mainly known as 1seg.

Blu-ray

Commercial Blu-ray discs encode the first 10 second long "FBI anti-piracy warning" in MPEG-2 regardless of the rest of the disc's encoding.

Patent Pool

MPEG LA, a private patent licensing organization, has acquired rights from over 20 corporations and one university to license a patent pool of approximately 640 worldwide patents, which it claims are the "essential" to use of MPEG-2 technology, although many of the patents have since expired. Where software patentability is upheld, the use of MPEG-2 requires the payment of licensing fees to the patent holders. Other patents are licensed by Audio MPEG, Inc. The development of the standard itself took less time than the patent negotiations. Patent pooling between essential and peripheral patent holders in the MPEG-2 pool is the subject of a study by the University of Wisconsin. Over half of the patents expired in 2012.

According to the MPEG-2 licensing agreement any use of MPEG-2 technology is subject to royalties. MPEG-2 encoders are subject to a royalty of \$2.00 per unit, decoders are subject to a royalty of \$2.00 per unit, and royalty-based sales of encoders and decoders are subject to different rules and \$2.50 per unit. Also, any packaged medium (DVDs/Data Streams) is subject to licence fees according to length of recording/broadcast. A criticism of the MPEG-2 patent pool is that even though the number of patents will decrease from 1,048 to 416 by June 2013 the license fee has not decreased with the expiration rate of MPEG-2 patents. Since January 1, 2010, the MPEG-2 patent pool has remained at \$2 for a decoding license and \$2 for an encoding license. By 2015 more than 90% of the MPEG-2 patents will have expired but as long as there are one or more active patents in the MPEG-2 patent pool in either the country of manufacture or the country of sale the MPEG-2 license agreement requires that licensees pay a license fee that does not change based on the number of patents that have expired.

Interlaced Video: Frame Picture and Field Picture

Broadcast television applications follows interlaced scanning in which a frame is partitioned into a set of odd-numbered scan lines (referred to as *odd field*) and a set of even numbered scan line (referred to as *even field*). If the input is interlaced, the output of the encoder consists of a sequence of fields that are separated by one field period.

MPEG-2 supports two new picture formats – *frame pictures*, and *field pictures*. In field picture, every field is coded separately. Every field is separated into non overlapping macroblock and DCT is applied on a field basis. In *frame pictures*, the two fields are coded together as a frame, similar to the conventional coding of progressive video sequence.

Frame pictures are preferred for relatively still images and field pictures give better results in presence of significant motion. It is possible to switch between the frame picture and the field picture on a frame-by-frame basis. Each frame picture or a field picture may be I-type, P-type or B-type.

Field and Frame Prediction

It is possible to predict a *field picture* from previously decoded field pictures. Each *odd field* (top field) is coded using motion compensated inter-field prediction based on the previously coded *even field* (bottom field). Each *even field* may either be predicted through motion compensation on a previously coded *even field* or from previously coded *odd field* belonging to the same picture. Within a field picture, all predictions are field predictions. Figure illustrates the field picture prediction mechanism.

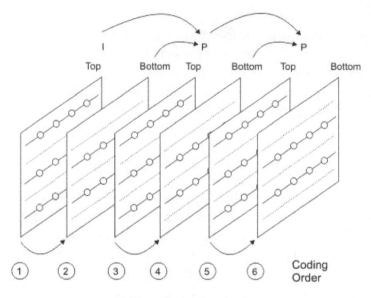

Field prediction in MPEG-2

Frame pictures can either have a frame prediction or field prediction and the prediction mode may be selected on a macroblock to macroblock basis. MPEG-2 also supports a *dual prime* prediction in which two independent predictions are made - one for the 8-lines which correspond to the odd (top)field, another for the 8 even (bottom)field lines.

Chrominance Format for MPEG-2

In digital video encoding, chrominance format describes the ratio between the horizontal spatial sampling frequencies of the luminance and chrominance components. The chrominance format is expressed as three numbers - the first represents the luminance (Y) sampling frequency, the second and the third represent chrominance U and V sampling frequencies respectively. By convention, the first number is always taken as 4.

In MPEG-1, both U and V are sampled at half the sampling rate of Y in both horizontal and vertical directions (i.e., there is one sample each of U and V for every four Y samples). It should have been called as 4:1:1, but is referred to as 4:2:0 since the relative positions of luminance and chrominance in these two formats differ. In 4:2:0, the chrominance samples are located in between the grids for luminance samples, as shown in figure (b), whereas in 4:1:1 format, the U and V samples have same spatial locations as that of Y, as illustrated in figure (a).

MPEG-2 not only supports the 4:2:0 format, but also the 4:2:2 format illustrated in figure (c), in which case, the chrominance sub-sampling is done in only one direction (horizontal), but in the vertical, the same sampling frequency as that of luminance is maintained.

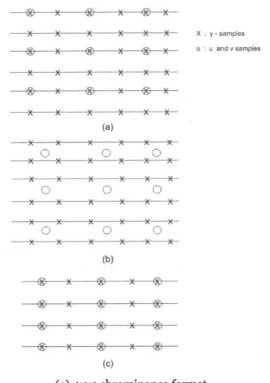

(a) 4:1:1 chrominance format
(b) 4:2:0 chrominance format
(c) 4:2:2 chrominance format

Scalability Support of MPEG-2

MPEG-2 standard supports scalability to provide interoperability between different services and to support receivers with different display capabilities. Receivers not having the capability to reconstruct full resolution video can decode only a subset of the layered bitstream to reconstruct a reduced resolution video.

The bit-stream is organized into layers having two or three hierarchies. The bottom of the hierarchy contains base layer, which every receivers and every application must make use of. Above the base layer, enhancement layers exist, which will be used by high-end applications.

The scalability support is of particular interest for SDTV (Standard Definition Television) and HDTV applications. Instead of providing separate bitstreams for SDTV and HDTV, one common scalable bitstream is provided. The SDTV applications can be addressed by the base-layer and only a combination of base- layer and enhancement layers can address the HDTV applications.

Figure illustrates the basic philosophy of a multi-scale video-coding scheme. Here, a downscaled version is encoded into a base-layer bitstream with reduced bit-rate. The reconstructed base-layer video is up-scaled spatially or temporally to predict the original input video. The prediction error is encoded into an enhancement layer bitstream. The scalable coding can be used to encode video with a suitable bit-rate allocated to each layer in order to meet the specific bandwidth requirement of the transmission channels or the storage media. Browsing through video databases or transmission of video over heterogeneous networks can benefit from the calability.

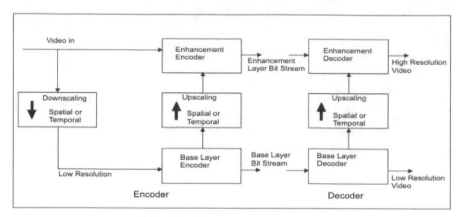

Multi-scale video encoding and deciding

MPEG-2 has standardized three scalable coding schemes: (a) signal-to-noise ratio (SNR) scalability, (b) spatial scalability and (c) temporal scalability – each of which are targeted to specific requirements.

Scalable Coding Schemes

We are going to discuss each of the three scalable coding schemes just mentioned.

SNR Scalability

SNR scalability is intended for use in video applications involving telecommunications, video services with multiple qualities. The SNR scalable algorithms use a frequency (DCT-domain) scalability technique in which both base-layer and the enhancement layers are encoded at the same spatial scale but using different quantization for DCT coefficients. At the base-layer, the DCT coefficients are coarsely quantized to achieve moderate image quality at reduced bit rate. The enhancement layer encodes the difference between the non- quanitized DCT coefficients and the coarsely quantized coefficients from the base-layer with fine quantization step-sizes. The SNR scalability is obtained as a straight forward extension to the main profile and obtains good coding efficiency.

Spatial Scalability

Spatial scalability is designed to support displays having different spatial resolution using one common layered bit-stream. This scheme best suits SDTV/HDTV applications. The base-layer encodes a spatially down-sampled video sequence and the enhancement layer encodes the extra information that would be necessary to support higher spatial resolution displays. The spatial scalability algorithm is based on the classical pyramidal approach for progressive image coding.

Temporal Scalability

Temporal scalability is intended for use in systems where a migration into the higher temporal resolution from a lower one may be necessary.

Temporal scalability is achieved by skipping certain fields/ frames at the base- layer. The skipped frames are then encoded at the enhancement layer. The enhancement layer forms its predictions from either the decoded picture at the base layer or from previous temporal prediction at the enhancement layer.

Temporal scalability can be used to accommodate both interlaced and progressive video. The base layer can be interlaced and the enhancement layer can be a progressive HDTV video sequence.

Data Partitioning in MPEG-2 Bit-stream

MPEG-2 bit-stream has a provision for data partitioning according to the priorities to support error concealment in presence of transmission or channel errors. Similar to the SNR scalability, the algorithm is based upon the separation of DCT coefficients in two layers with different error likelihood. This scheme is implemented with a very low complexity as compared to the scalable coding schemes.

MPEG-4

MPEG-4 is a method of defining compression of audio and visual (AV) digital data. It was introduced in late 1998 and designated a standard for a group of audio and video coding formats and related technology agreed upon by the ISO/IEC Moving Picture Experts Group (MPEG) (ISO/IEC JTC1/SC29/WG11) under the formal standard ISO/IEC 14496 – *Coding of audio-visual objects*. Uses of MPEG-4 include compression of AV data for web (streaming media) and CD distribution, voice (telephone, videophone) and broadcast television applications.

Background

MPEG-4 absorbs many of the features of MPEG-1 and MPEG-2 and other related standards, adding new features such as (extended) VRML support for 3D rendering, object-oriented composite files (including audio, video and VRML objects), support for externally specified Digital Rights Management and various types of interactivity. AAC (Advanced Audio Coding) was standardized as an adjunct to MPEG-2 (as Part 7) before MPEG-4 was issued.

MPEG-4 is still an evolving standard and is divided into a number of parts. Companies promoting MPEG-4 compatibility do not always clearly state which "part" level compatibility they are referring to. The key parts to be aware of are MPEG-4 Part 2 (including Advanced Simple Profile, used by codecs such as DivX, Xvid, Nero Digital and 3ivx and by QuickTime 6) and MPEG-4 part 10 (MPEG-4 AVC/H.264 or Advanced Video Coding, used by the x264 encoder, Nero Digital AVC, QuickTime 7, and high-definition video media like Blu-ray Disc).

Most of the features included in MPEG-4 are left to individual developers to decide whether or not to implement. This means that there are probably no complete implementations of the entire MPEG-4 set of standards. To deal with this, the standard includes the concept of "profiles" and "levels", allowing a specific set of capabilities to be defined in a manner appropriate for a subset of applications.

Initially, MPEG-4 was aimed primarily at low bit-rate video communications; however, its scope as a multimedia coding standard was later expanded. MPEG-4 is efficient across a variety of bitrates ranging from a few kilobits per second to tens of megabits per second. MPEG-4 provides the following functions:

- Improved coding efficiency over MPEG-2

- Ability to encode mixed media data (video, audio, speech)

- Error resilience to enable robust transmission

- Ability to interact with the audio-visual scene generated at the receiver

Overview

MPEG-4 provides a series of technologies for developers, for various service-providers and for end users:

- MPEG-4 enables different software and hardware developers to create multimedia objects possessing better abilities of adaptability and flexibility to improve the quality of such services and technologies as digital television, animation graphics, the World Wide Web and their extensions.

- Data network providers can use MPEG-4 for data transparency. With the help of standard procedures, MPEG-4 data can be interpreted and transformed into other signal types compatible with any available network.

- The MPEG-4 format provides end users with a wide range of interaction with various animated objects.

- Standardized Digital Rights Management signaling, otherwise known in the MPEG community as Intellectual Property Management and Protection (IPMP).

The MPEG-4 format can perform various functions, among which might be the following:

- Multiplexes and synchronizes data, associated with media objects, in such a way that they can be efficiently transported further via network channels.

- Interaction with the audio-visual scene, which is formed on the side of the receiver.

Profiles and Levels

MPEG-4 provides a large and rich set of tools for encoding. Subsets of the MPEG-4 tool sets have been provided for use in specific applications. These subsets, called 'Profiles', limit the size of the tool set a decoder is required to implement. In order to restrict computational complexity, one or more 'Levels' are set for each Profile. A Profile and Level combination allows:

- A codec builder to implement only the subset of the standard needed, while maintaining interworking with other MPEG-4 devices that implement the same combination.

- Checking whether MPEG-4 devices comply with the standard, referred to as conformance testing.

Licensing

MPEG-4 contains patented technologies, the use of which requires licensing in countries that acknowledge software algorithm patents. Over two dozen companies claim to have patents covering MPEG-4. MPEG LA licenses patents required for MPEG-4 Part 2 Visual from a wide range of companies (audio is licensed separately) and lists all of its licensors and licensees on the site. New licenses for MPEG-4 System patents are under development and no new licenses are being offered while holders of its old MPEG-4 Systems license are still covered under the terms of that license for the patents listed.

AT&T is trying to sue companies such as Apple Inc. over alleged MPEG-4 patent infringement. The terms of Apple's QuickTime 7 license for users describes in paragraph 14 the terms under Apple's existing MPEG-4 System Patent Portfolio license from MPEG LA.

In MPEG-4, audio and video data are *content based*, which allow independent access and manipulation of audio-visual objects in the compressed domain. Transformation of existing objects (re-positioning, scaling, and rotations), addition of new objects, removal of existing objects etc. are all within the scope of manipulation. The object manipulations are possible through simple operations performed on the bit stream. The audio-visual objects are layered and each layer is encoded into an elementary stream (ES) of bits.

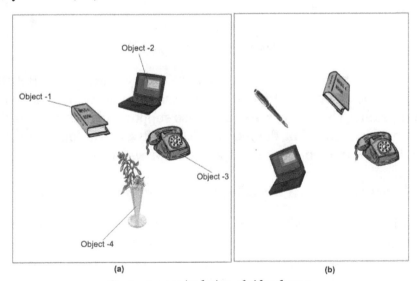

Content - manipulation of video frame.
The contents shown in (a) original and (b) reconstructed scene

Figure illustrates the concepts of content based representation of data. Each of the contents (objects) shown in figure (a) are encoded and decoded independently. While reconstructing the scene in figure (b), some objects have been re-positioned, rotated or deleted and new objects added. As mentioned, the bit-stream is *object layered* as the shape and transparency of each object as well as the spatial coordinates and additional parameters that describe object scaling, rotation etc are described in the bit-stream of each object layer. The receiver can either reconstruct the object in its entirety or do some manipulation at the bit stream level to present the object in a different way. These capabilities are given to both natural and synthetic video objects and the reconstructed scene can have a combination of both.

Toolbox Approach of MPEG-4

The MPEG-4 has followed a different approach towards the standardization of algorithms, as compared to MPEG-1 and MPEG-2. In the two earlier standards, complete algorithms for audio, video and system aspects were standardized. MPEG-4 in contrast, follows a *toolbox approach* in which tools are standardized. Video tools include a complete algorithm, or individual modules such as shape coding, motion compensation, texture coding etc. These independent coding tools can be bound together using the MPEG-4 Systems Description Language (MSDL). The MSDL is also transmitted with the bit stream and it specifies the structure and the rules for the decoder.

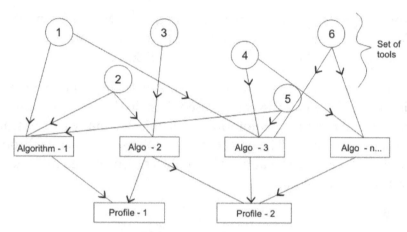

MPEG-4 "Toolbox" approch

The toolbox approach, illustrated in the figure offers flexibility to address variety of requirements. For example, the tools and algorithms for high compression applications and error-prone environments can not be the same. The tool box approach also supports future expandability and missing software tools can be downloaded at the receiver. The software implementation of the standard also facilitates implementation on general purpose DSP processors.

Video Object Representation and Encoding Layers

To achieve content-based interactivity, MPEG-4 has standardized on the video object representation. A sequence is composed of one or more audio visual objects (AVO). AVOs can be either an audio object resulting out of speech, music, sound effects, etc or a *video object* (VO) representing a specific content, such as a talking sequence of head-and-shoulder images of a person or a moving object, static/moving background etc. A video object may be present over a large collection of frames. A snapshot of a video object in one frame is defined as the *video object plane* (VOP) and is the most elementary form of content representation.

For content representation using VOPs, an input video sequence is segmented into a number of arbitrarily shaped regions (VOPs). Each of the regions may possibly cover particular image or video content of interest. The shape and the location of the region can vary from frame to frame. The shape, motion and texture information of the VOPs belonging to the same VO is encoded and transmitted into a Video Object Layer (VOL). Since typically there are several video objects, the bit stream should also include information on how to combine the different VOLS to reconstruct the video.

Snapshot of a video sequence

Binary alpha-plane

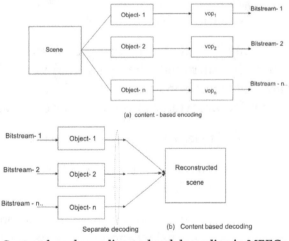

Content based encoding and and deconding in MPEG - 4

First figure shows a snapshot (frame) of a Video sequence, segmented into an arbitrarily shaped foreground VOP, and a background VOP2. Second figure shows a binary alpha-plane for the same frame, which is a binary segmentation mask specifying the location of the foreground content VOP. The last figure illustrates the scheme of content-based encoding and decoding. The scene is first segmented into a number of VOPs, each of which specifies particular image sequence content and is coded into a separate VOL. It is possible to reconstruct the original video if all the VOLs are considered. However, contents can be decoded by considering only a subset of all VOLs and this allows content based interactivity. Each VOL encoding has three components –

- Shape (contour) coding

- Motion estimation and compensation

- Texture coding

We may note that the frame-based functionalities of MPEG-1 and MPEG-2 form a subset of content based functionalities supported in MPEG-4. While MPEG-4 supports multiple VOPs, the former two standards support only one VOP containing the entire picture of fixed rectangular size.

VOP Window and Shape-adaptive Macroblock Grid

To encode shape, motion and texture information in arbitrarily shaped VOPs, the concept of VOP image window and a shape adaptive macro block grid has been introduced.

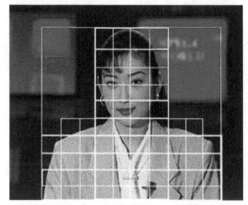

VOP Window and VOP macroblocks

The VOP image window, as illustrated in figure is a rectangular window having size in multiples of 16 pixels in each image direction that surrounds the foreground VOP. This window is adjusted to collocate with the top-most and left- most border of the VOP. The position of the VOP image window is defined with respect to a reference window of constant size by specifying a shift parameter.

The VOP image window is composed of macro block of size 16 x 16 pixels, which are of three types:

- Macroblocks which do not belong to the VOP at all. These are inactive macroblock with respect to the VOP and are not encoded in the VOL.

- Macroblocks which partly belong to the VOP. These are the boundary macroblocks for the VOP and require some special consideration during its encoding.

- Macroblocks which fully belong to the VOP. The are the standard macroblock for the VOP.

The last two categories of macroblocks are the active macroblocks and the grids that define those are referred to as the shape-adaptive macroblock grid marked in figure. This plays a major role in VOP encoding.

Encoding of VOPs

As already mentioned, the VOLs compose the bit-streams for the VOPs and their encoding have three major components, namely the shape, motion and texture. We are now going to discuss each of these in the context of content based functionalities of MPEG-4.

Shape Coding in MPEG-4

Since video objects in MPEG-4 are of arbitrary shape, encoding of shapes form an essential part of encoding. Whether a pixel belongs to the VOP or not is specified by a binary map known as alpha plane which has an entry of "1" if the pixel belongs to VOP and is "0" otherwise.

Shape coding techniques may be broadly classified as (a) contour based and (b) bit-map based. The contour based techniques extract and encodes a description of the closed contour enclosing the shape. The bit-map based techniques are applied directly to the binary alpha-plane, within the conventional block-based framework.

The contour based technique adopted in MPEG-4 is the vertex-based coding that approximates the shape using a polygonal approximation. First, the longest axis of the shape is found and its two end points are used as the initial polygon. For each polygon line, it is checked if the approximation lies within the tolerance. If not, a new vertex is inserted at the point of largest prediction error. Each new polygon side is checked again for approximation and the process is iteratively repeated.

Bit map based shape coding techniques may be broadly categorized as:

- Modified Read (MR) approach, used in fax

- Context based arithmetic encoding (CAE), which has been adopted in JBIG standard.

The MPEG-4 standard has adopted CAE for encoding the bit-map of binary alpha planes. The pixels of alpha-planes are grouped into binary alpha block (BAB) of size 16 x 16 pixels. BABs may be intra-coded using CAE or inter-coded using motion compensation and CAE.

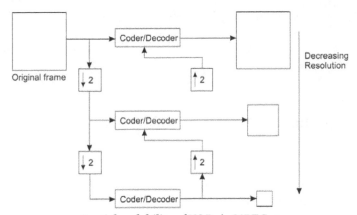

Spatial scalability of VOPs in MPEG-4

Motion Estimation in VOPs

The shape-adaptive macroblock grid is used for motion estimation in VOPs. The standard macroblock within the grid are motion compensated, following the approaches adopted in the earlier two MPEG standards. However, a different approach is adopted for the contour macroblocks. An image padding method is employed in the reference for these macroblocks, which can be seen as an extrapolation of pixel values outside the VOP based on the values inside the VOPs. After padding the reference VOP, a *polygon matching technique* is employed for motion estimation and compensation. "Polygon" refers to the part of the contour macroblock which belongs to the active area inside the VOP frame to be coded and excludes the pixels outside this area.

Based on the motion estimation and motion compensation philosophy, three types of VOPs can be defined :

- *I-VOP* : These are the intra-coded VOPs, similar to the intra coded frames (I-picture) where no motion estimation is employed and only texture coding is done.

- *P-VOP* : These VOPs use forward prediction for motion compensation, very similar to the P-picture.

- *B-VOP:* These VOPs are bi-directionally predicted, very similar to the B- picture.

It may be noted that the encoding of standard I-picture, P-pictures and B-pictures are still possible in MPEG-4 for the special case of single, rectangular VOPs.

Texture Coding

Texture coding is to be performed on the I-VOP or the residual errors after the motion compensation in the P-VOPs and B-VOPs. For texture coding too, the shape adaptive macroblock grid is used. For each macroblock, a maximum of four 8 x 8 luminance blocks and two 8 x 8 chrominance block are employed.

Special adaptation is required for the contour blocks, where image padding technique is used to fill the macro block content outside a VOP before applying the DCT in intra-VOP. For motion compensated coding of P-VOPs, the contents of the pixels outside the active VOP area are set to128.

Multiplexing of Shape, Motion and Texture Information

The video object layer (VOL) is formed by multiplexing the encoded VOP information in the following order:

- Shape encoding

- Motion vector encoding

- Texture coding

Two different encoding mechanisms are supported by MPEG-4. One is a joint motion vector, along with DCT coefficient encoding procedure to achieve high compression efficiency at very low bit rates. The second mechanism is to separately encode the motion vectors and the DCT coefficients.

Spatial and Temporal Scalability of MPEG-4

We have seen the scalability supports in the MPEG-2 standard, which can be used to make the lower resolution decoders (receivers) work from a scalable or layered bit stream. The same concept is extended to the encoding of arbitrarily shaped VOPs in MPEG-4. In this case, each VOP can be encoded to multiple number of VOLs of which only one forms the base layer and the remaining ones compose the enhancement layers. The layered bitstream has a major advantage in terms of prioritized transmission and error resiliency.

Two types of scalabilities are supported in VOP encoding process- one is the spatial scalability and the other is the temporal scalability.

Spatial Scalability

This is very similar to the spatial scalability support in MPEG-2. Here, multi resolution representations of the VOPs are formed by spatially downsampling the input video signal into a number of levels. The lowest resolution level supports the base-layer bit stream and the subsequent upper resolutions are predicted by upsampling from the lower resolution of the VOP. The spatial scalability concept is illustrated in figure.

Temporal Scalability

Very similar to the temporal scalability concepts for pictures in MPEG-2, the MPEG-4 standard supports temporal scalability for the VOPs. Like the spatial scalability temporal scalability too generates a layered bit stream in which the base-layer is formed by temporally subsampling the video objects and the enhancement layers are obtained by temporal prediction from the lower layers.

Using the MPEG-4 VOP temporal scalability approach, it is possible to have different frame rates for different video objects. For example, the foreground object may have a higher frame rate as compared to the relatively stationary background.

Sprite Coding in MPEG-4

The sprite coding is an important feature of MPEG-4. The object based coding in MPEG-4 essentially requires video segmentation algorithm to extract the foreground from the background. This idea is extended to spite coding, in which the background is reconstructed and transmitted separately from the foreground, using a very sophisticated motion analysis and prediction strategies.

Sprite, also referred to *panorama* assumes a flat, static background. As the camera pans rotates or zooms over the scene, the spite coder learn more information about the background. By estimating the camera parameters from the successive frames, the background content of each frame can be added to or deleted from the panorama.

In the spite coding approach of MPEG-4, the large, static panorama picture is first transmitted to the receiver. For each frame, camera parameters are transmitted separately, which facilitates extraction of frame backgrounds from the panorama. The foreground is encoded separately and the receiver composes the scene from the separately transmitted foreground and the background.

Since sprite-coding requires only one time transmission of the background, substantial coding gain is usually achieved as compared to the usual block based encoding of the entire scene.

Facial Feature Animation Capabilities of MPEG-4

The sprite coding concepts can be extended to the model based video coding for head-and-shoulder video sequences. Such model based coding techniques use a 3-D wire mesh model of a human head and shoulders. A sprite image of a person is mapped on to the 3-D surface to represent the texture details of the person.

Both model and human –face sprites are required to be sent by the transmitter to the receiver in the beginning and subsequently, for each frame, only a few parameters, that represent the motion of the person are to be transmitted. Transmission of 2 to 6 motion parameters per frame is sufficient for excellent predictions of the face region.

The MPEG-4 uses a similar concept to animate synthetically generated faces. There are some specific control points in the wire mesh model to which motion parameters can be imparted to create the impression of a "talking head".

References

- Chiariglione, Leonardo (October 21, 1989), Kurihama 89 press release, ISO/IEC, archived from the original on August 5, 2010, retrieved 2008-04-09

- Chiariglione, Leonardo (March 2001), Open source in MPEG, Linux Journal, archived from the original on 2011-07-25, retrieved 2008-04-09

- Herre, Jurgen (October 5, 2004), From Joint Stereo to Spatial Audio Coding (PDF), Conference on Digital Audio Effects, p. 2, archived from the original (PDF) on April 5, 2006, retrieved 2008-04-17

- Pan, Davis (Summer 1995), A Tutorial on MPEG/Audio Compression (PDF), IEEE Multimedia Journal, p. 8, archived from the original (PDF) on 2004-09-19, retrieved 2008-04-09

- B/MAE Project Group (September 2007), EBU evaluations of multichannel audio codecs (PDF), European Broadcasting Union, archived from the original (PDF) on 2008-10-30, retrieved 2008-04-09

- J. Johnston, Transform Coding of Audio Signals Using Perceptual Noise Criteria, IEEE Journal Select Areas in Communications, vol. 6, no. 2, pp. 314-323, Feb. 1988

- Quint, Dan; Amit Gandhi. "Economics of Patent Pools When Some (but not all) Patents are Essential". Working Paper. Retrieved 2009-10-11

- "ISO/IEC 14496-23:2008 – Information technology — Coding of audio-visual objects — Part 23: Symbolic Music Representation". ISO. Retrieved 2009-10-30

5

Wavelet and Wavelet Coding

Wavelet is a wave-like oscillation, created to be used in signal processing. They can be used to examine spatial frequency contents at different resolutions. Due to this, they can perform multi-resolution analysis of images. Multi-resolution analysis is a design method of discrete wavelet transforms and justification for fast wavelet transforms' algorithm. The chapter on wavelet and wavelet coding offers an insightful focus, keeping in mind the complex subject matter.

Wavelet

A wavelet is a wave-like oscillation with an amplitude that begins at zero, increases, and then decreases back to zero. It can typically be visualized as a "brief oscillation" like one recorded by a seismograph or heart monitor. Generally, wavelets are intentionally crafted to have specific properties that make them useful for signal processing. Wavelets can be combined, using a "reverse, shift, multiply and integrate" technique called convolution, with portions of a known signal to extract information from the unknown signal.

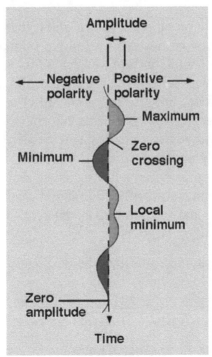

Seismic wavelet

For example, a wavelet could be created to have a frequency of Middle C and a short duration of roughly a 32nd note. If this wavelet were to be convolved with a signal created from the recording of a song, then the resulting signal would be useful for determining when the Middle C note was being played in the song. Mathematically, the wavelet will correlate with the signal if the unknown signal contains information of similar frequency. This concept of correlation is at the core of many practical applications of wavelet theory.

As a mathematical tool, wavelets can be used to extract information from many different kinds of data, including – but certainly not limited to – audio signals and images. Sets of wavelets are generally needed to analyze data fully. A set of "complementary" wavelets will decompose data without gaps or overlap so that the decomposition process is mathematically reversible. Thus, sets of complementary wavelets are useful in wavelet based compression/decompression algorithms where it is desirable to recover the original information with minimal loss.

In formal terms, this representation is a wavelet series representation of a square-integrable function with respect to either a complete, orthonormal set of basis functions, or an overcomplete set or frame of a vector space, for the Hilbert space of square integrable functions. This is accomplished through coherent states.

Name

The word *wavelet* has been used for decades in digital signal processing and exploration geophysics. The equivalent French word *ondelette* meaning "small wave" was used by Morlet and Grossmann in the early 1980s.

Wavelet Theory

Wavelet theory is applicable to several subjects. All wavelet transforms may be considered forms of time-frequency representation for continuous-time (analog) signals and so are related to harmonic analysis. Almost all practically useful discrete wavelet transforms use discrete-time filterbanks. These filter banks are called the wavelet and scaling coefficients in wavelets nomenclature. These filterbanks may contain either finite impulse response (FIR) or infinite impulse response (IIR) filters. The wavelets forming a continuous wavelet transform (CWT) are subject to the uncertainty principle of Fourier analysis respective sampling theory: Given a signal with some event in it, one cannot assign simultaneously an exact time and frequency response scale to that event. The product of the uncertainties of time and frequency response scale has a lower bound. Thus, in the scaleogram of a continuous wavelet transform of this signal, such an event marks an entire region in the time-scale plane, instead of just one point. Also, discrete wavelet bases may be considered in the context of other forms of the uncertainty principle.

Wavelet transforms are broadly divided into three classes: continuous, discrete and multiresolution-based.

Continuous Wavelet Transforms (Continuous Shift and Scale Parameters)

In continuous wavelet transforms, a given signal of finite energy is projected on a continuous family of frequency bands (or similar subspaces of the L^p function space $L^2(R)$). For instance the signal may be represented on every frequency band of the form $[f, 2f]$ for all positive frequencies $f > 0$. Then, the original signal can be reconstructed by a suitable integration over all the resulting frequency components.

The frequency bands or subspaces (sub-bands) are scaled versions of a subspace at scale 1. This subspace in turn is in most situations generated by the shifts of one generating function ψ in $L^2(\mathbf{R})$, the *mother wavelet*. For the example of the scale one frequency band [1, 2] this function is

$$\psi(t) = 2\text{sinc}(2t) - \text{sinc}(t) = \frac{\sin(2\pi t) - \sin(\pi t)}{\pi t}$$

with the (normalized) sinc function. That, Meyer's, and two other examples of mother wavelets are:

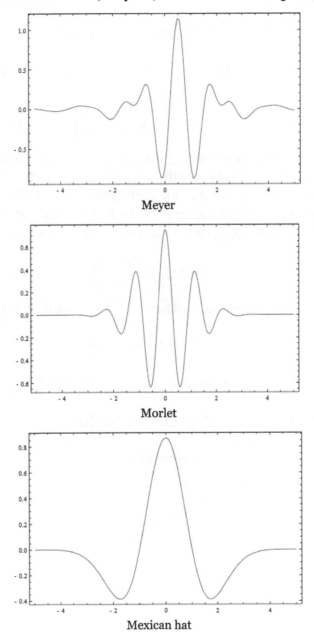

Meyer

Morlet

Mexican hat

The subspace of scale a or frequency band [1/a, 2/a] is generated by the functions (sometimes called *child wavelets*)

$$\psi_{a,b}(t) = \frac{1}{\sqrt{a}}\psi\left(\frac{t-b}{a}\right),$$

where a is positive and defines the scale and b is any real number and defines the shift. The pair (a, b) defines a point in the right halfplane $\mathbb{R}_+ \times \mathbb{R}$.

The projection of a function x onto the subspace of scale a then has the form

$$x_a(t) = \int_{\mathbb{R}} WT_\psi\{x\}(a,b) \cdot \psi_{a,b}(t)db$$

with *wavelet coefficients*

$$WT_\psi\{x\}(a,b) = \langle x, \psi_{a,b} \rangle = \int_{\mathbb{R}} x(t)\psi_{a,b}(t)dt.$$

For the analysis of the signal x, one can assemble the wavelet coefficients into a scaleogram of the signal.

Discrete Wavelet Transforms (Discrete Shift and Scale Parameters)

It is computationally impossible to analyze a signal using all wavelet coefficients, so one may wonder if it is sufficient to pick a discrete subset of the upper halfplane to be able to reconstruct a signal from the corresponding wavelet coefficients. One such system is the affine system for some real parameters $a > 1$, $b > 0$. The corresponding discrete subset of the halfplane consists of all the points $(a^m, na^m b)$ with m, n in Z. The corresponding *child wavelets* are now given as

$$\psi_{m,n}(t) = \frac{1}{\sqrt{a^m}} \psi\left(\frac{t - nb}{a^m}\right).$$

A sufficient condition for the reconstruction of any signal x of finite energy by the formula

$$x(t) = \sum_{m \in \mathbb{Z}} \sum_{n \in \mathbb{Z}} \langle x, \psi_{m,n} \rangle \cdot \psi_{m,n}(t)$$

is that the functions $\{\psi_{m,n} : m, n \in \mathbb{Z}\}$ form an orthonormal basis of $L^2(\mathbb{R})$.

Multiresolution based Discrete Wavelet Transforms

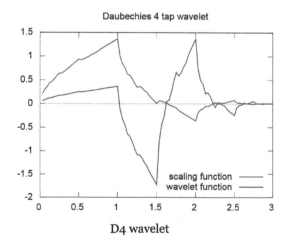

D4 wavelet

In any discretised wavelet transform, there are only a finite number of wavelet coefficients for each bounded rectangular region in the upper halfplane. Still, each coefficient requires the evaluation of an integral. In special situations this numerical complexity can be avoided if the scaled and shifted wavelets form a multiresolution analysis. This means that there has to exist an auxiliary function, the *father wavelet* φ in $L^2(\mathbb{R})$, and that a is an integer. A typical choice is $a = 2$ and $b = 1$. The most famous pair of father and mother wavelets is the Daubechies 4-tap wavelet. Note that not every orthonormal discrete wavelet basis can be associated to a multiresolution analysis; for example, the Journe wavelet admits no multiresolution analysis.

From the mother and father wavelets one constructs the subspaces

$$V_m = \text{span}(\phi_{m,n} : n \in \mathbb{Z}), \text{ where } \phi_{m,n}(t) = 2^{-m/2}\phi(2^{-m}t - n)$$

$$W_m = \text{span}(\psi_{m,n} : n \in \mathbb{Z}), \text{ where } \psi_{m,n}(t) = 2^{-m/2}\psi(2^{-m}t - n).$$

The father wavelet V_i keeps the time domain properties, while the mother wavelets W_i keeps the frequency domain properties.

From these it is required that the sequence

$$\{0\} \subset \ldots \subset V_1 \subset V_0 \subset V_{-1} \subset V_{-2} \subset \ldots \subset L^2(\mathbb{R})$$

forms a multiresolution analysis of L^2 and that the subspaces $\ldots, W_1, W_0, W_{-1}, \ldots\ldots$ are the orthogonal "differences" of the above sequence, that is, W_m is the orthogonal complement of V_m inside the subspace V_{m-1},

$$V_m \oplus W_m = V_{m-1}.$$

In analogy to the sampling theorem one may conclude that the space V_m with sampling distance 2^m more or less covers the frequency baseband from 0 to 2^{-m-1}. As orthogonal complement, W_m roughly covers the band $[2^{-m-1}, 2^{-m}]$.

From those inclusions and orthogonality relations, especially $V_0 \oplus W_0 = V_{-1}$, follows the existence of sequences $h = \{h_n\}_{n \in \mathbb{Z}}$ and $g = \{g_n\}_{n \in \mathbb{Z}}$ that satisfy the identities

$$g_n = \langle \phi_{0,0}, \phi_{-1,n} \rangle \text{ so that } \phi(t) = \sqrt{2} \sum_{n \in \mathbb{Z}} g_n \phi(2t - n), \text{ and}$$

$$h_n = \langle \psi_{0,0}, \phi_{-1,n} \rangle \text{ so that } \psi(t) = \sqrt{2} \sum_{n \in \mathbb{Z}} h_n \phi(2t - n).$$

The second identity of the first pair is a refinement equation for the father wavelet φ. Both pairs of identities form the basis for the algorithm of the fast wavelet transform.

From the multiresolution analysis derives the orthogonal decomposition of the space L^2 as

$$L^2 = V_{j_0} \oplus W_{j_0} \oplus W_{j_0-1} \oplus W_{j_0-2} \oplus W_{j_0-3} \oplus \ldots$$

For any signal or function $S \in L^2$ this gives a representation in basis functions of the corresponding subspaces as

$$S = \sum_k c_{j_0,k} \phi_{j_0,k} + \sum_{j \leq j_0} \sum_k d_{j,k} \psi_{j,k}$$

where the coefficients are

$$c_{j_0,k} = \langle S, \phi_{j_0,k} \rangle \text{ and}$$

$$d_{j,k} = \langle S, \psi_{j,k} \rangle.$$

Mother Wavelet

For practical applications, and for efficiency reasons, one prefers continuously differentiable functions with compact support as mother (prototype) wavelet (functions). However, to satisfy analytical requirements (in the continuous WT) and in general for theoretical reasons, one chooses the wavelet functions from a subspace of the space $L^1(\mathbb{R}) \cap L^2(\mathbb{R})$. This is the space of measurable functions that are absolutely and square integrable:

$$\int_{-\infty}^{\infty} |\psi(t)| dt < \infty \text{ and } \int_{-\infty}^{\infty} |\psi(t)|^2 dt < \infty.$$

Being in this space ensures that one can formulate the conditions of zero mean and square norm one:

$\int_{-\infty}^{\infty} \psi(t) dt = 0$ is the condition for zero mean, and

$\int_{-\infty}^{\infty} |\psi(t)|^2 dt = 1$ is the condition for square norm one.

For ψ to be a wavelet for the continuous wavelet transform, the mother wavelet must satisfy an admissibility criterion (loosely speaking, a kind of half-differentiability) in order to get a stably invertible transform.

For the discrete wavelet transform, one needs at least the condition that the wavelet series is a representation of the identity in the space $L^2(\mathbb{R})$. Most constructions of discrete WT make use of the multiresolution analysis, which defines the wavelet by a scaling function. This scaling function itself is a solution to a functional equation.

In most situations it is useful to restrict ψ to be a continuous function with a higher number M of vanishing moments, i.e. for all integer $m < M$

$$\int_{-\infty}^{\infty} t^m \psi(t) dt = 0.$$

The mother wavelet is scaled (or dilated) by a factor of a and translated (or shifted) by a factor of b to give (under Morlet's original formulation):

$$\psi_{a,b}(t) = \frac{1}{\sqrt{a}} \psi\left(\frac{t-b}{a}\right).$$

For the continuous WT, the pair (a,b) varies over the full half-plane $\mathbb{R}_+ \times \mathbb{R}$; for the discrete WT this pair varies over a discrete subset of it, which is also called *affine group*.

These functions are often incorrectly referred to as the basis functions of the (continuous) transform. In fact, as in the continuous Fourier transform, there is no basis in the continuous wavelet transform. Time-frequency interpretation uses a subtly different formulation (after Delprat).

Restriction:

(1) $\dfrac{1}{\sqrt{a}} \int\limits_{-\infty}^{\infty} \varphi_{a1,b1}(t) \varphi\left(\dfrac{t-b}{a}\right) dt$ when a1 = a and b1 = b,

(2) $\Psi(t)$ has a finite time interval

Comparisons with Fourier Transform (Continuous-time)

The wavelet transform is often compared with the Fourier transform, in which signals are represented as a sum of sinusoids. In fact, the Fourier transform can be viewed as a special case of the continuous wavelet transform with the choice of the mother wavelet $\psi(t) = e^{-2\pi it}$. The main difference in general is that wavelets are localized in both time and frequency whereas the standard Fourier transform is only localized in frequency. The Short-time Fourier transform (STFT) is similar to the wavelet transform, in that it is also time and frequency localized, but there are issues with the frequency/time resolution trade-off.

In particular, assuming a rectangular window region, one may think of the STFT as a transform with a slightly different kernel

$$\psi(t) = g(t-u)e^{-2\pi it}$$

where $g(t-u)$ can often be written as $\text{rect}\left(\dfrac{t-u}{\Delta_t}\right)$, where Δ_t and u respectively denote the length and temporal offset of the windowing function. Using Parseval's theorem, one may define the wavelet's energy as

$$E = \int_{-\infty}^{\infty} |\psi(t)|^2 \, dt = \frac{1}{2\pi} \int_{-\infty}^{\infty} |\hat{\psi}(\omega)|^2 \, d\omega$$

From this, the square of the temporal support of the window offset by time u is given by

$$\sigma_t^2 = \frac{1}{E} \int |t-u|^2 |\psi(t)|^2 \, dt$$

and the square of the spectral support of the window acting on a frequency ξ

$$\sigma_\omega^2 = \frac{1}{2\pi E} \int |\omega - \xi|^2 |\hat{\psi}(\omega)|^2 \, d\omega$$

Multiplication with a rectangular window in the time domain corresponds to convolution with a $\text{sinc}(\Delta_t\omega)$ function in the frequency domain, resulting in spurious ringing artifacts for short/localized temporal windows. With the continuous-time Fourier Transform, $\Delta_t \to \infty$ and this convolution is with a delta function in Fourier space, resulting in the true Fourier transform of the signal $x(t)$. The window function may be some other apodizing filter, such as a Gaussian. The choice of windowing function will affect the approximation error relative to the true Fourier transform.

A given resolution cell's time-bandwidth product may not be exceeded with the STFT. All STFT basis elements maintain a uniform spectral and temporal support for all temporal shifts or offsets, thereby attaining an equal resolution in time for lower and higher frequencies. The resolution is purely determined by the sampling width.

In contrast, the wavelet transform's multiresolutional properties enables large temporal supports for lower frequencies while maintaining short temporal widths for higher frequencies by the scaling properties of the wavelet transform. This property extends conventional time-frequency analysis into time-scale analysis.

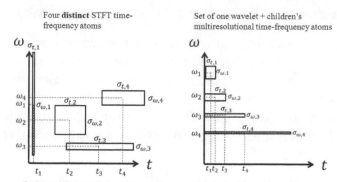

STFT time-frequency atoms (left) and DWT time-scale atoms (right). The time-frequency atoms are four different basis functions used for the STFT (i.e. four separate Fourier transforms required). The time-scale atoms of the DWT achieve small temporal widths for high frequencies and good temporal widths for low frequencies with a single transform basis set.

The discrete wavelet transform is less computationally complex, taking $O(N)$ time as compared to $O(N \log N)$ for the fast Fourier transform. This computational advantage is not inherent to the transform, but reflects the choice of a logarithmic division of frequency, in contrast to the equally spaced frequency divisions of the FFT (Fast Fourier Transform) which uses the same basis functions as DFT (Discrete Fourier Transform). It is also important to note that this complexity only applies when the filter size has no relation to the signal size. A wavelet without compact support such as the Shannon wavelet would require $O(N^2)$. (For instance, a logarithmic Fourier Transform also exists with $O(N)$ complexity, but the original signal must be sampled logarithmically in time, which is only useful for certain types of signals.)

Definition of a Wavelet

There are a number of ways of defining a wavelet (or a wavelet family).

Scaling Filter

An orthogonal wavelet is entirely defined by the scaling filter – a low-pass finite impulse response (FIR) filter of length $2N$ and sum 1. In biorthogonal wavelets, separate decomposition and reconstruction filters are defined.

For analysis with orthogonal wavelets the high pass filter is calculated as the quadrature mirror filter of the low pass, and reconstruction filters are the time reverse of the decomposition filters.

Daubechies and Symlet wavelets can be defined by the scaling filter.

Scaling Function

Wavelets are defined by the wavelet function $\psi(t)$ (i.e. the mother wavelet) and scaling function $\varphi(t)$ (also called father wavelet) in the time domain.

The wavelet function is in effect a band-pass filter and scaling it for each level halves its bandwidth. This creates the problem that in order to cover the entire spectrum, an infinite number of levels would be required. The scaling function filters the lowest level of the transform and ensures all the spectrum is covered.

For a wavelet with compact support, $\varphi(t)$ can be considered finite in length and is equivalent to the scaling filter g. Meyer wavelets can be defined by scaling functions.

Wavelet Function

The wavelet only has a time domain representation as the wavelet function $\psi(t)$. For instance, Mexican hat wavelets can be defined by a wavelet function.

History

The development of wavelets can be linked to several separate trains of thought, starting with Haar's work in the early 20th century. Later work by Dennis Gabor yielded Gabor atoms (1946), which are constructed similarly to wavelets, and applied to similar purposes. Notable contributions to wavelet theory can be attributed to Zweig's discovery of the continuous wavelet transform in 1975 (originally called the cochlear transform and discovered while studying the reaction of the ear to sound), Pierre Goupillaud, Grossmann and Morlet's formulation of what is now known as the CWT (1982), Jan-Olov Strömberg's early work on discrete wavelets (1983), Daubechies' orthogonal wavelets with compact support (1988), Mallat's multiresolution framework (1989), Akansu's Binomial QMF (1990), Nathalie Delprat's time-frequency interpretation of the CWT (1991), Newland's harmonic wavelet transform (1993) and many others since.

Timeline

- First wavelet (Haar wavelet) by Alfréd Haar (1909)

- Since the 1970s: George Zweig, Jean Morlet, Alex Grossmann

- Since the 1980s: Yves Meyer, Stéphane Mallat, Ingrid Daubechies, Ronald Coifman, Ali Akansu, Victor Wickerhauser

Wavelet Transforms

A wavelet is a mathematical function used to divide a given function or continuous-time signal into different scale components. Usually one can assign a frequency range to each scale component. Each scale component can then be studied with a resolution that matches its scale. A wavelet transform is the representation of a function by wavelets. The wavelets are scaled and translated copies (known as "daughter wavelets") of a finite-length or fast-decaying oscillating waveform (known as the "mother wavelet"). Wavelet transforms have advantages over traditional Fourier transforms for representing functions that have discontinuities and sharp peaks, and for accurately deconstructing and reconstructing finite, non-periodic and/or non-stationary signals.

Wavelet transforms are classified into discrete wavelet transforms (DWTs) and continuous wavelet transforms (CWTs). Note that both DWT and CWT are continuous-time (analog) transforms. They can be used to represent continuous-time (analog) signals. CWTs operate over every possible scale and translation whereas DWTs use a specific subset of scale and translation values or representation grid.

There are a large number of wavelet transforms each suitable for different applications. The common wavelet-related transforms onesare listed below:

- Continuous wavelet transform (CWT)

- Discrete wavelet transform (DWT)

- Fast wavelet transform (FWT)

- Lifting scheme & Generalized Lifting Scheme

- Wavelet packet decomposition (WPD)

- Stationary wavelet transform (SWT)

- Fractional Fourier transform (FRFT)

- Fractional wavelet transform (FRWT)

Generalized Transforms

There are a number of generalized transforms of which the wavelet transform is a special case. For example, Joseph Segman introduced scale into the Heisenberg group, giving rise to a continuous transform space that is a function of time, scale, and frequency. The CWT is a two-dimensional slice through the resulting 3d time-scale-frequency volume.

Another example of a generalized transform is the chirplet transform in which the CWT is also a two dimensional slice through the chirplet transform.

An important application area for generalized transforms involves systems in which high frequency resolution is crucial. For example, darkfield electron optical transforms intermediate between direct and reciprocal space have been widely used in the harmonic analysis of atom clustering, i.e. in the study of crystals and crystal defects. Now that transmission electron microscopes are capable of providing digital images with picometer-scale information on atomic periodicity in nanostructure of all sorts, the range of pattern recognition and strain/metrology applications for intermediate transforms with high frequency resolution (like brushlets and ridgelets) is growing rapidly.

Fractional wavelet transform (FRWT) is a generalization of the classical wavelet transform in the fractional Fourier transform domains. This transform is capable of providing the time- and fractional-domain information simultaneously and representing signals in the time-fractional-frequency plane.

Applications of Wavelet Transform

Generally, an approximation to DWT is used for data compression if a signal is already sampled, and the CWT for signal analysis. Thus, DWT approximation is commonly used in engineering and computer science, and the CWT in scientific research.

Like some other transforms, wavelet transforms can be used to transform data, then encode the transformed data, resulting in effective compression. For example, JPEG 2000 is an image compression standard that uses biorthogonal wavelets. This means that although the frame is overcomplete, it is a *tight frame*, and the same frame functions (except for conjugation in the case of complex wavelets) are used for both analysis and synthesis, i.e., in both the forward and inverse transform.

A related use is for smoothing/denoising data based on wavelet coefficient thresholding, also called wavelet shrinkage. By adaptively thresholding the wavelet coefficients that correspond to undesired frequency components smoothing and/or denoising operations can be performed.

Wavelet transforms are also starting to be used for communication applications. Wavelet OFDM is the basic modulation scheme used in HD-PLC (a power line communications technology developed by Panasonic), and in one of the optional modes included in the IEEE 1901 standard. Wavelet OFDM can achieve deeper notches than traditional FFT OFDM, and wavelet OFDM does not require a guard interval (which usually represents significant overhead in FFT OFDM systems).

As a Representation of a Signal

Often, signals can be represented well as a sum of sinusoids. However, consider a non-continuous signal with an abrupt discontinuity; this signal can still be represented as a sum of sinusoids, but requires an infinite number, which is an observation known as Gibbs phenomenon. This, then, requires an infinite number of Fourier coefficients, which is not practical for many applications, such as compression. Wavelets are more useful for describing these signals with discontinuities because of their time-localized behavior (both Fourier and wavelet transforms are frequency-localized, but wavelets have an additional time-localization property). Because of this, many types of signals in practice may be non-sparse in the Fourier domain, but very sparse in the wavelet domain. This is particularly useful in signal reconstruction, especially in the recently popular field of compressed sensing. (Note that the short-time Fourier transform (STFT) is also localized in time and frequency, but there are often problems with the frequency-time resolution trade-off. Wavelets are better signal representations because of multiresolution analysis.)

This motivates why wavelet transforms are now being adopted for a vast number of applications, often replacing the conventional Fourier transform. Many areas of physics have seen this paradigm shift, including molecular dynamics, chaos theory, ab initio calculations, astrophysics, density-matrix localisation, seismology, optics, turbulence and quantum mechanics. This change has also occurred in image processing, EEG, EMG, ECG analyses, brain rhythms, DNA analysis, protein analysis, climatology, human sexual response analysis, general signal processing, speech recognition, acoustics, vibration signals, computer graphics, multifractal analysis, and sparse coding. In computer vision and image processing, the notion of scale space representation and Gaussian derivative operators is regarded as a canonical multi-scale representation.

Wavelet Denoising

Suppose we measure a noisy signal $x = s + v$. Assume s has a sparse representation in a certain wavelet bases, and $v \sim \mathcal{N}(0, \sigma^2 I)$

So $y = W^T x = W^T s + W^T v = p + z.$.

Most elements in p are 0 or close to 0, and $z \sim \mathcal{N}(0, \sigma^2 I)$

Since W is orthogonal, the estimation problem amounts to recovery of a signal in iid Gaussian noise. As p is sparse, one method is to apply a Gaussian mixture model for p.

Assume a prior $p \sim a\mathcal{N}(0,\sigma_1^2)+(1-a)\mathcal{N}(0,\sigma_2^2)$, σ_1^2 is the variance of "significant" coefficients, and σ_2^2 is the variance of "insignificant" coefficients.

Then $\tilde{p} = E(p/y) = \tau(y)y$, $\tau(y)$ is called the shrinkage factor, which depends on the prior variances σ_1^2 and σ_2^2. The effect of the shrinkage factor is that small coefficients are set early to 0, and large coefficients are unaltered.

Small coefficients are mostly noises, and large coefficients contain actual signal.

At last, apply the inverse wavelet transform to obtain $\tilde{s} = W\tilde{p}$

Scaling Functions and Functional Subspace

Any function $f(x)$ can be analyzed as a linear combination of real-valued expansion functions $\varphi_k(x)$

$$f(x) = \sum_k \alpha_k \varphi_k(x) \quad (1)$$

where k is an integer index of summation (finite or infinite), the α_k s are the real-valued expansion coefficients and $\{\varphi_k(x)\}$ forms an expansion set.

Let us compose a set of expansion functions $\{\varphi_{r,s}(x)\}$ through integer translations and binary scalings of the real, square-integrable function $\varphi(x)$, so that

$$\varphi_{r,s}(x) = 2^{r/2}\varphi(2^r x - s) \quad (2)$$

where, $r, s \in Z$ (the integer space) and $\varphi(x) \in L^2(R)$(the square-integrable real space). In the above eqautions, s controls the translation in integer steps and r controls the amplitude, as well as the width of the function in the x-direction. Increasing r by one decreases the width by one-half and increases the amplitude by $\sqrt{2}$ In other words, the index r scales the function and the set of functions $\{\varphi_{r,s}(x)\}$ obtained through equation (2) are referred to as scaling functions. By a wise choice of $\varphi(x)$ the set of functions $\{\varphi_{r,s}(x)\}$ can be made to cover the entire square-integrable real space $L^2(R)$. Hence, if we choose any particular scale, say r = r_0, the set of functions $\{\varphi_{r_0}(x)\}$ obtained through integer translations can only cover a subspace of the entire $L^2(R)$. The subspace V_{r_0} so spanned is defined as the functional subspace of $\{\varphi_{r_0}(x)\}$ at a given scale r_0. Since the width of the set of functions $\{\varphi_{r_0+1,s}(x)\}$ is half of that of the set of functions $\{\varphi_{r_0,s}(x)\}$ the latter can be analyzed by the former, but not the other way. Hence, the functional subspace spanned by $\{\varphi_{r_0+1,s}(x)\}$ contains the subspace $\{\varphi_{r_0,s}(x)\}$ that is, the subspace spanned by the scaling functions at lower scales is contained within the subspace spanned by those at higher scales and is given by the following nested relationship

$$V_{-\infty} \subset \cdots \subset V_{-1} \subset V_0 \subset V_1 \subset V_2 \subset \cdots \subset V_\infty \quad (3)$$

This subspace relationship is illustrated in figure.

The expansion functions of subspace V_r can be expressed as a weighted summation of the functions of subspace V_{r+1} as $V_0 \subset V_1 \subset V_2$ follows

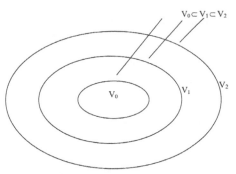

$$V_0 \subset V_1 \subset V_2$$

Subspace Relationship of Scaling Functions

$$\varphi(x) = \sum_n h_\varphi(n)\sqrt{2}\varphi(2x - n) \quad (4)$$

where the $h_\varphi(n)$ are the wavelet function coefficients.

Let us consider the example of unit amplitude, unit width Haar scaling function, shown in the figure.

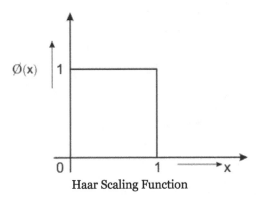

Haar Scaling Function

and mathematically defined as

$$\varphi(x) = \begin{cases} 1 \ for \ x \in [0,1) \\ 0 \ otherwise \end{cases} \quad (5)$$

By the mathematical definition of scaling functions, given in equation (1),

$$\varphi_{0,0}(x) = \varphi(x) \quad (6)$$

The functional subspace V_0 is spanned by the set $\{\varphi_{0,s}(x)\}$, each functional element of which represents a translated version of $\varphi_{0,0}(x)$ by an integer s. To obtain any scaled and translated version $\varphi_{r,s}(x)$ of the scaling function from $\varphi_{0,0}(x)$, it follows from the scaling function definition given in equation (2) that

(a) its amplitude should be $2^{r/2}$,

(b) its width should be $2^{-r/2}$,

(c) it should be positioned at $s.2^{-r/2}$

Figures below show a few examples of these.

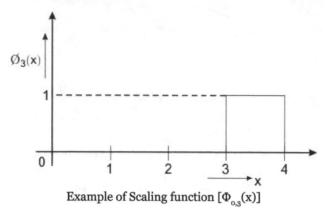

Example of Scaling function [$\Phi_{0,3}(x)$]

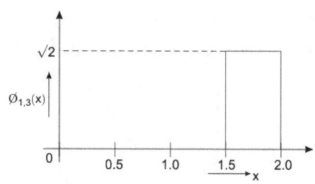

Example of Scaling function [$\Phi_{1,3}(x)$]

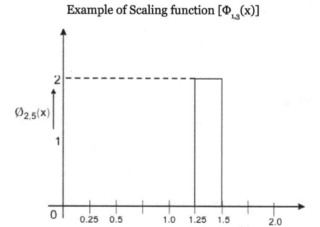

Example of Scaling function [$\Phi_{2,5}(x)$]

Wavelet Functions:

A set of integer translated and binary scaled functions $\{\psi_{r,s}(x)\}$ that spn the difference subspace between two adjacent scaling functions subspace is defined as a set of wavelet functions. If we consider two adjacent subspaces V_r and V_{r+1}, the set of wavelets spanning the subspace W_r within these are given as

$$\psi_{r,s}(x) = 2^{r/2}\psi(2^r x - s) \quad (7)$$

where, $s \in Z$ and $\psi(x) \in L^2(R)$. It may be noted that although the functional forms of equations (2) and (7) are the same, the scaling functions and the wavelet functions differ by their spanning subspaces. The relationship between scaling and wavelet function spaces is illustrated in the figure.

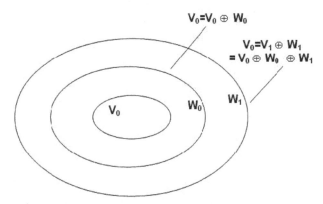

Relationship between Scaling and wavelet Functions.

and is given by

$$V_{r+1} = V_r \oplus W_r \quad (8)$$

where $\oplus$ indicates union of subspaces.

By recursively applying equation (7) to compute V_r, we can express the total measurable square-integrable space $L^2(R)$ as

$$L^2(R) = V_0 \oplus W_0 \oplus W_1 \oplus \cdots\cdots \quad (9)$$

Again, by repetitively applying equation (8) in (9), we can obtain alternative forms of expansion as

$$\begin{aligned}
L^2(R) &= V_1 \oplus W_1 \oplus W_2 \oplus \cdots\cdots \\
&= V_2 \oplus W_2 \oplus W_3 \oplus \cdots\cdots \quad (10) \\
&= V_{r_0} \oplus W_{r_0} \oplus W_{r_0+1} \oplus \cdots
\end{aligned}$$

Suppose that a function $f(x)$ to be analyzed belongs to the subspace V_1 but not V_0. In that case, the scaling functions of V_0 make a crude approximation of $f(x)$ and the wavelet functions of W_0 provide the details. In this sense, the scaling functions analyze $f(x)$ into its low-pass filtered form and the wavelet functions analyze $f(x)$ into its high-pass filtered form.

Since wavelet spaces reside within the spaces spanned by the next higher scaling functions, any wavelet function can be expressed as a weighted sum of shifted double-resolution scaling functions as follows

$$\psi(x) = \sum_n h_\psi(n)\sqrt{2}\varphi(2x-n) \quad (11)$$

where the $h_\psi(n)$ are the wavelet function coefficients. Using the conditions that the wavelets span the orthogonal complement spaces in the figure below and the integer wavelet translates are orthogonal, it is possible to obtain relationship between $h_\varphi(n)$ and $h_\psi(n)$. Using the definition of Haar scaling function given in equation(5) and the solutions of $h_\varphi(n)$ and $h_\psi(n)$, the corresponding Haar wavelet function is obtained as

$$\psi(x) = \begin{cases} 1 & 0 \le x < 0.5 \\ -1 & 0.5 \le x < 1 \\ 0 & elsewhere \end{cases} \quad (12)$$

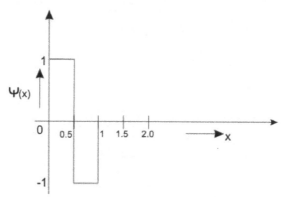

Haar Wavelet function

shows equation (12) graphically. By the definition of equation (7),

$$\psi_{0,0}(x) = \psi(x) \quad (13)$$

Like the scaling functions, we can obtain binary scaled and integer shifted versions of wavelets by applying equation (7). Figures below show few such examples.

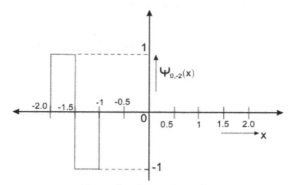

Example of Haar Wavelet

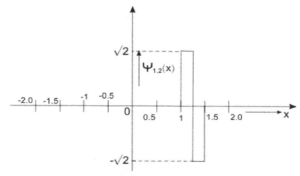

Example of Haar Wavelet

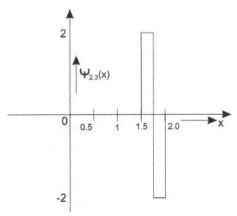

Example of Haar Wavelet [$\Psi_{2,3}(x)$]

The wavelet series:

In accordance with the functional subspace relationships shown in equation (10) and the definition of expansion functions in equation (1), any function $f(x) \in L^2(R)$ can be expressed as a series summation of scaling functions and wavelet functions as

$$f(x) = \sum_s a_{r_0,s} \varphi_{r_0,s}(x) + \sum_{r=r_0}^{\infty} \sum_s b_{r,s} \psi_{r,s}(x) \qquad (14)$$

where, $a_{r_0,s}$ and $b_{r,s}$ are the corresponding expansion coefficients. In the above equation, the first term of the expansion involving the scaling functions provide approximations to $f(x)$ at scale r_0 and the second term of expansion involving the wavelet functions add details to the approximation at r_0 and its higher scales. If the expansion functions form an orthonormal basis, which is often the case, the coefficients can be calculated as

$$a_{r_0,s} = \int f(x) \varphi_{r_0,s}(x) dx \qquad (15)$$

$$b_{r,s} = \int f(x) \psi_{r,s}(x) dx. \qquad (16)$$

As an example, let us consider the wavelet series expansion of the following function:

$$f(x) = \begin{cases} e^x & 0 \le x < 1 \\ 0 & otherwise \end{cases}. \qquad (17)$$

using Haar scaling and wavelet functions.

By applying equations (15) and (16) on the function defined in (17), the expansion coefficients are obtained as follows:

$$a_{0,0} = \int_0^1 e^x \varphi_{0,0}(x) = \int_0^1 e^x \, dx = e^x \big|_0^1 = e - 1 \qquad (18)$$

$$b_{0,0} = \int_0^1 e^x \psi_{0,0}(x) = \int_0^{0.5} e^x \, dx - \int_{0.5}^1 e^x dx = 2e^{0.5} - (e+1). \qquad (19)$$

$$b_{1,0} = \int_0^1 e^x {}_{1,0}(x) = \int_0^{0.25} \sqrt{2} e^x \, dx - \int_{0.25}^{0.5} \sqrt{2} e^x \, dx = 2\sqrt{2} e^{0.25} - \sqrt{2}(e^{0.5} + 1) \qquad (20)$$

$$b_{1,1} = \int_0^1 e^x \psi_{1,1}(x) = \int_{0.5}^{0.75} \sqrt{2}e^x \, dx - \int_{0.75}^1 \sqrt{2}e^x \, dx = 2\sqrt{2}e^{0.75} - \sqrt{2}(e + e^{0.5}) \quad (21)$$

Using the coefficients obtained in equations (18) to (21), the function f(x) can be realized as

$$f(x) = a_{0,0}\varphi_{0,0}(x) + b_{0,0}\psi_{0,0}(x) + b_{1,0}\psi_{1,0}(x) + b_{1,1}\psi_{1,1}(x) + \quad (22)$$

In this, we have presented the basic theory of the scaling and wavelet functions. It is shown that these functions can analyze a continuous valued, square-integrable signal in multiple resolutions. The scaling functions provide approximations or low-pass filtering of the signal and the wavelet functions add the details at multiple resolutions or perform high-pass filtering of the signal. Although the theory is presented for continuous, one-dimensional signals, it may be extended for discrete two-dimensional signals, which we require for multi- resolution image analysis and coding.

Multiresolution Analysis

A multiresolution analysis (MRA) or multiscale approximation (MSA) is the design method of most of the practically relevant discrete wavelet transforms (DWT) and the justification for the algorithm of the fast wavelet transform (FWT). It was introduced in this context in 1988/89 by Stephane Mallat and Yves Meyer and has predecessors in the microlocal analysis in the theory of differential equations (the *ironing method*) and the pyramid methods of image processing as introduced in 1981/83 by Peter J. Burt, Edward H. Adelson and James L. Crowley.

Definition

A *multiresolution analysis* of the Lebesgue space $L^2(\mathbb{R})$ consists of a sequence of nested subspaces

$$\{0\} \ldots \subset V_1 \subset V_0 \subset V_{-1} \subset \ldots \subset V_{-n} \subset V_{-(n+1)} \subset \ldots \subset L^2(\mathbb{R})$$

that satisfies certain self-similarity relations in time/space and scale/frequency, as well as completeness and regularity relations.

- *Self-similarity* in *time* demands that each subspace V_k is invariant under shifts by integer multiples of 2^k. That is, for each $f \in V_k, m \in \mathbb{Z}$ the function g defined as $g(x) = f(x - m2^k)$ also contained in V_k.

- *Self-similarity* in *scale* demands that all subspaces $V_k \subset V_l, k > l$, are time-scaled versions of each other, with scaling respectively dilation factor 2^{k-l}. I.e., for each $f \in V_k$ there is a $g \in V_l$ with $\forall x \in \mathbb{R} : g(x) = f(2^{k-l}x)$.

- In the sequence of subspaces, for $k > l$ the space resolution 2^l of the *l*-th subspace is higher than the resolution 2^k of the *k*-th subspace.

- *Regularity* demands that the model subspace V_o be generated as the linear hull (algebraically or even topologically closed) of the integer shifts of one or a finite number of generating functions ϕ or $\phi_1, \ldots, \phi_r$. Those integer shifts should at least form a frame for the subspace $V_0 \subset L^2(\mathbb{R})$, which imposes certain conditions on the decay at infinity. The generating functions are also known as scaling functions or father wavelets. In most cases one demands of those functions to be piecewise continuous with compact support.

- *Completeness* demands that those nested subspaces fill the whole space, i.e., their union should be dense in $L^2(\mathbb{R})$, and that they are not too redundant, i.e., their intersection should only contain the zero element.

Important Conclusions

In the case of one continuous (or at least with bounded variation) compactly supported scaling function with orthogonal shifts, one may make a number of deductions. The proof of existence of this class of functions is due to Ingrid Daubechies.

Assuming the scaling function has compact support, then $V_0 \subset V_{-1}$ implies that there is a finite sequence of coefficients $a_k = 2\langle \phi(x), \phi(2x-k) \rangle$ for $|k| \leq N$, and $a_k = 0$ for $|k| > N$, such that

$$\phi(x) = \sum_{k=-N}^{N} a_k \phi(2x-k).$$

Defining another function, known as mother wavelet or just the wavelet

$$\psi(x) := \sum_{k=-N}^{N} (-1)^k a_{1-k} \phi(2x-k),$$

one can show that the space $W_0 \subset V_{-1}$, which is defined as the (closed) linear hull of the mother wavelet's integer shifts, is the orthogonal complement to V_0 inside V_{-1}. Or put differently, V_{-1} is the orthogonal sum (denoted by $\oplus$) of W_0 and V_0. By self-similarity, there are scaled versions W_k of W_0 and by completeness one has

$$L^2(\mathbb{R}) = \text{closure of } \bigoplus_{k \in \mathbb{Z}} W_k,$$

thus the set

$$\{\psi_{k,n}(x) = \sqrt{2}^{-k} \psi(2^{-k}x - n) : k, n \in \mathbb{Z}\}$$

is a countable complete orthonormal wavelet basis in $L^2(\mathbb{R})$.

Theory of Subband Coding

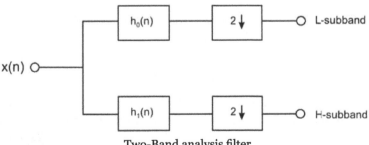

Two-Band analysis filter

Before we discuss about the subband analysis of images, let us first consider the simplest example of a band-limited one-dimensional signal, having a cut-off frequency $\omega_c = \pi$, that is, exactly half of the sampling frequency $\omega_s = 2\pi$. Suppose, we pass this signal through a bank of two digital filters

– the first one being a low-pass filter having impulse response $h_0(n)$ and upper cut-off frequency $\omega_0 = \pi / 2$ and the second one being a high-pass filter having impulse response $h_1(n)$ and lower cut-off frequency $\omega_1 = \pi / 2$.

Figure above shows the block diagram of the filter bank, which essentially analyzes the signal into two subbands, whose spectral responses are as shown in the figure below.

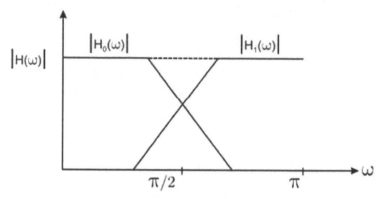

Spectral response of two-bands of analysis filter.

Since the filter banks perform subband analysis, the filters are known as analysis filters.

If we perform subband analysis on N samples of an input sequence $x(n)$ for n=0,1,...,N-1, both the low-frequency and high-frequency analysis filter outputs will have N samples. However, it should be noted that since the bandwidth of the signal at each of the analysis filter outputs is only one-half of the original signal, the analysis filter outputs can be sampled at half the original Nyquist rate. In other words, half of the samples at the analysis filter outputs are redundant and hence every one out of two consecutive samples at the filter output can be dropped. Therefore, the analysis filter outputs are downsampled by a factor of two, as shown in the block diagram.

Two-band Synthesis of Signals

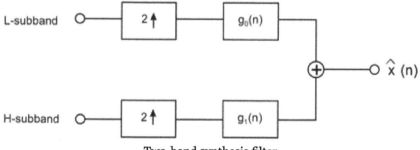

Two-band synthesis filter.

Synthesis is just the reverse of analysis, as shown in the above figure. The low-pass and high-pass filtered subbands are first upsampled by a factor of two, so that each of the subband filters, having impulse responses $g_0(n)$ and $g_1(n)$ respectively for low and high subbands, generate N samples for an input sequence of length N samples. The outputs of these two filters are added to generate the reconstructed sequence $\hat{x}(n)$ for $n = 0,1, N - 1$ Since the two filter outputs do the synthesis of the signal, these filters are known as *synthesis filters*. The two- band analysis and synthesis can be shown in the form of a combined block diagram of the next figure.

Conditions for Perfect Reconstruction in Analysis- Synthesis Filters

We are now going to derive the necessary conditions for perfect reconstruction in analysis-synthesis filters. For a perfect reconstruction, we must have $x(n) = \hat{x}(n)$ for $n = 0,1, \dots, N-1$ and to achieve this, the analysis and the synthesis filters must fulfill some conditions. Since, filtering involves convolution in the time (or spatial) domain and multiplication in the transform-domain, it is easier to derive the conditions of perfect reconstruction in transform-domain and we use the z- transforms for this purpose. The choice of z-transform is motivated by the fact that it can handle sampling-rate changes, as required by us due to the involvement of down-sampling in analysis and up-sampling in synthesis.

z-transform of Down-sampled Sequence

The z-transform of the original sequence $x(n)$, $n = 0,1,2,\dots$ is given by

$$X(z) = \sum_{n=-\infty}^{\infty} x(n) z^{-n}$$

where, z is a complex variable. Down-sampling $x(n)$ by a factor of two preserves every alternate samples of the original sequence, i.e. $x(2n)$ for $n = 0,1,2,\dots$. Its z-transform is therefore given by

$$
\begin{aligned}
X_{down}(z) &= \sum_{n=-\infty}^{\infty} x(2n) z^{-n} \\
&= x(0)z^0 + x(2)z^{-1} + x(4)z^{-2} + \cdots + x(-2)z^1 + x(-4)z^2 + \cdots \\
&= \frac{1}{2}\left[x(0)z^0 + x(1)z^{-1/2} + x(2)z^{-1} + \dots + x(-1)z^{1/2} + x(-2)z^1 + \cdots \right] \\
&\quad + \frac{1}{2}\left[x(0)z^0 - x(1)z^{-1/2} + x(2)z^{-1} - \cdots - x(-1)z^{1/2} + x(-2)z^1 + \cdots \right] \\
&= \frac{1}{2}[X(z^{1/2}) + X(-z^{1/2})]
\end{aligned}
$$

z-transform of up-sampled Sequence

In the process of up-sampling, zeros are added for every odd sample and thus, up-sampling a given sequence $x(n)$ for $n = 0,1,2,\dots$ can be expressed in terms of the samples of given sequence as

$$
x^{up}(n) = \begin{cases} x\left(\dfrac{n}{2}\right) & for\ n = 0,2,4,\dots \\ 0 & otherwise \end{cases}
$$

The z-transform of the up-sampled sequence may be expressed as

$$
\begin{aligned}
X^{up}(z) &= x(0)z^0 + x(1)z^{-2} + x(2)z^{-4} + \cdots + x(-1)z^2 + x(-2)z^4 + \cdots \\
&= X(z^2)
\end{aligned}
$$

Without using any analysis or synthesis filter, if we simply cascade a down- sampler and an up-sampler, then the z-transform of the reconstructed sequence is given by combining above equations as

$$\hat{X}(z) = \frac{1}{2}[X(z) + X(-z)].$$

The second term of the above equation represents the z-transform of the aliased version of the signal $\hat{x}(n)$. Its inverse z-transform is given by

$$Z^{-1}[X(-z)] = (-1)^n x(n)$$

z-transform of Subband Coding/decoding:

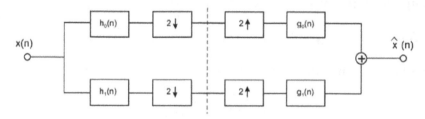

Analysis-synthesis of 2-band decomposition and reconstruction

With this background, we can now consider the block-diagram of figure and write the z-transform of the reconstructed signal by using earlier equation and using the property that convolution in time (or spatial) domain is multiplication in frequency domain as

$$\hat{X}(z) = \frac{1}{2}G_0(z)[H_0(z)X(z) + H_0(-z)X(-z)]$$

$$+ \frac{1}{2}G_1(z)[H_1(z)X(z) + H_1(-z)X(-z)]$$

Rearranging the terms, we obtain

$$\hat{X}(z) = \frac{1}{2}[G_0(z)H_0(z)X(z) + G_1(z)H_1(-z)]X(z)$$

$$+ \frac{1}{2}[G_0(z)H_0(-z) + G_1(z)H_1(-z)]X(-z)$$

where the second term involving −z indicates the aliased components.

Conditions for Error-free Reconstruction of Signals

From above equation, it is easy to derive the necessary conditions for error-free reconstruction of the signal at the analysis-synthesis filter bank output. For errorfree reconstruction, we must ensure

$$X(z) = \hat{X}(z).$$

the conditions for which are obtained from equation above as

$$G_0(z)H_0(z) + G_1(z)H_1(z) = 2$$

and

$$G_0(z)H_0(-z) + G_1(z)H_1(-z) = 0.$$

Equation earlier ensures that there is no amplitude distortion in reconstruction and previous equation forces the condition that there is no aliasing. Both these equations can be combined in a matrix form as

$$[G_0(z) \; G_1(z)] \begin{bmatrix} H_0(z) & H_0(-z) \\ H_1(z) & H_1(-z) \end{bmatrix} = [2 \; 0].$$

We define $H_m(z) = \begin{bmatrix} H_0(z) & H_0(-z) \\ H_1(z) & H_1(-z) \end{bmatrix}$ as the analysis modulation matrix and hence, above equation can be rewritten as

$$[G_0(z) \; G_1(z)] H_m(z) = [2 \; 0]$$

Assuming that the matrix $H_m(z)$ is non-singular, we can take the transpose of both the sides of equation given above and then pre-multiply by $(H_m^T(z))^{-1}$, we obtain

$$\begin{bmatrix} G_0(z) \\ G_1(z) \end{bmatrix} = \frac{2}{\det(H_m(z))} \begin{bmatrix} H_1(-z) \\ -H_0(-z) \end{bmatrix}$$

Where $\det(H_m(z))$ is the determinate of the matrix $H_m(z)$.

The above equation reveals an interesting fact that $G_0(z)$ is a function of $H_1(-z)$ and $G_1(z)$ is a function of $H_0(-z)$, which means that the analysis and the synthesis filters are cross-modulated. For Finite Impulse Response (FIR) filters, the determinate of the matrix $H_m(z)$ is a pure delay and is given by $det(H_m(z)) = \alpha z^{-(2k+1)}$.

Neglecting the delay, letting α=2 and taking inverse transforms, we obtain

$$g_0(n) = (-1)^n h_1(n)$$

$$g_1(n) = (-1)^{n+1} h_0(n)$$

If α=-2, the above expressions are sign-reversed, i.e.

$$g_0(n) = (-1)^{n+1} h_1(n)$$

$$g_1(n) = (-1)^n h_0(n)$$

Hence, for error-free reconstruction, the FIR synthesis filters are cross-modulated copies of analysis filters, with one of the signs reversed.

Bi-orthogonality of Analysis-synthesis Filters

We define the product of the low-pass analysis and synthesis filter transfer functions as $P(z)$. Hence, from earlier equation, we get

$$P(z) = G_0(z)H_0(z) = \frac{2}{\det(H_m(z))} H_0(z)H_1(-z).$$

Also, noting that $\det(H_m(z)) = -\det(H_m(-z))$, we can obtain the product of the high-pass analysis and synthesis filter transfer functions from earlier equation as

$$G_1(-z)H_1(-z) = \frac{-2}{\det(H_m(z))} H_0(-z)H_1(-z) = P(-z) = G_0(-z)H_0(-z).$$

Thus, one of the conditions for error-free reconstruction, given by from earlier equation may be rewritten as

$$G_0(z)H_0(z) + G_0(-z)H_0(-z) = 2.$$

Taking the inverse z-transform of the above, we obtain

$$\sum_k g_0(k)h_0(n-k) + (-1)^n \sum_k g_0(k)h_0(n-k) = 2\delta(n).$$

Where $\delta(n)$ is unit impulse function having value of unity for $n = 0$ and zero otherwise.

Since, all odd-indexed terms get cancelled, as per above given equation and the even-indexed terms add up in the left-hand side, it is possible to write above given equation in a different form as

$$\sum_k g_0(k)h_0(2n-k) = \langle g_0(k), h_0(2n-k) \rangle = \delta(n).$$

Again, using above equation and changing z to -z, it is also possible to rewrite equation as

$$G_1(z)H_1(z) + G_1(-z)H_1(-z) = 2.$$

From the above equation, we can similarly derive

$$\langle g_1(k), h_1(2n-k) \rangle = \delta(n)$$

Taking earlier equation as the starting point, we can also derive two other conditions

$$\langle g_0(k), h_1(2n-k) \rangle = 0.$$

$$\langle g_1(k), h_0(2n-k) \rangle = 0.$$

The four conditions given in equations above can be expressed in a combined form of bi-orthogonality condition as

$$\langle g_i(k), h_j(2n-k) \rangle = \delta(i-j)\delta(n), \quad i,j = \{0,1\}$$

Thus, the bi-orthogonality of analysis and synthesis filter responses is essentially the condition for error-free reconstruction.

Bi-orthogonality conditions are fulfilled by following classes of filters: Quadrature Mirror Filters (QMF), Conjugate Quadrature Filters (CQF) and Orthonormal filters. For each class, a prototype filter is constructed, based on the filter specifications and then the other analysis and synthesis filters are derived from the prototype. For QMF and CQF, the readers are referred to the references provided. The orthonormal class of filters requires some special mention. These filters not only satisfy bi-orthogonality, but also orthonormality, as given by

$$\langle g_i(n), g_j(n+2m) \rangle = \delta(i-j)\delta(m), \quad i,j = \{0,1\}.$$

For orthonormal filters, the impulse response of analysis filters $h_0(n)$, $h_1(n)$ and synthesis filter $g_1(n)$ can be obtained from $g_0(n)$ as

$$g_1(n) = (-1)^n g_0(2K - 1 - n)$$
$$h_i(n) = g_i(2K - 1 - n)$$

where 2K is the number of taps in FIR filter. Examples of orthonormal FIR filters include the Smith and Barnwell filters, Daubechies filters and Vaidyanathan and Hoang filters. The impulse responses of four 8-tap Daubechies FIR filters, whose coefficients of low-pass analysis filters are shown in the table below. Other filters are derived through above equation.

Table: Coefficients of Daubechies 8-tap low-pass analysis filter

$h_0(0)$	-0.01059740
$h_0(1)$	0.03288301
$h_0(2)$	0.03084138
$h_0(3)$	-0.18703481
$h_0(4)$	-0.02798376
$h_0(5)$	0.63088076
$h_0(6)$	0.71484657
$h_0(7)$	0.23037781

Subband Decomposition of Images

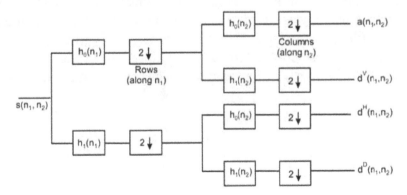

Four-band analysis of images

The idea of subband coding can be extended for two-dimensional signals, if the one-dimensional filters used for analysis and synthesis can be used as two-dimensional separable filters. Figure shows the block diagram of a two dimensional four-band analysis filter bank used for subband coding. The two-dimensional signal, i.e. images having discrete set of samples $s(n_1, n_2)$ are first analyzed into low-frequency and high-frequency subbands through FIR analysis filters along the n_1-direction, i.e. along the rows (vertically) and then down-sampled by factors of 2. Each of the resulting subbands are then analyzed into the low and high-frequency subbands along the n_2-direction, i.e. along the columns (horizontally) and we thus obtain four subbands, each of which is further sub-sampled by a factor of two.

Thus, each of the subbands shown in the figure above contain only one-fourth of the original samples in the pixel array. The resulting subband outputs $a(n_1, n_2), d^V(n_1, n_2), d^H(n_1, n_2)$ and $d^D(n_1, n_2)$ contain the approximation, the vertical details, the horizontal details and the diagonal details respectively. In terms of resulting images, these subbands are generally expressed as LL, LH, HL and HH, where the first letter indicates the filter applied in the horizontal direction ("L" for low-pass and "H" for high-pass) and the second letter indicates the filter applied in the vertical direction.

The above principle of four-band decomposition may be applied to one or more of the subbands. Any of the resulting subbands obtained may be further split into four subbands and so on.

Example of 4-band decomposition of an image using Daubechies 8-tap FIR filter.

Figure above shows an example of the 4-band decomposition of an image using Daubechies 8-tap FIR filter. The block diagram of synthesis filter banks to reconstruct the image is shown in the figure below. It is the mirror of the analysis filter banks of the previous figure and require an up-sampling by a factor of two before filtering the signal. If the filters satisfy the conditions of bi-orthogonality, the reconstruct is going to be exact. In practice, the image compression systems perform quantization of the subband coefficients and thus, the reconstructed image contains quantization errors.

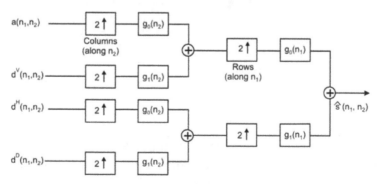

Synthesis of four subbands

References

• Ali Akansu and Richard Haddad, Multiresolution Signal Decomposition: Transforms, Subbands, Wavelets, Academic Press, 1992, ISBN 0-12-047140-X

- Press, WH; Teukolsky, SA; Vetterling, WT; Flannery, BP (2007), "Section 13.10. Wavelet Transforms", Numerical Recipes: The Art of Scientific Computing (3rd ed.), New York: Cambridge University Press, ISBN 978-0-521-88068-8

- Burrus, C.S.; Gopinath, R.A.; Guo, H. (1997). Introduction to Wavelets and Wavelet Transforms: A Primer. Prentice-Hall. ISBN 0-13-489600-9

- Akansu, A.N.; Haddad, R.A. (1992). Multiresolution signal decomposition: transforms, subbands, and wavelets. Academic Press. ISBN 978-0-12-047141-6

- Ramazan Gençay, Faruk Selçuk and Brandon Whitcher, An Introduction to Wavelets and Other Filtering Methods in Finance and Economics, Academic Press, 2001, ISBN 0-12-279670-5

Permissions

We would like to thank the editorial team for lending their expertise to make the book truly unique. They have played a crucial role in the development of this book. Without their invaluable contributions this book wouldn't have been possible. They have made vital efforts to compile up to date information on the varied aspects of this subject to make this book a valuable addition to the collection of many professionals and students.

This book was conceptualized with the vision of imparting up-to-date and integrated information in this field. To ensure the same, a matchless editorial board was set up. Every individual on the board went through rigorous rounds of assessment to prove their worth. After which they invested a large part of their time researching and compiling the most relevant data for our readers.

The editorial board has been involved in producing this book since its inception. They have spent rigorous hours researching and exploring the diverse topics which have resulted in the successful publishing of this book. They have passed on their knowledge of decades through this book. To expedite this challenging task, the publisher supported the team at every step. A small team of assistant editors was also appointed to further simplify the editing procedure and attain best results for the readers.

Apart from the editorial board, the designing team has also invested a significant amount of their time in understanding the subject and creating the most relevant covers. They scrutinized every image to scout for the most suitable representation of the subject and create an appropriate cover for the book.

The publishing team has been an ardent support to the editorial, designing and production team. Their endless efforts to recruit the best for this project, has resulted in the accomplishment of this book. They are a veteran in the field of academics and their pool of knowledge is as vast as their experience in printing. Their expertise and guidance has proved useful at every step. Their uncompromising quality standards have made this book an exceptional effort. Their encouragement from time to time has been an inspiration for everyone.

The publisher and the editorial board hope that this book will prove to be a valuable piece of knowledge for students, practitioners and scholars across the globe.

Index